Hist

PROPHETIC
SONS AND DAUGHTERS

Female Preaching and Popular
Religion in Industrial
England

DEBORAH M. VALENZE

PRINCETON UNIVERSITY PRESS

PRINCETON, NEW JERSEY

For
my father
and the memory of
my mother

And it shall come to pass afterward, that I will pour out my spirit upon all flesh; and your sons and your daughters shall prophesy, your old men shall dream dreams, your young men shall see visions.

JOEL 2:28

CONTENTS

CONTENTS

PART III

FROM THE COUNTRY TO THE TOWN

PART IV

POPULAR CULTURE AND RELIGION

MAPS

ILLUSTRATIONS

ACKNOWLEDGMENTS

THIS BOOK owes much to the people who helped me over a long period of time. My earliest interest in popular religion was influenced by Eric Hobsbawm, who taught me how to observe the past and never doubted my discoveries. I am deeply grateful to him for his insights and encouragement. The book grew out of a doctoral dissertation helpfully guided by Eugene C. Black; it is much the better for his thoughtful reading. I owe special thanks to Joan Wallach Scott, who provided invaluable help in conceptualizing the project and whose own work in the history of women inspired my efforts in the field. John Walsh read carefully all that I wrote and was always a source of deep learning and unfailing advice. Jim Obelkevich and Raphael Samuel were generous friends and sympathetic critics throughout the course of my attempts to link social with religious history. Karen Fields and John Brewer read chapters and made useful suggestions; Bernard Wasserstein, David D. Gilmore, Jeffrey Cox, Phyllis Mack, Gill Burke, and Dorothy Thompson added to my understanding of the material I faced. I am also indebted to Kim Hays, Charles Kletzsch, and Doris Walsey Shay for innumerable conversations about my work, and to my colleagues in the Humanities Department at Worcester Polytechnic Institute for their unwavering support. Peter Onuf's thorough and creative response to an earlier version of the manuscript helped me rethink the subject matter more forcefully; and Thomas Laqueur and Clarissa Atkinson offered meticulous, illuminating readings that greatly improved the book. Herb Heidt produced the maps with great creativity and patience. I would also like to thank Gail Ullman for the editorial advice that she administered so reassuringly.

In aiding the research for the book, I wish to thank Michael Collinge, Frank Prochaska, and Patrick Joyce for numerous and varied bits of information. I am also grateful to D. Colin Dews and Christine Dews of Leeds, John and Maisie Crimlisk of Filey, Tom, Ida, and Marjorie Abel of Warrington, Arthur Jarratt of Hull, and Ursula Vogel. They were kind enough to share their private collections, their homes, and their time with me during my travels to archives. The staff of the North Library of the British Library were especially patient and helpful; I am also indebted to Mr. D. Woodward Riley of the John Rylands University Library of Manchester and the staff of the Methodist Archives and Research Center, the Institute of Historical Research, London, the Hull Central Library, the Leeds Central Library, including the Sheepscar branch, the Manchester City Library, Huddersfield Central Library, the Bodleian Library, Widener Library of Harvard University, and the Boston Public Library. The research and writing of this book would not have been possible without generous grants from the Fulbright-Hays Commission in 1978–79 and the American Association of University Women in 1980–81. The maps for the book were partially funded by the Humanities Department of Worcester Polytechnic Institute through a grant from the Mellon Foundation. I am also grateful to the Boston YWCA for donating office space, which enabled me to work on a large portion of the manuscript.

Most of all, I am grateful to my husband, Michael Timo Gilmore. His care, love, and understanding, as well as his example, made all the difference to my work. He will understand why I have dedicated the book to others.

PROPHETIC SONS AND DAUGHTERS

Cottage religion in industrial England—
selected regions

INTRODUCTION

THIS STUDY began as a general investigation of the religion of laboring people in nineteenth-century England. I wanted to know how religion shaped or was shaped by the experiences of laboring life—how work, family, and community related to belief and practice. Social historians interested chiefly in political consciousness or class relations had imposed a bias on the field; while important, neither approach enabled me to get beyond a superficial or abstract understanding of the role religion played during this period. Were political and class considerations foremost in the minds of working-class adherents? Or did religion represent other ways of experiencing and interpreting the nineteenth-century world?

Religion created consensus. This is the interpretation of the *created consensus.* Victorian Age, handed down by its foremost historians. Halévy pointed out the conservative political influence of religion, while G. M. Young called evangelicalism "the strongest binding force in England."[1] More recent historians have elaborated on these themes. Viewing evangelicalism as a homogenous set of beliefs, some have celebrated its liberal, progressive aspects, while others have criticized its power to mute popular protest and prevent revolution. Even while challenging Halévy's conclusions, many have shared his conceptual bias towards politics. Political consciousness is often seen as the enlightened heir to religion, finally enabling the less powerful to shake off the control of hegemonic classes.

Religion undoubtedly provided one means of cultural con-

---

[1] *Victorian England: Portrait of an Age* (London: Oxford University Press, 1960), p. 5. The view of evangelicalism as part of an established consensus has influenced most textbook definitions of Victorian religion. See also Elie Halévy, *History of the English People in the Nineteenth Century*, vol. 1, rev. ed. (1913; London: Ernest Benn, 1960), p. 458.

3

trol in the hands of the middle and upper classes in Britain; but instrumental interpretations of religion derive, at least in part, from ignorance. Until recently, the history of religion in Britain did not extend beyond the study of institutions and great men: the health of the Church of England and the aims of prominent and powerful reformers defined the field. Figures like Hannah More, William Wilberforce, and John Wesley crowded the theological landscape and trained attention upon "institutional neglect" and "humanitarian awakening." As a result, the late eighteenth century seemed strangely dissevered from the turbulent, popular vitality of the seventeenth. For most studies, excepting some on Methodism, "popular" appeared altogether irrelevant to a discussion of religion.[2]

A major reversal of this historiographical pattern began with Edward Thompson's *The Making of the English Working Class*. Tracing the history of dissenting tradition from the seventeenth century, Thompson depicted a critical struggle between radical and normative religion through the Revolutionary and Napoleonic era.[3] And yet religion seemed inextricably tied to a persistent "whiggish" interpretation of social history. Questions of elite politics and religion still defined working-class

[2] See Ford K. Brown, *Fathers of the Victorians* (Cambridge: Cambridge University Press, 1961); Ernest M. Howse, *Saints in Politics* (Toronto: University of Toronto Press, 1952); Maurice Quinlan, *Victorian Prelude*, reprint (1945; Hamden, Conn.: Archon Books, 1965); Paul Sangster, *Pity My Simplicity: The Evangelical Revival and the Religious Education of Children, 1738–1800* (London: Epworth Press, 1963); W. L. Burn, *The Age of Equipoise* (London: George Allen & Unwin, 1964).

[3] (New York: Vintage Books, 1963). In depicting this struggle, Thompson uncovered obscure forms of popular belief that had not yielded to new pressures. Previously neglected or regarded as eccentric, these systems of belief now enjoyed a renaissance of historical study: millenarians like Richard Brothers and Joanna Southcott, Owenites, Muggletonians, Swedenborgians, and others demonstrated that the orthodox Christianity of industrial England had not triumphed over all autonomous activity among the masses. See also J.F.C. Harrison, *The Second Coming: Popular Millenarianism, 1780–1850* (New Brunswick, N.J.: Rutgers University Press, 1979); James K. Hopkins, *A Woman to Deliver Her People: Joanna Southcott and English Millenarianism in an Era of Revolution* (Austin, Texas: University of Texas Press, 1982).

history, sustaining categories of orthodox and unorthodox, respectable and radical, traditional and modern. Thompson's arguments, despite their freshness, breathed new life into Halévy's thesis by identifying religious revivalism with political reaction. A "chiliasm of despair" followed on the heels of periods of working-class political activism and "took over just at the point where 'political' or temporal aspirations met with defeat." Religion again was a function of political history, at least with regard to the "mainstream" of English society.[4]

Convinced that religion encompassed more of this mainstream than supposed, I tried to determine a way of gaining access to working-class experience. All laborers, religious or not, witnessed fundamental changes in nineteenth-century society and culture. Might religion provide a sensitive indicator of economic and social influences on laboring life?[5] Historians of Continental Europe have had less trouble extending the realm of the religious to encompass a wider sphere of social experience. Mircea Eliade, Natalie Zemon Davis, Carlo Ginzburg, and others have transcended concepts like "social control" by calling attention to fundamental cultural assumptions underlying the sacred realm. Through these "manifestations of the sacred" in everyday life, attitudes towards work, family, and power relations become accessible.[6] My intention, then,

[4] Thompson, *Making of the English Working Class*, p. 389. For an insightful critique of Thompson, see Hans Medick, "Plebeian Culture in the Transition to Capitalism," *Culture, Ideology and Politics: Essays for Eric Hobsbawm*, Raphael Samuel and Gareth Stedman Jones, eds. (London: Routledge & Kegan Paul, 1983), pp. 87–9.

[5] Several such treatments of the social history of religion have provided a foundation for this study, among them essays by John Walsh, including "Methodism and the Mob in the Eighteenth Century," *Popular Belief and Practice*, Studies in Church History, vol. 8, G. J. Cuming and Derek Baker, eds. (Cambridge: Cambridge University Press, 1972), pp. 213–27; Eric J. Hobsbawm, *Primitive Rebels* (New York: Norton, 1959); Thomas W. Laqueur, *Religion and Respectability: Sunday Schools and Working Class Culture, 1780–1850* (New Haven: Yale University Press, 1976); James Obelkevich, *Religion and Rural Society* (Oxford: Clarendon Press, 1976).

[6] See Kaspar von Greyerz, "Conference Report: The Social History of Religion," *Social History* 7 (1982): 207.

was to uncover the sacred world view of laborers and relate it to contemporary economic and social change.

A scarcity of sources influenced the focus of my research. Obviously, few working-class accounts of the period existed, and much of what survived was unhelpful. Working-class autobiography, temperance biography, and Victorian memoirs revealed too little about ordinary laboring life while reiterating truisms of nineteenth-century reform. These were the very sources that had promoted the political biases of the past by creating formulaic models of consensus and progress. I searched instead for information on persons less whiggishly heroic and exemplary. From religious sources, I isolated what I thought was most authentically working-class. The Methodist sects, comprised almost exclusively of laborers, published obituaries and memoirs reporting factual material on rank-and-file followers and preachers. The accounts revealed circumstances of birth, childhood, occupation, and places of residence in extraordinary detail. Combined with spiritual writings, denominational histories, and local histories, these data would enable me to explore the lives of religious laborers.

This new material suggested important revisions of textbook generalizations about Victorian religion and society. Rather than demonstrating an uncritical acceptance of the new industrial order, the lives of sectarian Methodists revealed tortuous struggles to control and at times resist change. Their religious ethos was rooted in the old world of work, not the new; many persisted in occupations outmoded by technological change in order to preserve independence. Migration and impoverishment further alienated sectarians from the society of their superiors. For these laborers, religion became a means of overturning middle-class ideals of piety, reciprocity, and progress. In doctrine and behavior, popular evangelicals rejected deference and dependence in favor of Old Testament *ressentiment*, vociferous demonstrations of piety, and relentless reproofs of their employers and neighbors. Far from celebrating progress, they resisted it in their speech and dress as well as through their work.

6

An accumulating stock of biographies produced another discovery: among the obituaries of leading sectarians there were a considerable number of female preachers. I knew of the existence of women preachers through two or three brief treatments of the subject; but the women I was finding were not those famous "exceptions" working at the right hand of John Wesley.[7] These were humble women with little education and no connection to prestigious religious circles. Despite the singularity and extent of their work, their obituaries seemed to understate their achievement. I decided to set them aside until I had a surer sense of their numerical significance, and when their number exceeded two hundred, I faced the task of fitting them into the general picture of popular evangelicalism that was already taking shape.

Women's work in religion in itself was not especially unusual. A long tradition of pious *noblesse oblige* existed to help the poor and provide for their salvation, and, during the Victorian era, such efforts grew to an unprecedented height. But female preaching was different. As Edward Lytton Bulwer pointed out, "The aristocratic world does not like either clergymen, or women, to make too much noise."[8] These evangelists were, then, doubly offensive. Unlike the more dignified ladies of charitable institutions, sectarian women travelled widely on their own and spoke publicly and freely to audiences of both sexes. Rather than deferring to official clergymen, they contradicted and reproached them. Female preachers were remarkably strong-willed. They took up occupations and abandoned them according to the spirit, and, when necessary, relied upon networks of followers for modest means of support. Risking their physical well-being and reputations, labor-

---

[7] The only treatment of women preachers has been by Methodist historians, viz., Wesley F. Swift, "The Women Itinerant Preachers of Early Methodism," *Proceedings of the Wesley Historical Society* 28–9 (1952-3): 89–94; 76–83, and Leslie F. Church, *More About the Early Methodist People* (London: Epworth Press, 1949), chap. 4.

[8] *England and the English* reprint, Classics of British Literature Series (1833; Chicago: University of Chicago Press, 1970), p. 188.

ing women preachers strove to establish their own models of female piety.

But what prompted this repudiation of conventional religion? Was female preaching simply "ranting" by "women of the lower classes,"[9] or did these women have something worthwhile to say? Only a close examination of the social context of popular evangelicalism could address these questions and militate against ahistorical explanations of their significance. Though female preaching has recurred over time, it has not had the same meaning in widely disparate settings. Ronald Knox's assertion that "from the Montanist movement onwards, the history of enthusiasm is largely a history of female emancipation" is epigrammatic but unenlightening.[10] It is tempting to see female preaching as an expression of an individualistic ethos. According to this theory, women seeking power within sectarian communities reflected the general breakdown of traditional authority in wider society. Such arguments are not totally without merit. During the Civil War period, as Keith Thomas has shown, female sectarian preaching was part of a general challenge to the established order, including that of the family.[11] But models of "possessive individualism" associated with industrial capitalism have invested the history of women and the family with a noisome bias; the acquisitive motivations attributed to women are patently exaggerated and anachronistic. Hence, one must proceed with caution when viewing the attitude of women in religion as instrumental, in effect forming a silhouette of men in the market economy. Such an interpretation fails to make sense of the many ways

[9] Olive Anderson, "Women Preachers in Mid-Victorian Britain: Some Reflexions on Feminism, Popular Religion and Social Change," *Historical Journal* 11 (1969): 469. Anderson focuses on women of the middle class who assumed a more private "respectable" role in leading church groups during the second half of the century.

[10] Ronald Knox, *Enthusiasm* (New York: Oxford University Press, 1950), p. 20, quoted in Keith Thomas, "Women and the Civil War Sects," *Past & Present* 13 (1958): 50.

[11] Thomas, "Women," passim.

INTRODUCTION

in which religion maintained old arrangements and values; indeed, this "modernized" view tends to undervalue the very world created and inhabited by women.

The involvement of women in religion helps us to shift our focus from the marketplace to the domestic sphere during the transition to early industrialism. The home did not always readily adapt to changes taking place in the public world of capitalism. In a study of the bourgeoises in northern France, Bonnie G. Smith has argued that the home became the locus of preindustrial values that were directly opposed to the march of progress. As industrialization forced the retreat of women from economic production, bourgeois mothers redirected their energies towards creating a separate, "natural" domestic world rooted in reproduction and womanhood. Through religion, women established a corrective to the excessive rationalism and individualism of the new industrial era.[12]

The world of women and domestic life could challenge the institutions and values articulated at the center of society. Smith rightly directs attention away from political and economic institutions to the diffused power within the relationships of women and their families. As bearers of cultural values and transmitters of class attitudes, women constituted a formidable force capable of massive reformist efforts. Their charitable activities, schools, and religious literature sought to shape the public sphere according to a design distinctly different from the utilitarian purposes of industrialists. Religion gave women effective means of extending their influence, in the form of a domestic and personal ideology, throughout the larger nineteenth-century world.[13]

In contrast to their French counterparts, middle-class Englishwomen promoted a personal ideology that was apparently more compatible with laissez-faire capitalism. Philanthropy often perpetuated old-style paternalism in new settings. Han-

[12] Bonnie G. Smith, *Ladies of the Leisure Class: The Bourgeoises of Northern France in the Nineteenth Century* (Princeton, N.J.: Princeton University Press, 1981).
[13] See, for example, Frank J. Prochaska, *Women and Philanthropy in Nineteenth-Century England* (Oxford: Clarendon Press, 1980).

nah More, "probably the most influential woman of her day"[14] as a result of her philanthropic work, zealously enforced a discipline suited to a quiescent work force. Were sectarian women preachers simply reinforcing the ideology of their masters and mistresses? Were their concerns, expressed in the familiar form of religious belief and behavior, the same as those of wealthier Victorian women? Female preachers reveal the important relationship between religion and the context of laboring life, for their appearance calls attention to alterations in the laboring household caused by economic and social change. Their different experiences as working women, wives, and mothers informed their roles as preachers. Here, the chronology of popular evangelicalism becomes significant: Methodist sectarianism, reaching its height between the years 1790 and 1850, provides an unmatched view of industrialization and the growth of capitalism in the countryside. As a home-based "cottage religion," its beliefs and practices were thoroughly implicated in new developments. Changes within the village agrarian economy, including the spread and decline of domestic industries, transformed relations forming the base of cottage religion. The expansion of towns and cities also influenced the spread of popular evangelicalism. The upheaval and migration, poverty and unemployment, solitude and family life of cottage evangelicals were part of a general transformation of English society. In helping to define new household arrangements, gender roles, and reproductive behavior, women preachers fashioned a unique domestic ideology grounded in working-class experience.

Despite the threat to their reputations and physical and material welfare, women preachers spoke publicly on a regular basis. Even in the opinion of sectarian leaders, who were wont to restrain overzealous female comrades for the sake of a fragile public image, the work of these women was an incontestable

[14] Ibid., p. 6. See also William Wilberforce, *A Practical View of the Prevailing Religious System of Professed Christians* (London, 1834), p. 54; and Laqueur, *Religion and Respectability*, esp. chap. 7.

necessity. In many ways, female preachers resembled their male counterparts: they were strong-willed, vociferous, meddling, and persistent in their work. But in other ways, they excelled: they overturned conventional standards of privacy, and, more important, propriety. In their "unnatural" pastoral role, women preachers brought the private lives of labor into public view. Their womanhood underscored demands for domestic security and traditional village accountability. Moreover, by breaking the rules, as it were, of an institution historically controlled by men, women preachers allied their sectarian cause with the general political and social unrest of the early Victorian period.

In the 1850s, the number of female preachers began to decline. Their dramatic rise and subsequent retreat reflected changes taking place in institutional religion and in the wider society. Cottage preaching flourished during a specific preindustrial phase of popular evangelicalism, when public and private converged within the domestic framework of laboring life. Inside the home, cottage religion borrowed and absorbed all kinds of popular belief and practice; once inside the chapel, this syncretism, along with the public role of women, declined. By mid-century, an established Victorian religion had reached full-blown maturity, and cottage religion was swept into the now respectable evangelical mainstream. The loss of a foundation in cottage and village life meant a loss of a basis of protest. The distinctive theology of popular preachers, rooted in the experiences of laboring life, became subsumed under deceptively similar but empty Victorian formulae. Angry and critical asceticism became pious abstinence; cottage solidarity became conservative domesticity. Most revealing of all, female assertiveness became unacceptable. The grievances of women and their families no longer reached the pulpit, but instead, were defined in private and personal terms. The domestic welfare of laborers, once considered a public concern, was now seen as the concern of Victorian individuals.

Cottage religion nevertheless survived, but economic and social developments transformed its public image. The upheavals of the first part of the nineteenth century had subsided by the 1850s: unemployment and migration had declined, political radicalism had temporarily receded, and rising prosperity offered a delayed reward for the difficult transition to factory industry. Sectarian Methodism evolved into a chapel-based denomination in many cities and towns, reflecting the gradual *embourgeoisement* of its membership. As these circumstances changed, popular preachers suggested fewer associations with plebeian culture. Whatever criticism or protest remained appeared in indirect and oblique form. Coming to the fore was a new generation of popular preachers who, as national or trans-Atlantic figures, reduced the rich experiences of their predecessors to simple common denominators.

The following chapters examine the emergence of cottage religion during the first half of the nineteenth century. I have avoided recounting the entire history of Methodist sectarianism, even though the sects provide the basis for cottage religion; I also have omitted discussion of church and chapel attendance, assuming that the reader, if interested, will look elsewhere for institutional religious history. Instead, I have focused upon the development of the domestic ideology so central to popular religion. Part I establishes the interconnection between popular culture and cottage religion and shows how that relationship led to the shaping of a domestic ideology of survival. Female preaching became an ideal vehicle for expressing this ideology. Part II elaborates on the role of women in rural society during the early years of Methodist sectarianism. The lives of female preachers in chapter six offer vivid illustrations of common people responding to dramatic economic and social change; their histories underline the corrosive effects of agrarian capitalism and industrialization on laboring families. Unemployment and migration brought rural women in contact with towns, and chapters seven and eight point ahead to the ways in which cottage evangelicals adapted religion to new settings. Part II concentrates on the preservative and resistant role of cottage religion in industrial towns, where domestic ideology became associated with village values

and independence from a new Victorian society. The movement from country to town did not spell the end of cottage
religion, however. The final case study of a Yorkshire fishing
village develops more general insights into popular religion
and historical change and suggests comparisons with other
places in other times.

PART I

THE POPULAR CHALLENGE TO ESTABLISHED RELIGION

ONE

Popular Evangelicalism in Historical Perspective

THE EVANGELICAL REVIVAL was "the result of the confluence of many tributaries" within the religious life of the eighteenth century.[1] The movement was international in scope and lasting in impact. Its most influential and well-known product was British Methodism; but John Wesley was only one of the several Anglican divines who, for as many reasons, experienced profound spiritual conversions and turned outward to carry their messages to others. A multitude of societies and sects rose from such beginnings, distinguished from seventeenth-century predecessors by an intensified interest in "evangelism on a wider front" and diminished concern for "niceties of creed, liturgy and church polity." Their simultaneous reaction against the rationalism and religious indifference of the age resulted in a widespread campaign to rekindle the spiritual life of the masses.[2]

A tradition of dissent also contributed to the impetus of the new evangelicalism. Though considerably weakened by world-weariness, dissent still inspired religious independence and a critique of English government and church in the eighteenth century. "Liberty of conscience was the one great value the common people had preserved from the Commonwealth," Ed-

[1] W. E. Gladstone, *Gleanings of Past Years* (1879), vii, 205, quoted in John Walsh, "Origins of the Evangelical Revival," *Essays in Modern English Church History*, G. V. Bennett and J. D. Walsh, eds. (New York: Oxford University Press, 1966), p. 135. Much of the following discussion of the Evangelical Revival is taken from Walsh's excellent study.

[2] Walsh, "Origins," p. 154; Alan D. Gilbert, *Religion and Society in Industrial England* (London: Longman, 1976), part 2.

ward Thompson has pointed out. "The countryside was ruled by the gentry, the towns by corrupt corporations, the nation by the corruptest corporation of all; but the chapel, the tavern and the home were their own." The Revolutionary era gave the democratic core of dissent new life; radical religious and moral principles once again animated reform movements. Just as dissenters changed into political radicals in the 1790s, so the poor expressed their discontent in a loosely organized millenarian movement. An undercurrent of religious enthusiasm was remindful of the Civil War years, when, as Hobbes observed, "Every man, nay, every boy and wench that could read English thought they spoke with God Almighty, and understood what he said."[3]

The growth of Methodism and New Dissent insured that the Church of England would never enjoy a monopoly of religious life. By the time of Wesley's death, the movement was destined to separate from the Established Church, despite the original intentions of its founder. When an internal struggle for the right to administer Holy Communion, which inevitably spelled schism, joined with a more general popular radicalism, continuance within the Church became impossible. The break signified more than a simple doctrinal difference. "Teachers of [established religion] . . . have already lost their hold on the public mind," one critic observed, "and they will lose it more and more."[4] As Methodism, and other forms of New Dissent, reached out to sectors of the population untouched by the Church, "a large competing religious culture" emerged as a challenge to the passive consensus underlying the social order. A new era of religious and social relations had come into being.[5]

[3] Quoted in Christopher Hill, *The Century of Revolution, 1603–1714* (New York: Norton, 1961), p. 173; Edward P. Thompson, *The Making of the English Working Class* (New York: Vintage Books, 1963), pp. 51–2.

[4] *A Treatise on the Causes which have contributed, and do contribute to the increase of Methodists and Dissenters* (Macclesfield, 1813), p. 37.

[5] Gilbert, *Religion and Society*, p. 51; W. R. Ward, *Religion and Society in England, 1790–1850* (New York: Schocken Books, 1973), pp. 28–9; Robert Currie, *Meth-*

Reform was also taking place within the Church of England; new-found piety and fervor inspired major philanthropic efforts and a concern for the poor. But unlike the Methodist movement, established Evangelicalism derived its leadership and style from the upper classes and strove to avoid all that Methodism emphasized. The Clapham Sect, probably the most famous group within the Church, decried current trends towards religious "enthusiasm." Feeling in religion, cautioned William Wilberforce, "resides in a man's own bosom, and shuns the observation of the multitude." A "practical," dutiful Christianity operated in the public sphere instead. The foremost task of religion was "to promote the preservation . . . of political communities"; Methodism, in contrast, was seen as a dangerous influence on the lower orders. Wilberforce's system of ethics and moral precepts depended on a strict social hierarchy: rules "regulat[ing] the conduct of the higher classes" would, in turn, reinforce the political order. For Evangelicals of the Church, religion gave the state security and conscience.[6]

Two conflicting trends thus appeared in the burgeoning evangelical movement of the late eighteenth century. One perpetuated the democratizing impulse of Wesley's spiritual revolution and appealed to the lower classes for initiative and direction. This popular evangelicalism struggled against the confinements of conventional institutional religion, often eschewing formal worship for spontaneous and heterodox practices. The other trend sought social harmony and political order through class-based morality, a strategy increasingly evident in Victorian institutional religion. Ironically, the drive towards hierarchical authority and propriety gradually dominated Wesleyan Methodism itself and divided the new-born denomination. The conservative element within Methodist

---

odism Divided: A Study in the Sociology of Ecumenicalism (London: Faber and Faber, 1968), pp. 28–31.

[6] Geoffrey Best, "The Evangelicals and the Established Church in the Early Nineteenth Century," *Journal of Theological Studies*, N.S., X (1959): 63–78; William Wilberforce, *A Practical View of the Prevailing Religious System of Professed Christians* (London, 1797), pp. 410–1; 399; 11.

leadership became more prominent after the death of Wesley in 1791, when the Connexion gravitated towards a more authoritarian government and slowly hardened into a hierarchical, church-like organization. Admittedly, its metamorphosis from sect to denomination took place over several decades and had much to do with institutional growth generated by rising membership. But during the years of public disorder and popular radicalism following the 1790s, connexional policy revealed a new determination, undiminishing in later years, to suppress and control popular religion. By the 1820s, the aims of Wesleyanism had changed "from feeding and guiding to teaching and ruling" its adherents.[7]

Rank-and-file followers were not always aware of the doctrinal and constitutional disputes taking place above them, but certain unmistakable changes aroused popular disapproval. In 1815, Wesleyan ministers were calling for higher salaries, and, in 1818, they adopted the previously shunned title of "Reverend." The *embourgeoisement* of the Wesleyan ministry figured frequently in the harangues of William Cobbett, whose keen eye for hypocrisy found the betrayal of principle and social origin offensive. "For many years," he railed,

> they were little better, in appearance, than beggars. Their places of preaching were under trees, in hovels, barns and other buildings very little better than barns. For a long while, they not only possessed no political influence; but they were scarcely protected from mud and rotten eggs flying from the hands of the bigotted or the ignorant. By degrees, they crept upwards. . . . They quitted the tree, the hovel and the barn; and saw themselves elevated in elegant pulpits and stately temples.[8]

[7] W. R. Ward, "Popular Religion and the Problem of Control, 1790–1830," *Popular Religion and Practice*, Studies in Church History, vol. 8, G. J. Cuming and Derek Baker, eds. (Cambridge: Cambridge University Press, 1972), p. 255; Currie, *Methodism Divided*, pp. 48–53; Bernard Semmel, *The Methodist Revolution* (New York: Basic Books, 1973).

[8] Cobbett's *Weekly Political Register*, January 13, 1821, p. 83.

Though maintaining links with the poor, Wesleyans comprised a more prosperous body of followers by 1830. Connexional leadership came to resemble the ministry of established institutionalized religions and thus abandoned one of the original goals of the early movement. Followers wishing to revive "primitive Methodism" would have to look elsewhere for support.[9]

More than a half-dozen groups broke away from Wesleyanism between 1795 and 1815 and chose to retain, at least for several decades, a pre- or semi-institutional form. Tension between ministers and people echoed the struggle between Wesleyans and the Church: once the right to administer the sacrament was established, controversy over *who* should administer it erupted. Lay leaders and congregations, angered by what they saw as the growing tyranny and arrogance of high-ranking ministers, pressed for greater authority within Methodist societies. As lay preachers discovered the power of their own appeal among the masses, particularly in rural areas, secession became inevitable. The Independent Methodists broke away in 1796, the Methodist New Connexion in 1797, the Primitive Methodists in 1812, and the Bible Christians in 1815, to name only the major associations. Many other groups separated on account of localized conflicts over chapel building, finances, and means of worship. No single sect attained the numerical strength of Wesleyan Methodism, and combined, the various new groups hardly amounted to half the Wesleyan total of 500,000 in 1851. Their significance was nonetheless great: the laborers and artisans making up the overwhelming majority of membership also directed the sects' activities and thus made a unique contribution to religious and social history.[10]

While Methodist sectarianism represented a reaction against Wesleyanism as it strove to make peace with Church and state,

[9] Edward P. Stigant, "Methodism and the Working Class, 1760–1821" (M.A. thesis, Keele, 1968); Ward, *Religion and Society*, esp. chap. 6; Thompson, *Making of the English Working Class*, p. 397.

[10] Currie, *Methodism Divided*, pp. 54–6.

it was more than just a product of church history. Religion played a large part in village culture, and as economic and social changes influenced the lives of laborers, attitudes towards church and chapel became significant in new ways. Antipathy towards established religion indicated a rejection of existing power relations within nation and village; adherence to a popular evangelicalism outside Church and chapel could mean a desire for self-expression or an alternative vision of community and family relations. The locus of truly popular religious activity was the home, where generational, seasonal, and personal changes governed practice and belief. Domestic religion, more than anything else, distinguished the sects from institutional Victorian evangelicalism.

The centrality of the domestic sphere alone was not unique to Methodist sectarianism. A new domestic ideology pervaded the prescriptive literature and philanthropic ventures of the day. Late eighteenth-century Evangelicalism set the stage for Victorian domesticity, emphasizing the sanctity of the nuclear family and home as a model for society. In her prolific advice to the female sex, Hannah More elevated women to the position of moral and social guardians of the family, and advocated their education and activity as crucial support for an authoritarian family and state. John Wesley dwelt upon metaphors of family and household to represent an ideal community of believers. But the domesticity of popular religion differed sharply from these notions. While established Evangelicals designated the home a cloistered "place apart" where carefully prescribed restrictions were in force, particularly with regard to women, popular religion recognized the *domus* as part of a wider universe. The household was the locus of economic and social relations intrinsic to laboring life, and no distinction between home and work, or work and life, obtained. Women, furthermore, derived modes of behavior and power in sectarian Methodism from their place within and outside the home. Primitive Methodists like Elizabeth Moore (b. ca. 1788), a Lincolnshire local preacher for forty years, managed cottage societies and evangelized while working to support their families. Moore, a widow, was no fragile Victorian woman, but was known instead for what her obituary euphemistically called her "considerable force of character." Popular evangelicals inhabited a world far from the middle-class model, and they tailored their religion to meet the need for hard effort to survive in a harsh environment.[11]

The sects adopted and expanded the domestic practices of early Methodism. Before Wesleyan Methodism became a distinct movement, houses and cottages had taken the place of chapels, providing services that otherwise were nonexistent in many areas. Necessity rather than choice usually dictated location. Preaching took place in barns, dye-houses, sheds, abandoned rooms, and open spaces outdoors when private homes were not available. In some instances, such unlikely places also shielded worshippers from local persecution. The improvised arrangements that preceded chapelbuilding depended upon management by followers as much as by leaders and preachers. What these "cottage societies" lacked in security and status, they gained in appeal as local-based, democratically run associations. Without exception, the founders of the sects gained experience and confidence from early affiliation with Methodist cottage societies.[12]

Sectarians were quick to recognize all the advantages of location outside church and chapel. Domestic preaching services incorporated local and private affairs into religion in a way that institutionalized services could not. In weekday serv-

[11] "Memoir of Mrs. Elizabeth Moore," *Primitive Methodist Magazine*, 1870, p. 300; Walter E. Houghton, *The Victorian Frame of Mind, 1830–1870* (New Haven: Yale University Press, 1957), p. 343; John Wesley, "On Friendship and the World," *Sermons*, ii, pp. 526–7, quoted in Gilbert, *Religion and Society*, p. 88; Hannah More, *Strictures on the Modern System of Female Education*, 2 vols. (London, 1799), 1:7.

[12] W. J. Townsend, H. B. Workman, G. Eayrs, eds., *A New History of Methodism*, 2 vols. (London, 1909), Book 1; George W. Dolbey, *The Architectural Expression of Methodism* (London: Epworth Press, 1964), chap. 2; Leslie F. Church, *The Early Methodist People* (New York: The Philosophical Library, 1949), p. 30; John Walsh, "Methodism at the End of the Eighteenth Century," *History of the Methodist Church in Great Britain*, II (London: Epworth Press, 1965).

ices, when itinerants were not scheduled, local preachers took charge and seldom restricted the range of concerns addressed in their sermons. Unlike itinerants, they possessed intimate knowledge of their listeners' lives, and, in domestic settings, neither preachers nor followers could ignore the material circumstances surrounding them. An account of an early Wesleyan domestic service in Slaithwaite, a weaving village in the West Riding, revealed how much contemporary experiences influenced cottage religion:

> The preachings used to be in the weekdays on the Wednesday nights at some brother's or sister's house. This particular one for John [o' Charlotte's] was at Clough House, in a large roomy house, with the furniture and work-things all put back, and forms added to sit on. On this occasion, after duly opening with singing and prayer, and a lesson, the time of the sermon came, which was "Owe thou no man anything"; but, do what he could, our friend John could get no forrarder, and after struggling with it a long time with no better result, old Anthony Hoyle gave out a hymn. A prayer was said, then the pipes were brought out, and in the discussion which followed some one said, "Whatever did ta tak yond text for, John, because it is unkindly said that tha owes Jim Clay some money, and he cannot get paid.[13]

The story, however inaccurate in detail, conveys a sense of religion far different from the institutional Wesleyanism evolving in towns and some villages by the late eighteenth century. Unprofessional preaching, in noninstitutional surroundings, encompassed the immediate, tangible, and private aspects of life. Cottage religion shared a great deal with folk traditions in its use of local habit and material concerns, and, like village

[13] John Sugden, *Slaithwaite Notes of the Past and Present*, 3rd ed. (Manchester, 1905), p. 133. Charlotte was John's wife; his nickname could be a reference to the rather forbidding power of her personality. According to Sugden, Charlotte was "remarkable for her short cuts at truth, religious or otherwise" (p. 132).

customs, it could express antagonism as well as unanimity. While learned theology lost this immediacy in abstraction and elocution, cottage religion remained rooted in rural community life through concrete language and local dialect.

Besides preaching services in the home, early Wesleyanism had established the precedent of cottage class meetings. Wesley himself recognized the importance of small independent societies in carrying out the work begun by scarce itinerants. Cottage-based class meetings originated in 1742 as a means of financially sustaining a society in Norfolk, but it was not long before members discovered other, more spiritual benefits arising from the shared enterprise. Under the guidance of an appointed class leader, members related personal experiences and problems in order to deepen their understanding of daily life. The meetings promoted a feeling of spiritual equality. They were less like "courts of inquiry" (as Methodist band meetings were) and more "like family circles."[14] Indeed, meetings often took place in the homes of class leaders, men and women who assumed a role that combined household with spiritual responsibilities. The ability to set a tone of domestic intimacy, to elicit private reflections, and to generalize from the particulars of worldly circumstances made the class leader a prophet among his or her neighbors. Together members and leaders eschewed impersonal formalities and developed styles of worship suited to local needs.

Cottage meetings counterbalanced preaching services with their dynamic, nearly chaotic quality. While preaching by a visiting itinerant demanded some formality and deference to the spoken word, prayer and class meetings strove to avoid the implicit hierarchy of "sermonizing." Instead, members prayed freely and responded spontaneously to the revelations of others. During prayer at meetings of "the true Old Methodist stamp," a Yorkshire historian recalled, "others would respond to almost every sentence" so that "at times it was

[14] Church, *Methodist People*, p. 156.

difficult to discover who was praying."[15] Cottage meetings were, like revivalist preaching services, notoriously noisy. The full flavor of democracy rose in part from the meeting place itself; even the humblest of members could host the gathering, and when an old farm laborer or a village blacksmith offered his home, anything was possible.[16] A Lincolnshire clergyman complained that it was difficult to stay abreast of "those more private assemblies, which are generally known by the name of classed [sic] meetings, and at which those persons preside who do not take upon themselves the name of Teachers or Preachers."[17]

"Few, who have been truly awakened to a sense of religion, will be long content without having, if possible, the ordinances of the Gospel in their own neighborhood, and a church in their own house." That prophesy, made by early Wesleyans, became realized to a far greater extent within the Methodist sects of the nineteenth century. Cottage religion was the centerpiece of a new popular evangelicalism spreading throughout the countryside by 1820. "It was a common saying in some places in those days," recalled one sectarian, " 'Only let the Bible Christians get into the hearts of the people, and they will soon get into their houses.' " Followers often preferred the atmosphere of cottage meetings to that of the chapel; many Yorkshire societies, still based in cottages decades after their founding date, gave ample evidence of this.[18] Cottage services engendered a more flexible, intimate mood than most chapel worship. When "the pipes were brought out," ritual easily turned to neighborly talk. Women, moreover, eagerly took

[15] John Sykes, *Slawit in the 'Sixties. Reminiscences of the moral, social, and industrial life of Slaithwaite* (Huddersfield, 1926), pp. 246–7, quoted from J. Sykes, *Life of William Schofield* (Huddersfield, 1882).

[16] For example, see J. Jackson Wray, *Nestleton Magna. A Story of Yorkshire Methodism* (London, 1885), pp. 66ff.

[17] Ward, *Religion and Society*, p. 51.

[18] "Memoir of Luke Barton," *Bible Christian Magazine*, 1880, p. 549; William Jessop, *An Account of Methodism in Rossendale and the Neighbourhood* (Manchester, 1881), p. 41; see also John Lyth, *Glimpses of Early Methodism in York and the Surrounding District* (York, 1885), esp. pp. 292–3.

advantage of new leadership opportunities offered by cottage religion. While the Wesleyan administration, and indeed the leadership of all other nineteenth-century religions, remained an exclusively male prerogative, women assumed prominent and vocal roles in sectarian Methodism. During the industrial transformation of England, both men and women recognized the valuable potential of cottage meetings: through religion of the household, popular evangelicals could mobilize efforts to preserve a way of life as well as a way of worship.

TWO

Domesticity and Survival

DURKHEIM OBSERVED that religious man's "rites are, in part, means destined to aid him in imposing his will upon the world."[1] The symbols and rites of popular evangelicalism, like those of all religions, were rooted in the material circumstances that surrounded the participants. In many respects, this faith was typical in its concentration upon space, time, and nature; its specificity emerges, however, in the ways in which followers idealized ordinary activity and rendered sacred the ordinary features of laboring life. The imagery of their hymns, sermons, and journals provides a symbolic language through which the domestic and social world of popular evangelicalism becomes accessible. By elevating domestic space, cottage evangelicals found a way of combatting physical and economic hardship while sanctifying their struggle to survive.

In expressing the laboring experience, popular evangelicalism dwelt upon two principal themes: the sanctification of the home and the embarkation upon a spiritual pilgrimage. Worldly travails thus gained coherence and significance through religion. These subjects had been addressed by ancient and primitive religions and were proven to be rich in symbolic potential. "Even the most habitual gesture," Mircea Eliade has pointed out,

> can signify a spiritual act. The road and walking can be transfigured into religious values, for every road can symbolize the "road of life," and any walk a "pilgrimage," a perigrination to the Center of the World. If possessing a house implies having assumed a stable situation in the world, those who have renounced their houses, the pil-

[1] Emile Durkheim, *The Elementary Forms of the Religious Life*, Joseph Ward Swain, trans. (1915; New York: Free Press, 1965), p. 105.

28

grims and ascetics, proclaim by their "walking," by their constant movement, their desire to leave the world, their refusal of any worldly situation. The house is a "nest," and, as the *Pañcavimsha Brāhmana* says (XI, 15, 1), the "nest" implies flocks, children, and a "home"; in a word, it symbolizes the world of the family, of society, of getting a living.[2]

Sectarian Methodism similarly transformed displacement into religious virtue. Its principal doctrines, illustrated vividly in its sermons and hymns, alternated between idealization of the home and renunciation of material satisfaction. Each denomination produced its own hymnology, which included many original hymns added to standard numbers culled from Wesley and Watts. These hymns were quite literally songs of experience, or, as one Primitive Methodist historian explained, "of an experimental nature—experience set to metre and rhyme." The themes of domestic security and pilgrimage, common to most hymnology, appeared in a multitude of forms:

I am a Christian pilgrim, a sinner saved by grace,
I travel to Mount Zion, my final resting-place;
Through many a storm and trial by Help divine I'm come,
And soon shall rest for ever in heaven, my happy home.
  Sing glory, hallelujah, the Lord is with us still,
  The little cloud increases that rose upon Mow Hill.[3]

The Female Revivalist hymnal included another statement of this theme:

I am a Pilgrim here below,
  A stranger wand'ring to and fro:
The world's a wilderness to me,
  There's nothing here but vanity.
[verse four]
I'm trav'ling to my native home,

[2] *The Sacred and the Profane* (New York: Harcourt Brace Jovanovich, 1959), pp. 183–4.
[3] Frederick B. Paston, "Introduction," in Arthur Patterson, *From Hayloft to Temple* (London, 1903), x.

With many a weary step I come,
Through much distress I slowly move
To my eternal rest above.[4]

And the Primitive Methodists and Female Revivalists shared
yet another:

We seek a glorious rest above,
  A land of endless light,
A heaven of happiness and love,
  A city out of sight.

We seek a house not made with hands
  Where pleasures never die,
Which on a sure foundation stands,
  Eternal in the sky.[5]

The hymns disclosed images of unreality as well as disguised
truths. What did not exist—material security and stability—
appeared in an idealized form. Heaven thus became domestic
and changeless, while earthly existence presented "storms,"
"battles," "snares," and untold miseries along the way. No
hymn was complete without literal, descriptive verses that
counterbalanced ethereal images. Rather than withdrawing
into an imaginary world, sectarian hymnology echoed rhythms
underlying material life.

Through these images and rhythms, hymns *dramatized* laboring life. The emphasis is important, for followers were
acutely aware of a process unfolding in each hymn. The idea
of a pilgrimage suggested change and offered promise, not
necessarily in the afterlife (though this belief was crucially
important), but in the "days of grace" that came through association.[6] The "vale of tears" and sexual repression so often

---

[4] *A Selection of Hymns for the Female Revivalists* (Leeds, 1828), No. 54.

[5] *A Selection of Hymns for the Use of the Female Revivalists* (Dewsbury, 1824),
No. 184; I. Dorricott and T. Collins, *Lyric Studies* (London, [1891]), p. 219. "It
is a valued hymn," the editors noted, ". . . but it does not seem to have got
beyond a denominational circle."

[6] See, for example, Primitive Methodist and Bible Christian hymn "Haste

stressed in recent interpretations of hymns were mom
images within a longer process. The nineteenth-century ruɪ ɐ.
world depended upon regeneration; images of sowing and
reaping, rising and falling, breath and blood referred to familiar repetitions. Production and reproduction figured large
in the minds of plebeian sectarians. "For the Lord's work is to
subdue the earth and renew it," wrote Hugh Bourne, leader
of the Primitive Methodists, "and man has fellowship in this
work by faith." What had been, perhaps, the sexual repression
of a John Wesley became the ebb and flow of lifeblood for
thousands of laboring women and men.[7]

At the center of the sectarian world was the *domus*, the household which served as a center of family life and work. Religion
reflected the wide variety of ways in which the household
served as an organizational unit in the laboring world.[8] Like

---

again, ye days of grace": Haste again, ye days of grace, / When assembled in
one place; / Signs and wonders mark'd the hour! / All were fill'd and spoke
with power; / Hands uplifted, eyes o'erflowed, / Hearts enlarged, self destroy'd!
/ All things common now we'll prove, / All our common stock be love.

Hugh Bourne, *A General Collection of Hymns and Spiritual Songs, For Camp
Meetings, Revivals,* &c. (Bingham, 1819), No. 13.

[7] John Walford, *Memoirs of Hugh Bourne,* W. Antliff, ed. (London, 1855), p.
236. Cf. Thompson, *Making of the English Working Class,* pp. 369–74; Michael
R. Watts, *The Dissenters* (Oxford: Clarendon Press, 1978), pp. 418–21.

[8] "The interdependence of work and residence, of household labor needs,
subsistence requirements, and family relationships constituted the 'family economy.'" Louise A. Tilly and Joan W. Scott, *Women, Work and Family* (New York:
Holt, Rinehart, and Winston, 1978), p. 12. This definition of the household
economy also demarcates the basis of peasant society. As Teodor Shanin explained in his work on Russian peasantry, "The household's production activities primarily consisted of strenuous efforts by its members to make ends meet,
i.e., to feed the family and to meet dues and taxes. Serious rural underemployment (both total and seasonal) was partly tempered by peasants' supple-
mentary employment in crafts and trades. . . . The consumption-determined
aims, the traditional methods of production, the use of family labour, the low
marketability of the product and the lack of checking and control by systematic
bookkeeping in money terms made the peasant household a production unit
very different from a 'rational' capitalistic enterprise." From "A Russian Peasant
Household at the Turn of the Century," in *Peasants and Peasant Societies,* Teodor
Shanin, ed. (Harmondsworth: Penguin, 1971), p. 32.

the *domus* of thirteenth-century Cathars, the sectarian household earned its place in religious life through its vital connection to all aspects of daily activity. In cottage religion, as in rural industry, family and society were one, and religion helped to sustain the organizational basis through times of stress. Religion rendered sacred and public many aspects of the laboring household: the interdependence of family members; the equalization of work roles of men, women, and children; distinctive rhythms of work and leisure; and a resistance to middle-class culture, which threatened behavior necessary for economic survival. In its foremost tenets of equality of believers and solidarity of the faithful, sectarianism reaffirmed the culture of the cottage economy.

From its meeting place on the hearth, cottage religion absorbed from the household as much as it returned to the community. Syncretism became crucial to the special history of this "religion of the hearth." Welsh Methodism, which often functioned as a folk religion, sheds light on the phenomenon. By interacting with household structures, religion strengthened the "older foundations of Welsh culture" and "renewed the life of *cefn gwlad*, the dispersed neighbourhood." Rotating from house to house, gatherings pulled together scattered small farmers, whose social and economic existence became increasingly marginal in Welsh life in the nineteenth century. Religion also gave the Welsh language new legitimacy and importance in the face of a growing industrial and urban culture. Similarly, sectarian Methodism conferred official status upon informal associations and elevated everyday features of English laboring life that were under assault by changes in the agrarian economy. The attempts of marginal people to preserve domestic and personal relations in their work gained cosmic significance. The sanctity of the household—its invulnerability, autonomy, and strategic importance—was a continuing theme in both religion and work.[9]

9 I owe thanks to John Walsh for pointing out this comparison. Alwyn D. Rees, *Life in a Welsh Countryside* (Cardiff: University of Wales Press, 1951), pp.

Sectarian religion thus strengthened and preserved the *domus*. Followers articulated beliefs rooted in their domestic and family lives, and, in doing so, they shaped a cohesive theology. Sermons aimed at reinforcing the ties that bound families, neighbors, and congregations together. "And I will raise up for them a plant of renown." (Ezekiel 34:29) "Rejoice, O young man, in thy youth; and let thy heart cheer thee in the days of thy youth, and walk in the ways of thine heart, and in the sight of thine eyes: but know thou, that for all these things God will bring thee into judgment." (Eccles. 11:9) "Then shall the righteous shine forth as the sun in the kingdom of their Father." (Matt. 13:43)[10] Like most religious bodies, sectarian Methodism strove to secure its future through a younger generation. But the context of cottage religion rendered this traditional concern particularly urgent, as changes in the rural economy and industrial capitalism presented declining economic opportunity and the necessity of migration.

Religion redefined private, domestic concerns as public and political issues. Every aspect of behavior and thought, from the personal and domestic to the public and communal, became significant. By definition, sectarianism required a thorough, uncompromising commitment that made no distinction between inward and outward or private and public. Followers scrutinized themselves and each other in fear that a lapse in one sphere might infect the other. The selfishness of individuals, for example, might extend to their families and communities. The main goal of the gospel, according to the Female Revivalists of Leeds, was to "counteract this [selfish] tendency."

129–30; Trefor M. Owen, "Chapel and Community in Glan-llyn, Merioneth," *Welsh Rural Communities*, Elwyn Davies and Alwyn D. Rees, eds. (Cardiff: University of Wales Press, 1962), pp. 185–248; E. T. Davies, *Religion in the Industrial Revolution in South Wales* (Cardiff: University of Wales Press, 1965).

[10] Martha Williams, *Memoirs of the Life and Character of Ann Carr* (Leeds, 1841), pp. 57–8; Hugh Bourne's sermon to children, reprinted in John Simpson, *Recollections of the Late Rev. Hugh Bourne* (London, 1859), pp. 15–7; Jane Garbutt, *Reminiscences of the Early Days of Primitive Methodism in Hull* (Hull, 1886), p. 31. See also "Family Hymn," *Primitive Methodist Magazine* [hereafter *PMM*], 1821, p. 286.

Hypocrisy was the quintessential crime against sectarian authenticity. "Mere professors" of religion sometimes appeared religious, but in truth, "the Self is too prominent; either [in] Self-conceit or Self-interest." "Their religion," continued one critic, "seems more for shew than use. If you catch them off their guard in private, they are not the same men that they are in public." Sectarians could not tolerate such two-sidedness.[11]

The practices of sectarianism, as much as the beliefs, rendered public the private world of cottagers. Followers were obliged to articulate their concerns at every opportunity. "Then they that feared the Lord, spake often one to another" (Malachi 3:16–7) formed the basis of a sermon that decisively converted a mining village, and for good reason. The networks of gossip, neighborly favors, courtship, family, and employment readily assimilated sectarianism.[12] Circuits and societies within Primitive Methodism and Bible Christianity depended upon family networks to extend their missions; the societies, in turn, kept distant kin in touch and facilitated the migration that became so commonplace during the first half of the nineteenth century. The public activity and speech of sectarians represented much more than the mere profession of piety. Religion reenacted important family and community activities and rituals that specific economic changes had undermined.[13]

Through their role in the household economy, high status and power accrued to women. As Michelle Zimbalist Rosaldo has argued from cross-cultural evidence, the status of women is lowest when "a firm differentiation between domestic and public spheres" isolates women and also devalues the household, but highest when "neither sex claims much authority and the focus of social life itself is the home."[14] By forcing

[11] "Apostacy in Professors of Religion," *PMM*, 1819, p. 112.
[12] "Remembrance of Primitive Methodism in Weardale," *PMM*, 1882, pp. 525–6. See also Gerald Sider, "Christmas Mumming and the New Year in Outport Newfoundland," *Past & Present* 71 (1976): 102–25.
[13] See Part II below.
[14] Michelle Zimbalist Rosaldo, "Women, Culture and Society: A Theoretical

"public" economic activity into the domestic realm, cottage industry obscured the division between public and private. Necessity demanded more equal work roles and sometimes eliminated the sexual division of labor. As cottage industry expanded into the countryside and changes in landholding dispossessed cottagers, men often had to "return to the household" to continue working. The domestic sphere became central to survival. As "the vanguard of the peasant household industries," women contributed essential labor power, management, and reproductive capacities to the cottage economy.[15] It was only natural that they should interpret and speak for this domestic culture through religion.

Empowered by pressing necessity, women cottagers adopted brave and sometimes brazen stances in the "plebeian public" arena of religion. The contrast to contemporary religious and social mores struck observers all over Europe as shocking. "Women and men [cottagers] . . . frequently smoke on their way to church and the sacrilegious sort of people do so even during the sermon," a critic noted in nineteenth-century Zurich.[16] The autonomy of cottage culture easily led to antinomianism; sexual and moral rebellion became an integral part of plebeian culture as it interacted with bourgeois capitalism. The female preachers of sectarian Methodism similarly rejected standards of proper public behavior belonging to respectable religion. The boundary between home and church did not exist for them. Through sectarian Methodism, they were able to reestablish the age-old relationship between production for survival and religion.

The title "mother in Israel," bestowed upon females who showed exemplary courage and devotion to the cause, pointed

Overview," *Women, Culture and Society*, Michelle Zimbalist Rosaldo and Louise Lamphere, eds. (Stanford: Stanford University Press, 1974), p. 36.

[15] K. Wittfogel, *Wirtschaft und Gesellschaft Chinas* (Leipzig, 1931), p. 656, quoted in Peter Kriedte, Hans Medick, Jürgen Schlumbohn, *Industrialization before Industrialization*, Studies in Modern Capitalism (Cambridge: Cambridge University Press, 1981), p. 62.

[16] H. Strehler, *Beiträge zur Kulturgeschichte der Zürcher Landschafte* (Phil. Diss., Zürich, 1934), p. 37, quoted in Kriedte, *Industrialization*, n. 158, p. 248.

to the importance of women in sectarian Methodism. The domestic allusion called up images of nurturer and protector, provider and healer; like religious ritual itself, it linked together spiritual and domestic spheres. Spiritual mothers were often witness to or responsible for the conversion of souls. Hence, women preachers sometimes earned the title through their evangelical successes. Other women became noted for their hospitality and assistance in particularly hard-pressed mission areas. In cottage religion, where settings had such a decisive influence upon the content and meaning of worship, these women shaped the development of new societies. A "mother in Israel" was far more distinguished than the ordinary "Sister," a form of address applied to every female sectarian; and the fact that no analogous "Father" title existed (all men were "Brothers") underscored the importance and power ascribed only to women.

More than in any other form of contemporary religion, women assumed an active, public role in sectarian Methodism. How, then, did this role conform to a maternal image? Christian religion traditionally reserved a place for women in the role of virgin/mother, an image that Protestantism literally destroyed with the Reformation. Sectarian Methodism revived the model but gave it a radical "new" meaning by reaching back to the Old Testament. Few women of the Old Testament, in fact, found their primary role in procreation. Rachel Adler has pointed out that many leading female figures, such as Rachael, Rebecca, and Sarah, were long barren; others, such as Eve and Lilith, were rebels who were more destructive than creative. The four mothers of the Old Testament (Sarah, Rebecca, Rachael, and Leah) found their calling through working alongside their chieftain husbands. There they assumed equality and strength as public counsellors, nurturing protectors, and inspired speakers. As Adler explains, the two single Biblical references to "a mother in Israel" occur in relation to this extra-familial leadership role. Both contexts ascribe a societal significance to the word "maternal."[17]

[17] "A Mother in Israel: Aspects of the Mother Role in Jewish Myth," *Beyond*

The best known reference occurs in Judges 5:6–7, in the Song of Deborah:

> In the days of Shamgar the son of Anath, In the days of Jael, the highways were unoccupied, and the travellers walked through byways. The inhabitants of the villages ceased, they ceased in Israel, until that I Deborah arose, that I arose a mother in Israel.

As a military leader, Deborah rescued the entire nation of Israel; both aspects of her role contradict the unaggressive and private nature of women in conventional nineteenth-century religion. More important, the epithet calls attention to the frequent use of Old Testament imagery in sectarianism. The "Hebraism of old Testament preaching" common to working-class sects "made all who took to it like the ancient prophets a stiff-necked people unwilling to bow down in the House of Rimmon."[18] Like the tribes of Israel, Methodist sectarians were uprooted in turbulent times; they also conceived of their mission as a combative struggle for survival, and women often assumed command.

A second Biblical use of "mother in Israel" lends another equally important dimension to the sectarian image. In II Samuel 20:1, a wise woman of the city of Avel of Bet Maacah rebuked the attacking armies of David with the words: "Thou seekest to destroy a city and a mother in Israel: why wilt thou swallow up the inheritance of the Lord?" In this context, the phrase referred to a place that was offering refuge (to an enemy of David), and it also suggested a relationship to "metropolis, or mother city."[19] Sectarian Methodism similarly sanctified a place, the home, which offered refuge to a besieged people. The combined imagery of motherhood and preserved territory represented perfectly the sectarian ideal of domesticity and the family.

Androcentrism, American Academy of Religion, Rita M. Gross, ed. (Missoula, Montana: Scholars Press, 1977), pp. 237–68. The following interpretation owes much to Adler's insights into this title.

[18] Eric J. Hobsbawm, *Primitive Rebels* (New York: Norton, 1959), p. 139.

[19] Adler, "A Mother in Israel," p. 247.

The ideal of sectarian domesticity came alive in the careers of female preachers. Elizabeth Gorse Gaunt, a Derbyshire local preacher, combined the characteristics of spiritual pilgrim and beneficent mother. Born in 1777 at Mackworth, near Mercaston, Derbyshire, Gaunt apparently came from a destitute family of agricultural laborers. She does not appear to have had any schooling, and owing to the monopoly of the Established Church at Mackworth, she remained "unacquainted with God, a stranger to conversion, and to those consolations which true religion affords." At "twelve or thirteen," Gaunt lost both parents; her unhappiness and "troubles increased" when she married an "unsteady" man some time later. The couple eventually moved to Hollington, an open parish and a notorious rural slum. Economic misery pervaded the place. In the midst of material hardship, Hollington provided the uncertain advantage of religious freedom. There Gaunt encountered Primitive Methodist missionaries, and soon "her mind was enlightened, her judgment informed, [and] her soul converted to God." Educated only by unremitting deprivation, she soon began "preach[ing] the unsearchable riches of Christ."[20]

Elizabeth Gaunt's experiences as laborer, mother, and wife provided the substance of her religious teachings; her new role grew out of her domestic circumstances, and she became the maternal pastor so special to cottage religion. "I . . . do not remember ever visiting her without being edified by her pious and motherly conversation," Hugh Bourne, founder of the Primitive Methodist Connexion, recalled at the time of her death. In conversation as well as in sermons, Gaunt translated her mundane struggle for survival into a holy striving for sectarian sainthood. Her life became a religious parable, a lesson in rewards granted to the faithful:

> . . . her family increasing and her husband remaining unsteady, she was reduced to such extreme poverty, that, in

[20] "Memoir of Elizabeth Gaunt," *PMM*, 1826, p. 138; *P.O. Directory*, 1855, p. 105; John Farey, *A General View of the Agriculture and Minerals of Derbyshire*, 3 vols. (London, 1811–17), 3:195.

her distress, she was driven into the fields, with her children by the hand, to partake of such fruits as the hedges produced; for which she used to fall down and return God thanks.

Her testimony included a miracle set in contemporary Hollington:

On one occasion, being so reduced as to have no food to supply the wants of hunger, her children crying for bread, she applied by prayer, to the Lord, who hath said, "Thy bread shall be given, and the water shall be sure." And, while engaged in prayer, it was as though a voice spoke to her, "Go to thy potatoe piece, thou hast plenty of potatoes." She answered, "How can this be, Lord, seeing they have been so lately set?" She applied to the Lord again, by prayer, and received the same answer. At length she went to see; and, to her surprise, found plenty. She brought some home and boiled them for herself and her family, and having asked a blessing, she said, "O how the Lord fills my soul with love to him!"

In place of loaves and fishes, Elizabeth's Biblical type revelation came in the shape of the commonplace potato.[21]

Women, more often than men, engaged in sacred ritual pertaining to food. Their familial and social roles required involvement in the production, preparation, and distribution of sustenance that naturally encouraged such acts. But more important to the rendering of food as sacred was the link between spirituality and physicality pungently experienced by women during their life cycles. Physical maturation, menstruation, procreation, and lactation impressed upon women an immediate sense of life and death, and hence, of the presence of the supernatural in daily life. Early Christian theology stressed a similar connection between the physical nature of woman and the flesh of Christ, a teaching which gave rise among women to widespread fasting and feasting as a means

[21] "Remarks by Hugh Bourne," *PMM*, 1826, pp. 139–40.

of mystical union with God. Though Protestantism had abandoned many formal rituals of Catholicism, sectarian religions often revived these practices in order to achieve higher forms of spirituality. Unmarried female preachers frequently expressed the wish to sever all ties to food; but Elizabeth Gaunt, as mother and wife, turned to prayer for the multiplication of provisions. Indeed, as a "mother in Israel," she searched for manna that would aid in maintaining her people.[22]

Elizabeth Gaunt's testimony conveyed a special message to laboring women. In harvesting potatoes and gleaning in open fields, Gaunt engaged in what Olwen Hufton has called an "economy of expedients." During times of financial hardship, poor working families devised strategies aimed at achieving a subsistence income; family members combined wages from assorted jobs, payments in kind, and anything obtained through begging and stealing in order to get by. As principal guardian of children and the household, the mother of the family "became the pivotal force" of such strategies: "She organized the family for the purpose of living on its wits." Primitive Methodism provided another strategy that contributed towards an economy of expedients and likewise thrust women into a central position in the family.[23]

Through religion, women found ideological support and inspiration for their campaign against economic defeat. Doctrines promoting family prayer, strong family ties, and education influenced their attitudes towards their spouses and children. One female preacher, Hannah Howe (b. 1811), of Stoney Middleton, converted to Primitive Methodism after hearing a preacher exhort his followers to domestic solidarity using Luke 11:21:

> When the strong man fully armed guardeth his court, his goods are in peace.

[22] For the importance of food in the religious practices of women, see Carolyn Bynum, "Holy Feast and Holy Fast: Food Motifs in the Piety of Medieval Women," unpublished paper.

[23] Olwen Hufton, "Women and the Family Economy in Eighteenth-Century France," *French Historical Studies* 9 (1975): 19.

Religion became an instrument of persuasion and even compulsion in the hands of women who sought domestic security. Practices that were beneficial for the religious society also aided the family. Preachers cited scriptural precedents for family prayer that depicted a religious community at its most fundamental level of organization:

> For I know him, that he will command his children and his household after him, and they shall keep the way of the Lord, to do justice and judgment; that the Lord may bring upon Abraham that which he hath spoken of him. [Genesis 18:19]
>
> And if it seem evil unto you to serve the Lord, choose you this day whom ye will serve; whether the gods which your fathers served that were on the other side of the flood, or the gods of the Amorites, in whose land ye dwell; but as for me and my house, we will serve the Lord. [Joshua 24:15]

Their aim of consolidating the family also sheds a different light upon Primitive Methodist attitudes towards child rearing. Preachers (particularly women preachers) were not only concerned with denominational survival and the maintenance of working-class culture when they advocated Sunday School training and careful guidance of children. The language and tone of articles like "A Treatise on the Duty of Parents" suggest an urgent need for supportive relationships between parents and children; such ties could prevent defection of family members to the "adversary the devil" that would undermine the household as well as the religious community.[24]

Primitive Methodism thus supplied women with reinforcement outside their own families. Because early Primitive Methodism used private houses for places of worship, hostels for preachers, and even Sunday Schools, women could bring re-

---

[24] *PMM*, 1823, pp. 3–4, 25–7; Rev. George Shaw, *John Oxtoby* (Hull, 1894), p. 86; "Memoir of Hannah Howe," *PMM*, 1849, pp. 9–11. Hannah's father was "for many years, an inveterate drunkard" until he converted to Primitive Methodism.

ligion directly into their homes. Once associated with Primitive Methodist societies, they could use religious contacts to domestic advantage. Members engaged in mutual visitation and donated material as well as spiritual support in times of sickness and indigence. The ministerial visit, most coveted of all, bestowed a myriad of intangible benefits upon the receiving household. Women could gain leverage with intransigent husbands through the aid of preachers passing through the neighborhood; or they could shepherd resisting children into the kitchen, where obliging itinerants would issue collective blessings and exhort all to behave. Such tactics did not always produce familial harmony. But the extraordinary attachment to visiting preachers so often displayed in memoirs of female followers suggests that both parties gained from the bargain.[25]

Such mutually beneficial arrangements enabled evangelists to secure bases for new religious societies. During formative years, local sponsorship could make the difference between survival or failure of a Primitive Methodist mission. Through the intercession of women, several Derbyshire societies originated in large households where an exchange took place. Hannah Woolley (b. ca. 1770) settled at Milford and raised a large family during the early years of Primitive missions there. By welcoming preachers into her house, she won local respect while gaining sectarian support in her new place of residence.

---

[25] Conversion to Methodism could disrupt as well as unite families. See John Walsh, "Methodism and the Mob in the Eighteenth Century," *Popular Belief and Practice*, Studies in Church History, vol. 8, G. J. Cuming and Derek Baker, eds. (Cambridge: Cambridge University Press, 1972), pp. 223–4. Obituaries of female followers, often drawn from their own testimony in later life, convey the intensity of their involvement with preachers and religious societies. Mrs. Martha Redman (b. 1800) "several times had the honour of cleaning the preachers' clothes when bedaubed by the persecutors." Mrs. Hannah Walton (b. 1804) was "a constant reader of Connexional literature," especially when too old to attend chapel. "No one could appreciate a ministerial visit more than she did . . . ," her obituary claimed. Both women lived in circuits where female preaching was common, a fact that undermines the implication that preachers provided women with a sexual or marital substitute. "Obituary of Mrs. Martha Redman," *PMM*, 1880, p. 185; "Memoir of Mrs. Hannah Walton," *PMM*, 1889, pp. 244–5.

For the elderly as well as for women with children, domestic services also offered the advantage of simple convenience. Rebecca Potter (b. 1746), an aging mother of eight and "a pattern of piety" in Alkmanton, risked—and lost—her membership in a Wesleyan society in order to hold Primitive Methodist meetings in her home. In many such cases, cottage religion grew out of a fortunate correspondence between private and public interests.[26]

The private world of cottage religion was clearly depicted in a later essay portrait of Hannah Yeomans, a Derbyshire woman. In "The Cottage Evangelist,"[27] preacher Charles Boden described a visit to the Yeomans' household that took place around 1860. Though highly subjective and sometimes verbose, his recollections suggest that many aspects of early nineteenth-century cottage religion still survived. The inaccessibility of her home at Hollington, even in the 1860s, was striking. Boden reached the Yeomans' cottage "by leaving the main road and going about half a mile out of the way, over the fields." Later, when Boden continued on to Yeaveley, Hannah escorted him part of the way, and together they "climbed the stiles, and went over the fields for about a mile and [a] half." The cottage itself, a way-station for numerous other preachers before Boden, was a simple one-storey structure,

> consisting of one room in which they lived, and another in which they slept, whilst the space between the ceiling and roof was utilised for common stores. There was a

[26] "Obituary of Hannah Woolley," *PMM*, 1857, p. 574; "Memoir of Rebecca Potter," *PMM*, 1825, pp. 85–9. See also "Memoir of Jane Green," *PMM*, 1852, p. 252, who left the Wesleyans in order to join Primitive Methodists because she was able to meet with her class in her own house at Colne Waterside.

[27] *Aldersgate Primitive Methodist Magazine*, 1900, pp. 278–81. The author of the article, the Rev. Charles H. Boden, was a frequent contributor of connexional biographies at the turn of the century. The above article appeared in a series entitled Lowly Heroes and Heroines of Primitive Methodism. By 1900 Boden must have been quite elderly, for he was already a travelling preacher in the Nottingham Circuit in 1852. His brother, J. Boden, painted a commissioned portrait of the Chartist John Skevington, also a Primitive Methodist, which was presented to Skevington in 1848 by Thomas Cooper. (Kendall, *History*, 1:227, 337.)

lean-to used for pantry and dairy. There was also a barn for the cow, and a sty for the pigs, which . . . replenished both purse and larder.[28]

The Yeomans obviously enjoyed greater prosperity than most Primitives had during earlier times in Hollington; their relative comfort enabled Hannah to participate more actively in visiting the sick and charity work than laborers without good wages or land. It is likely, though, that Hannah's famous hospitality had often substituted for monetary contributions to the local Primitive Methodist society. A preacher needier than Boden might have taken away food enough for days, a substantial aid to a circuit struggling to support its itinerants.

Boden unconsciously sized up the balance of power in the Yeomans' household in his description of its two chief members. William Yeomans "was a quiet, good, industrious man, who was never in a hurry" and "was always doing as he said, and seldom exceeding it."[29] Beside this rather lackluster stalwart, who admittedly suffered from caricature, Hannah proved to be the mainstay of the family. She acted as keeper of the house (Boden several times referred to it as hers) and principal guardian of their only child ("a boy, whom she dedicated to the service of the temple"). She apparently converted William as well as her son to Primitive Methodism; no one breathing the air beneath her roof could escape her "more than ordinary attachment to prayer." Her efforts, in her role as mother and spouse, might have passed for conventional female piety, but for a pertinacious streak, which took even Boden by surprise. She resolutely controlled every moment of his visit. Upon his arrival, she served him an early tea, and as soon as he finished, she donned "an antique cloak" and announced, "Now, child, I am ready."

I soon discovered that she was going to set me on the road [Boden recalled]—to prevent my being lost, and I

[28] "The Cottage Evangelist," p. 278.
[29] Ibid., p. 278.

also discovered that every attempt at dissuasion was utterly useless, for instead of yielding to my attempts ... , or answering me again, she said, "Now, child, thou'll say a word of prayer," to which I replied, "Yes, I'll pray first, and you pray after."

Boden obligingly accepted this single opportunity to take the lead.

Hannah's prayer followed; Boden aptly described it as "talking with God." In it, she revealed her major concerns:

O Lord, bless Thy servant; he's going to Y[eaveley] to preach, go with him, help him, and see him safe home tomorrow; and if he's got a wife bless her, and keep her safe while he's away, and if he's got any children, bless them, and bring them all to heaven, for Christ's sake, Amen.[30]

Boden was moved by the "beautiful simplicity" of Hannah Yeomans' liturgical style and impressed by her pastoral powers. He knew of her local claim to celebrity status; another minister had recommended her to him for "a choice bit of Connexional biography," imperative before the elderly "pilgrim" passed away. As cottage evangelist, the determined woman had invaded countless households and challenged hopeless circumstances for many years. In the early days of Primitive Methodism, Hannah "read and expounded the Scriptures" with Hugh Bourne at the home of a neighbor; for the next thirty years, she occupied a conspicuous place in domestic crises all around Hollington. Connexional obituaries, at best a haphazard record, testified to her ubiquitous presence in scattered references from 1820 through the 1840s. On a more immediate level, Hannah's visits promoted Primitive Methodism as effectively as the preaching of Elizabeth Gaunt; Hannah, too, was a mother in Israel.[31]

[30] Ibid., p. 279.

[31] See "Some Account of Ann Smith," *PMM*, 1821, pp. 103–4, a description of the death of a woman of Rodsley-Cote, Derbyshire, who died shortly after

The most legendary achievement of Hannah Yeomans was the "conversion" of the vicar of Lichfield and his wife. The vicar's wife chanced upon Hannah while visiting a sick parishioner, and after hearing the common woman pray, the lady wondered if "religion is something more than the endorsement of the Apostles' Creed, and prayer is something more than a formula." She persuaded the vicar to join her in a visit to the Yeomans' home. Boden's account of their exchange no doubt suffers from the embellishment of his sentimental pen, but the substance of Hannah's conversation with the vicar still conveys an accurate sense of the rift between high and low religion:

> The visit took place. The matter of conversion was canvassed. She told of her conversion, and of the "Spirit itself bearing witness with her spirit that she was a child of God." "But, Mrs. Y[eomans], we have been taught to believe our sins cannot be forgiven until death," said the vicar; to which she replied with the most becoming deference, "But, sir, if we die suddenly, as many do, how do matters stand then?"

The vicar eventually recognized that "religion not only furnishes a sublime theory but a supernatural experience," and the worthy couple underwent conversion, albeit of an Anglican variety. Boden then triumphantly traced Hannah Yeomans' humble influence upward to "the Legislative Assembly of the British Empire," as the evangelical vicar ultimately served as the chaplain to the House of Commons. Yet Hannah Yeomans' theological position was founded upon distinctly different circumstances. To "die suddenly," from occupational accidents or epidemics more prevalent among the poor, was but one tribulation that informed the daily lives of laborers. Evangel-

---

giving birth to a child in 1820. With the help of Hannah Yeomans, Primitive preachers found "a home in the family" of the Smiths for many years (p. 104). See also "Memoir of Elizabeth Black, of Shirley," *PMM*, 1842, pp. 135–6, who also received visits from Hannah Yeomans. She, too, entertained preachers and had "earned the title of a mother in Israel" (p. 136).

THREE

The Call for Cottage Religion and Female Preaching

THE IMAGERY AND SYMBOLS of popular evangelicalism vividly reflected the importance of women in laboring life and religion; as preachers they became quintessential models of piety among the laboring classes. Yet our understanding of women's work in religion is governed largely by middle-class standards. Susannah Wesley, Hannah More, and Mary Bosanquet determine our notions of eighteenth-century female piety through the many records produced by or about them. More commonly, historians associate religious activity in the nineteenth century with copious evidence of women in philanthropy. Alongside legions of lesser known women, Josephine Butler, Catherine Booth, and Octavia Hill leap to mind as typical examples of social reformers motivated by religious insight. Some similarities exist between these middle-class women and their laboring counterparts. Perhaps all of them scoured the pages of the Bible for inspiration and guidance, and many of them measured their universe according to what they found there. But such comparisons are limited and suggest too uniform an interpretation of intention. Not all women shared "those general ideas and attitudes about life which Victorians of the middle and upper classes would have breathed in with the air."[1] In places inaccessible to chroniclers of culture, in ways not in accordance with polite society, common women developed a unique form of female ministry, derived from specific circumstances of laboring life.

[1] Walter Houghton, *The Victorian Frame of Mind* (New Haven: Yale University Press, 1958), pp. xiii–xiv.

ical reformers might obscure these differences, but they could not remove them.[32]

Rooted in the sense of autonomy gained from laboring experience, the sectarian notions of home, work, and prayer sharply contrasted with contemporary Victorian values. The prescriptive mottos of Victorian Evangelicalism bore little relation to the aims of sectarian Methodism; while one proposed to inculcate the deference and discipline of an industrial society, the other sought to subvert such control. In sanctifying the cultural world of the *domus*, sectarian Methodism promoted a notion of work that was antithetical to modern industrial society. As a domestic religion linked to domestic concerns, sectarianism attempted to reconcile work and life. In their effort to combine spiritual avocations with daily occupations, followers resisted constraints of time, discipline, and the work place. They often achieved some freedom in domestic and handicraft industries; in traditional occupations such as domestic service and agricultural labor, they brought religion to bear upon every aspect of their work and thus rejected the prescribed deferential behavior expected of them. In many instances, their personal decisions jeopardized their economic survival and social advancement. But the struggle to protect domestic values and personal autonomy in work imposed a medieval maxim, *laborare est orare*, to work is to pray, upon increasingly secular, progressive conditions. Sectarian Methodism recapitulated a centuries-old theme important in ancient mythology as well as in religion: the belief that "what we do for our living—our work—ought somehow to dignify, perhaps glorify, certainly not mock, that living."[33]

[32] "The Cottage Evangelist," pp. 280–1.
[33] Joseph Cary, "Free Time," *A Way of Working*, D. M. Dooling, ed. (New York: Anchor Books, 1979), pp. 5–6, 8. On "the golden ages of faith and faithful labor," the author quotes Simone Weil: "There are numerous signs indicating . . . that long ago physical labor was preeminently a religious activity and consequently something sacred. The Mysteries—a religion that embraced the whole of pre-Roman antiquity—were entirely founded upon symbolical expressions concerning the salvation of the soul, drawn from agriculture. The

Rankled by the challenge, established Evangelicals tried to gain the upper hand by applying standards of Victorian respectability to lower-class upstarts. "Cottage Theologians," Evangelicals contended, preferred "ranter" religion out of ignorance and laziness. "I don't find I'm edified at all at Church," a Primitive Methodist woman confessed in an Evangelical tract, "because I can't understand what the Parson says half the time." Chapel-going, moreover, undermined laborers' productivity:

> . . . when I've been at Chapel to a prayer meeting, Jesus fills my mind so with glory, that I can't go to bed, and we sit up half the night, sometimes singing. And for days together sometimes, my master [i.e., husband] don't do any work hardly for praying, and studding about it.

A lady responded not with praise, but with disapprobation. The cottager and her husband, she warned, may end up in the workhouse.[34]

Victorian Britain assigned an increasingly narrow role to religion: church-going, Sunday Schools, and private piety became its central concerns, activities influenced by upper-class philanthropists whose "desire to educate the poor," E. M. Forster recalled, "[combined] . . . with the desire for a good supply of servants."[35] Sectarian religion continued to resist both secular compartmentalization and the hegemonic influence of the Established Church; while Victorian progress swept "respectable" religion along its path, sectarianism stood still. An account of a confrontation between the daughter of Sir Tatton Sykes, the esteemed estateholder of Sledmere (Yorks.), and Nancy Varey (b. 1792), an uncompromising Primitive Methodist, illuminates an enormous temporal and class divide. One

same symbolism is found again in the New Testament parables." From *The Need for Roots*, Arthur Will, trans. (New York: Harper Torchbook, Harper & Row, 1971), n.p. (Cary, p. 5.)

[34] M. F. L., *Cottage Theologians* (Oxford, 1835), pp. 8–9.
[35] E. M. Forster, *Marianne Thornton* (New York: Harcourt Brace, 1956), p. 253.

woman armed with tracts, the other with an undefe[r] tongue, they engaged in a religious battle. Miss Syk[es] traversed the village posting sheets upon cottage w[alls] read, "Do one good thing for God every day." When [hap]pened to meet Nancy Varey, she asked her what she [thought] of the handbills. According to legend, Nancy replied, "[They] are good, *varry good, as far as they gang*, but Miss, they d[on't] gang far eneuff . . . we owt to do ivverything for the Lo[rd]" Lecturing the young lady *in extenso* on Paul's Epistles, the Pr[im]itive matriarch registered a victory for the superior piety [of] the cottage.[36]

[36] Henry Woodcock, *Piety Among the Peasantry* (London, 1889), pp. 132–3. The Primitives at Sledmere laid claim to Sir Tatton's "horse-trainers, jockeys, grooms, a postboy, stableboys, butler, a coachman, a gardener, a cowherd, as well as shepherds, labourers, woodmen, tailors, blacksmiths, joiners, bricklayers, launderesses, dressmakers, and scullerymaids" (pp. 134–5).

The origins of female preaching, like cottage religion, lay in eighteenth-century Wesleyanism. These earlier preachers pioneered the methods adopted by nineteenth-century sectarians and established the theoretical basis of a female ministry. More important, their conflict with church authority and their close ties to laboring life implicated them in a struggle for an autonomous popular religion. Their efforts were not forgotten. Pamphlet literature and oral tradition elevated leading Wesleyan female preachers to mythic stature. Their symbolic images, as much as their actual behavior, contributed to the formation of sectarian Methodism.

The earliest leading Wesleyan women were people of standing in local religious and philanthropic circles. Social connections and social graces worked in their favor. Though Wesley initially opposed female preaching, his frequent and sometimes intimate correspondence with these women changed his mind. In the case of "an extraordinary call," Wesley admitted, a woman might speak publicly. Often the move from private to public work grew naturally out of charitable activity. Mary Bosanquet, later the wife of celebrated minister John Fletcher, began her preaching career in her own children's school and orphanage at Leytonstone (Essex) and then in Leeds. She and a "distinguished group of women" gained confidence and skill as they developed a practical piety along the lines of early Wesleyan tenets. Not satisfied with prayer and class meetings in towns, some women ventured into remote country regions neglected by appointed Wesleyan preachers. Their missions, however, never gained official status or respect equal to that of male itinerants. In all cases, female preachers depended upon assurances from Wesley and each other to continue their work on an *ad hoc*, irregular basis.[2]

At the same time, common women stimulated by the egalitarian spirit of cottage religion assumed powerful roles in

[2] Leslie F. Church, *More About the Early Methodist People* (London: Epworth Press, 1949), chap. 4; W. J. Townsend, H. B. Workman, George Eayrs, eds. *A New History of Methodism*, 2 vols. (London: Hodder and Stoughton, 1909), 1:322.

domestic services. As keepers of the household, they often initiated and promoted meetings. Their sense of familial responsibility translated easily into pastoral concern, and through their "zeal and moral courage," they became "an important factor in the plan of cottage prayer meetings" in many areas. The aggressiveness and originality of such women lit fires beneath more reticent members; in fact, no meddlesome effort was too excessive. Even the village scold found a welcoming place in cottage religion, where relentless reproofs earned unqualified distinction. Village women were not slow to recognize potential leverage in their new roles as evangelists. By giving a legitimate voice to women hitherto silent, obedient, or otherwise noisome, cottage religion hinted at a different domestic and social order.[3]

The revivalism of the 1790s brought the work of laboring women into a more favorable and official light. Though regarded as exceptional periods within religious history, revivals nevertheless provided an important forum for new people and ideas. Constraints of gender and class fell away as the egalitarianism and urgency of Wesleyan Methodist revivals enabled people of all ranks to preach. Ordinarily restricted to a separate or special sphere, women temporarily assumed a central place in all aspects of the movement. Laboring women sensitive to the hardships of the lower classes joined in the activity and extended the scope of evangelism beyond that of their middle-class predecessors. Their work foreshadowed a division, eventually demonstrated by the sects, between middle-class female philanthropists and female preachers.

Ann Cutler, known as "Praying Nanny," was perhaps the most famous of this new generation of Wesleyan female preachers. Born in 1759 at Ribchester near Preston, Lancashire, Cutler apparently came from a poor working family engaged in the cottage textile industry of the area. From her

---

[3] John Sykes, *Life of William Schofield* (Huddersfield, 1882), pp. 32–3. See also Church, *Methodist People*, pp. 168ff., on how class meetings "provided a great sphere of service for the women of Methodism."

early years, Cutler was "very strict in her morals and serious in her deportment." Her conversion to Methodism, occurring when she was twenty-six, only confirmed her longstanding habits of self-control. As "she laboured with her hands," her biographer reported, "she would retire twelve or fourteen times in the day, a few minutes at a time" to read the Scriptures and pray. The determined woman soon rose to the position of class leader among the Wesleyans and then began to move into a more public sphere of activity. Acknowledging what she believed was a special call from God, Cutler embarked upon a routine of house-to-house visiting. Neighbors seemed to accept her attentions, and the indefatigable Nanny earned a respected place among village celebrities.[4]

Connexional preachers, whether nervous or pleased, made room for the self-appointed itinerant. Revivalist William Bramwell delighted in Cutler's success and encouraged her to continue preaching. In his view, the singularity of her ministry and the peculiarity of her habits revealed divine will working through a humble vessel. As Cutler travelled through Yorkshire and into Derbyshire, her growing fame came to the attention of John Wesley himself, who, like Bramwell, decided to make the best of it. "There is something in the dealings of God with your soul," he wrote to Cutler in 1790, "which is out of the common way. . . . You may tell all your experiences to me at any time; but you will need to be cautious in speaking to others, for they would not understand what you say."[5] Wesleyanism had resuscitated a belief in miraculous signs of God's grace, and, with discretion, leaders admitted popular claimants into their circle. Praying Nanny promised to accept their guidance and, thus, in spite of her "strange" ways, received the sanction of official Wesleyanism.

Admitting Cutler could not have been easy, for her style

[4] William Bramwell, *A Short Account of the Life and Death of Ann Cutler* (Sheffield, 1796), pp. 9–14. See also *Memoir of the Life and Ministry of the Rev. William Bramwell, by members of his family* (London, 1848); Church, *More About the Early Methodist People*, p. 156.

[5] Bramwell, *Short Account*, p. 7.

was offensively bold. Praying Nanny had no truck with feminine virtues; the power of her approach rested upon a rejection of propriety and delicacy. When she first prayed in public, Cutler unleashed an extraordinarily loud voice. "Many were displeased," recalled Bramwell, "but some were *saved*." A spartan diet of herb tea and milk, an avowed commitment to celibacy, and, most marked of all, an intolerance of worldly conversation characterized her behavior. With the purposefulness of an inquiry commission, Cutler "used every prudent means" to influence penitents; directness, not tactfulness, was the shortest way to sinners' hearts. Rigorous questionings, exhortations, reproaches, and tears could last long into the night. Though shockingly intrusive, Cutler's strategies stimulated many conversions; wherever she went, a revival followed. Bramwell was impressed and amazed. Nanny Cutler, he believed, "had an uncommon sight into the people's states." Pointing to her meager diet, he could only conclude that "she was in an extraordinary way supported." A veritable combination of village scold, wise woman, and saint, Cutler capitalized on a village accommodation of eccentricity. Knowingly or not, Wesley had affixed his signature to practices that would preserve rural customs well into the nineteenth century.[6]

The ministry of women like Cutler must be distinguished from that of male preachers. Historians have placed Cutler within a limited context of Wesleyan politics, particularly in evaluating her role in the Great Yorkshire Revival of 1792–96. Following the death of Wesley, a hiatus in authority enabled several ministers to promote a full-scale revival, and Cutler could be seen as part of an effort involving many other adventurous evangelicals.[7] But female preachers shed a new, specifically female light upon Wesley's carefully developed ideal of pastor; their conception of pastoral duty was more general in scope and less theological in emphasis. Moving be-

[6] Ibid., pp. 9–10, 16.

[7] Ibid., pp. 9–11, 19–20; John Baxter, "The Great Yorkshire Revival, 1792–6: A Study of Mass Revival among the Methodists," *Sociological Yearbook of Religion* (1968), pp. 46–76.

54

yond the male-defined church or chapel, they worked in households and neighborhoods, particularly among the laboring classes. Sharing the status and class of her followers, Cutler challenged the hierarchy suggested by the male pastoral role.

Female evangelists, moreover, often ignored the restricted framework of revivals. Mary Barritt, another Bramwell protégée, played a leading role in expanding the scope of female preaching. Though contemporary accounts never noted any connection between them, Ann Cutler and Mary Barritt knew one another, once preached together in 1792, and covered much of the same territory for several years. Barritt, more than Cutler, sought to free female preaching from the confinement of exceptional status. The systematic nature of her work aroused opposition and concern in Wesleyan headquarters. Like Praying Nanny, Mary Barritt commanded a sizable popular following but encountered ambivalence among Wesleyan leaders. The dispute over her ministry led to the prohibition of all female preaching in 1803, a decision which gave impetus to the formation of the Methodist sects.

Mary Barritt was born in 1772 at Hay, Lancashire, two miles outside the village of Colne.[8] Hay was a rather somnolent place even in 1800. With characteristic uncharitableness, the Board of Agriculture described small farmers there as "extremely narrow" and not of the improving sort. Barritt's father was no exception, at least with regard to religion. He opposed the Methodistic bias of his wife, son, and two daughters until the

[8] Though several Methodist historians have referred briefly to Mary Barritt's career, none has dealt adequately with the details of her life. Passing reference is given to her memoirs, published by her husband, but only one copy of the book is, in fact, extant. The following account is based largely upon this volume. See Mrs. Mary Taft, *Memoirs of the Life of Mrs. Mary Taft; formerly Miss Barritt*, 2 vols. (London, 1827); see also Wesley F. Swift, "The Women Itinerant Preachers of Early Methodism," *Proceedings of the Wesley Historical Society* 28 (1952): 89–92. The Rev. Swift evidently owned the only known copy of Mary Barritt's *Memoirs*, which is now part of W.H.S.'s collection at Southlands College, Wimbledon. The spelling of "Barritt" varies according to sources; I have tried to follow that given in her own correspondence and memoirs.

day he died (when he wearily repented), even though his fury worked to his disadvantage. Mrs. Barritt had converted to Wesleyanism shortly after Mary's birth, and in spite of the violent protestations of her husband, shepherded her young children to services scattered around the countryside. Family strife notwithstanding, divine visitations and deliverances crowded into the Barritt household. Mary experienced conversion when she was twelve and thus made sense out of the calamities visited upon her home. Like Ann Cutler, she began calling from house to house to pray with neighbors. Her brother recently had become a Wesleyan preacher, and Mary likewise recognized her calling as a public minister. Before reaching seventeen, she organized her own prayer meetings, dismissing the threats of the Wesleyan superintendent, local preachers, and, of course, her father with unwavering determination. Saving souls, Barritt averred, was "the one talent God hath given me." So she persisted, and with such success that she drained the attendance of chapel services at Gisborn, eight miles away. Neighboring preachers must have felt relief when the brazen girl finally left home to join her brother and sister on the Isle of Man.[9]

The Yorkshire Revival, beginning in 1792, confirmed Barritt's hitherto unaccredited place in the Wesleyan ministry. She returned to Lancashire sometime that year and resumed speaking publicly at occasional love feasts, but her spirit was low and she needed encouragement. Praying Nanny administered the prodding that launched Mary's itinerancy. The revival was well under way, and both women seized the opportunity to travel widely and preach extensively. At Accrington, they jointly held a meeting lasting from nine in the morning till midnight that won them praise and fame. From that time, Barritt regularly received invitations to distant villages in Yorkshire and Lancashire. Ann Cutler died in 1794, shortly before the revival came to full fruition. But Barritt's success

[9] Taft, *Memoirs*, 1:3–24; W. Stevenson, *A General View of the Agriculture of Lancashire* (London, 1815), p. 117.

through the peak years of 1795–7 assured her a permanent place in northern Methodist circles. Speaking in chapels and town halls as well as in cottages and outdoors, Barritt achieved a popularity and stature unmatched by female preachers in later years.[10]

Barritt's success attested to the special appeal of a female ministry, and many marveled at her effectiveness. "Work in what way seems best to thine infinite wisdom," wrote Alexander Mather from Leeds after her visit there. "The people are coming about me like bees, to know if I [have] seen Mary," William Allen, a minister from Sherborn, reported after she left. William Bramwell expressed special pride in her work. "I am fully satisfied you are in your place," he confided after she assisted him in Sheffield. "I think I have seen this clearly since you came. Your way is open, numbers receive the power." Though he felt that an early death would terminate her career, he compared her to himself and noted, "You do more work in less time." To another minister, he wrote, "I never knew one man so much blessed as this young woman is in the salvation of souls." Even churchmen added their assent: in the Whitehaven Circuit, where she replaced her brother during his illness, three clergymen responded to her preaching with loud "Amen's."[11]

Reactions at the center of the Connexion were not as favorable. As Wesleyan leadership turned towards more conservative policies around 1800, revivalists (male and female alike) faced growing opposition. Barritt's journal admitted lit-

---

[10] Taft, *Memoirs*, 1:26; Swift, "Women Preachers," p. 92; Baxter, "Yorkshire Revival," Appendix, pp. 69–70.

[11] Taft, *Memoirs*, 1:87; William Bramwell to Miss Barritt, May 30, 1798, in *Memoir of William Bramwell*, pp. 199–200; William Bramwell to the Rev. J. Drake, n.d., 1800, Ibid., p. 206; Bramwell was not always so generous with praise in his letters to the young preacher; he sometimes assumed the role of supervisor in keeping watch over her personal habits. In one letter, he reprimanded her for preaching too far into the night. "Suppose you were to conclude sooner in the evening," he wrote, "go to rest sooner, and sometimes meet all that would come in the morning. A number . . . sink deep into sloth from your example of lying in bed." (Ibid., p. 209.)

tle of this, reporting only occasional difficulties since the start of her travels. Her decision to marry a fellow preacher in 1801, however, might have reflected a desire to strengthen her defenses. Zachariah Taft (b. 1773) was an obviously partisan "Minister of the olden stamp." As the son of a Derbyshire farmer who had been close friends with Wesley, Taft was marked for the ministry at an early age. His allegiance lay with "old" Methodists and common people. He, too, corresponded with Bramwell and supported popular revivalism.[12] While marriage promised support for Barritt, it foreshadowed trouble for Taft: their union cast his ministry into an unmistakably insubordinate light. In marrying Taft, Barritt gained an articulate and outspoken advocate and an opportunity to take her cause to the public.

Barritt and Taft faced resistance on all sides; even Bramwell, their friend and advisor, strongly opposed their marriage. When Barritt hinted at their intentions in a letter to Bramwell, the older preacher responded with emphatic words of discouragement:

> I am led to think that this proceeding [i.e., marriage] would prevent the design of the Almighty concerning you. Fully understand me: I do not mean that it is wrong to marry, but I think it would prevent in you the answering [of] that great end of your call. In the first place, your situation would become local. . . . You would soon become in a great degree useless. In the next place, you may have the cares of a family; but you would not have that influ-

---

[12] When Wesley visited the Taft family during the 1770s, he "laid hands" upon the three young boys. The youngest died soon after, but Zachariah and his older brother Henry fulfilled the prophetic touch by becoming ministers. When he was eighteen, Zachariah joined the Methodists while in London and preached his first sermon some time later at Stanton (Derbys.), where his parents were then living. *Methodist Magazine*, 1851, pp. 1120–1. See also Daniel M'Allum, *Memoirs of the Life, Character, and Death of the Rev. H. Taft* (Newcastle, 1824), Daniel M'Allum, Henry Taft's son-in-law, was also a renowned revivalist and a formative influence upon several prominent Primitive Methodist female preachers.

ence amongst members of your own sex. I conceive you
can only think of altering your state upon one ground—
and that is, "I am become obsolete! My work is done! I
am shut out! I can do no more! I am called to give it up!"
If you think so, I think differently.[13]

Bramwell offered a vigorous defense of celibate itinerancy,
though he had chosen a different way for himself. Wesley had
taken a similar stance on celibacy, and when Bramwell nevertheless married in 1787, Wesley temporarily suspended him
from the itinerancy.[14] Barritt, however, envisioned a different
ideal of the Methodist pastor. Marriage would not necessarily
restrict her movements and could enhance her ministry. Her
calling, she believed, was among entire families, not simply
young unmarried women. Now thirty, Barritt began to see a
new role for the woman preacher. Resisting the admonishment
of her long-standing patron, Barritt married Taft at Horncastle (Lincs.) on August 17, 1802, and from there, the couple
set out for Taft's new station in the Dover Circuit.[15]

Their move south hastened the end of official toleration of
female preaching. Trouble began when northern manners
met southern temperament at Taft's post in Kent. The circuit
made no effort to accommodate Taft's last-minute marriage.
When the couple arrived at their destination, they found a
room suitable for a single preacher. Differences in attitude
underlay the remonstrance, the Tafts soon discovered, for
their new hosts showed a restrained spirit and no zeal. Mary
"feared there was but little more than the form of religion
among those who attended" services; "so much looking at one
another" replaced any real involvement in worship, and "not
a wisper [sic] could be heard" except an occasional "amen" and
"reading of prayers." At Canterbury, moreover, "amens" came

[13] W. Bramwell to Miss Barritt [n.d.], *Memoir of Bramwell*, pp. 211–2.

[14] Ibid., p. 33, Bramwell later "expressed his conviction" that the Tafts'
"union was of God" (p. 122). On the issue of celibacy among Wesleyans, see
Henry Abelove, "The Sexual Politics of Early Methodism," unpublished paper.

[15] Taft, *Memoirs*, 2:42.

only from the gallery. The disaffection was mutual. Chapel leaders at Dover gave Taft firm advice on how to preach; his style, they contended, was too loud for Kentish tastes. Their animosity towards the Tafts was undisguised and promised to increase as the term of the couple continued.[16]

More serious problems arose when Mary Taft began to preach. Female evangelism was less common in the South, and the novelty created a tremendous sensation. According to newspaper reports, Mrs. Taft attracted crowds of "many hundreds" when she preached outdoors. But Dover leaders were distressed by the unwanted publicity. Just three months after the Tafts' arrival, the society split over the issue. The chairman of the Connexion district ordered Mrs. Taft to stop, but Zachariah defended her forcefully. The clash soon ignited a nationwide controversy, and the next spring, the central Conference dealt a death blow to Wesleyan female preaching.[17]

The Tafts met the Wesleyan prohibition with a vigorous campaign in defense of female preaching. Mary Taft continued speaking, while Zachariah published pamphlets, circulars, letters, petitions, and books on the ministry of women. The couple believed that the tenets of early Methodism were on their side. "O that God would revive his work of heart-felt religion and primitive Methodism amongst them!" Mary Taft complained to her husband while on a preaching tour.[18] In pamphlet defenses, Zachariah cited oft-quoted Old Testament passages on prophecy for support, along with additional evidence from John Locke's writings on Paul.[19] In 1819, Taft revived Bramwell's *Life of Ann Cutler*, adding an appendix providing more recent examples of the "extraordinary call" received by women. The famous biography now possessed the characteristics of folklore, promoting a vernacular style that

[16] Ibid., pp. 43–6.

[17] Ibid., pp. 59–83. The report was printed in the *Kentish Herald*, published in Canterbury, October 7, 1802. Ibid., p. 49.

[18] Ibid., p. 81.

[19] Z. Taft, *Thoughts on Female Preaching. With Extracts from the Writings of Locke, Martin, &c.* (Dover, 1803).

recalled village traditions and values. "Her method was very simple," Taft wrote of Cutler, "and perhaps far more primitive and apostolic than that which is generally practised."[20] With significant emphasis, he elevated humble spirituality over professionalism. Such writings were never without oblique attacks upon Wesleyanism. "If devils are cast out;" he advised all women wishing to preach, "souls saved; and the people willing to hear you; let no man stop you." Taft resurrected the "old Methodist" right of rebellion in the face of new Wesleyan leadership whose exclusivity betrayed the sectarian origins of the Connexion.[21]

The Tafts thus witnessed, but perhaps never fully comprehended, the slow process of class differentiation within Wesleyanism. Connexional leadership presented an increasingly respectable and middle-class model for ministerial behavior. Female evangelism violated this ideal and sustained an uncomfortably intimate relationship with lower-class life. Though Zachariah Taft came from a modest background, he was educated and respectable; Mary's origins were far more obscure. In her correspondence with the widow of the Reverend John Fletcher of Madeley, she revealed her interests as well as her lack of education. Around 1810, Mary wrote to inquire about the "Publick labours" of Mrs. Fletcher's "Maid." "[I] felt greevd," she confessed,

> to find in reeding the account of her in the Magazine that nothing wass said of her speaking for God or of her saving the seed of Etirnal life and I pirticlorly wished to know if you left out that part of her Life so preshous to me or the Editor had thought Proppor to omit that Part. . . . [I]

---

[20] "Advertisement" prefacing W. Bramwell, *A Short Account of the Life and Death of Ann Cutler* (York, 1827), p. 2.

[21] *The Scripture Doctrine of Women's Preaching: Stated and Examined* (York, 1820), p. 23. Taft also published a monumental two-volume compilation of over seventy-five biographical sketches in *Holy Women*, 2 vols. (London, 1825–1828), now in the John Rylands Library.

shall also be glad to know if you still labour for the Lord
and in what way . . .[22]

Like the Wesleyan model of female piety, Mary Taft visited
poorhouses and tended to the sick, but the extent of her involvement transcended mere charity and showed a true identification with working-class people. She sometimes spent the
night with penitents (including the poorer ones) and joined
the noisiest worshippers when they "rored [sic] out" during
services. The "Country People" in turn identified with Mrs.
Taft. Wherever she travelled, they came "in *Droves*," she reported, "saying come to us to us & so on . . ." The Tafts'
continuing involvement with the poor governed their activity
till their deaths. Never seeking official separation from the
Old Connexion, they nevertheless followed their own brand
of Methodist sectarianism.[23]

Ironically, Mary Taft's status as preacher-in-exile was well
suited to her work as a popular evangelist. Her irregular
preaching tours took her to places where established religion
and Wesleyanism were weak. Speaking in cottages, houses, and
outdoors, Mrs. Taft reached persons outside institutionalized
religion. Striking miners, distressed agricultural laborers, and
rural migrants avoided the chapel but accepted the Tafts. The
challenge to authority represented in Mary Taft's ministry

[22] Mary Taft, Epworth, Lincs., to Mrs. Fletcher, Madely [sic], Shrops., n.d.
[ca. 1803]. Methodist Archives/John Rylands Library, Manchester [hereafter
cited as MA/JRL]. Mrs. Fletcher also had spoken publicly among the Wesleyans
earlier in her life.

[23] Letter from Mary Taft, York, to Mr. Taft, Birstal, near Leeds, Feb. 2, 1808.
MA/JRL: Taft, *Memoirs*, 2:44. With the help of prominent ministers, including
John Pawson, Alexander Mather, and Samuel Bradburn, Taft continued to
defend Mary's work for years following the Wesleyan prohibition. See copy of
the circular letter from Z. Taft to all travelling preachers in the Wesleyan
Connexion, Birstal, near Leeds, July 1809, addressed to Mrs. Mary Fletcher,
Madely. MA/JRL. See also W. Swift, "Female Preachers," pp. 90–1. Jabez Bunting expressed his displeasure with Mary Taft's continuing work in 1833, but
her advocates at the Conference succeeded in retaining her under the category
of "special services preacher." See also Townsend, Workman, Eayrs, *History of
Methodism*, 1:413.

appealed to those without privilege or status. "I lived [as a] servant with Mr. James Robinson of Selstonwood nook," one member of a Birmingham congregation testified after hearing Mrs. Taft speak in 1841, "when forty years ago that woman came riding by and spoke to my master on the cornstack."[24] She brazenly ignored traditional social distinctions, and in the new setting of industrial cities, reminded her listeners of the "leveling" ethos implicit in rural religion. Mrs. Taft encountered many followers a second time, but in new locations; her pilgrimage mirrored theirs and became evidence of changing times.[25]

The ministry of Mary Taft substantially contributed to the growing divide between official Wesleyanism and popular evangelicalism. Though she and her husband remained within the Old Connexion, she nevertheless stood as an important figure in the rebellion against conventional religious authority. Zachariah continued to promote her work, and as a result, numerous "Spiritual Children" imbibed the different brand of faith provided by her ministry. She regularly upset the complacency of followers and preachers alike. "I feared she and some of the friends were in danger of going too far," recalled a local preacher at Hexham years after hearing her speak. "[But] ever since, I have found pleasure in [hearing] pious females speaking a word for God. My mind has got satisfied that those passages of holy writ has been misunderstood."[26] Not surprisingly, the Wesleyan Connexion refused to acknowledge her significant achievements. When she died shortly after Zachariah in 1851, the *Methodist Magazine* denied

[24] Mary Taft, Nottingham, to Mary Tooth, Madely, Nov. 8, 1841, MA/JRL.

[25] On apparent cases of migration, see Mary Anderson, Alford, Lincs., to Mary Taft, Horncastle, Oct. 13, 1811; Mary Taft, Sunderland, to Z. Taft, Birstal, June 14, 1809; Mary Taft, York, to Z. Taft, Birstal, Feb. 2, 1808; Mary Taft, Nottingham, to Mary Tooth, Madely, Nov. 8, 1841. On Mary's frequent house calls and successes in healing, see, e.g., Mary Taft, Nottingham, to Mary Tooth, Madely, June 13, 1841. On striking colliers, see Z. Taft, Castle Donnington, to M. Taft, [n.p.] Nov. 19, 1810; on distress in the countryside, see, e.g., Mary Taft [n.p.] to Mary Tooth, Madely, Nov. 20, 1842. MA/JRL.

[26] Mr. Stobart, Hexham, to Z. Taft [n.p.], May 17, 1828. MA/JRL.

her the standard biographical essay and published only a brief
notice:

> March 16th. At Sandiacre, in the seventy-ninth year of
> her age, Mrs. Mary Taft, widow of the late Rev. Zachariah
> Taft. For many years she had been "a mother in Israel."
> Early converted to God, she had much to endure from
> her own family on account of her religious decision. But
> this she bore with unflinching constancy. Mental energy,
> in a more than usual degree, was among her character-
> istics. She died, as she had lived, trusting in Christ, and
> rejoicing in God her Saviour.[27]

Had her advocate been alive, he might have published a final
pamphlet protesting this suppression of her many
achievements.

Perhaps the only female preacher known to the twentieth
century is Elizabeth Tomlinson, portrayed as Dinah Morris in
Adam Bede. George Eliot depicted Tomlinson, her aunt by marriage, with some accuracy. Samuel Evans first heard Betsey
Tomlinson speak as she made her way from Nottingham to a
village in Staffordshire in 1802, preaching from atop milkcarts
and wagons in precisely the same way as her fictional coun-
terpart. A Wesleyan local preacher himself, Evans shared
many of her values and goals. With much effort, he eventually
convinced Tomlinson that their commitment to preaching
would prosper through marriage, and, in 1804, the couple
wed and settled at Evans's native village of Roston.[28]

Like the Tafts, the Evanses' partnership encountered Wesleyan opposition to female preaching and popular evangelism;
more revealing, however, is the way in which Betsey Tomlin-

[27] *Methodist Magazine*, 1851, p. 604.

[28] No complete account of Elizabeth Tomlinson's life exists; the most detailed
information appears in an autobiographical sketch, "Mrs. Elizabeth Evans," in
Z. Taft, *Holy Women* (London, 1825), 1:145–58. See also Leslie F. Church, *More
About the Early Methodist People* (London: Epworth Press, 1949), pp. 160ff.;
H. B. Kendall, *History of the Primitive Methodist Church* (London, n.d.), 1:142–
4; Seth Bede, *Seth Bede "The Methody"* (London, 1859), pp. 14, 19.

son's origins and experiences point to a coherent basis for a female ministry. Owing to Zachariah Taft's efforts to publicize the work of women preachers, a detailed account of Tomlinson's life, including extracts from her journals, was published in 1825. From such sources, a clear picture of the interaction between her circumstances and the social and economic factors contributing to female preaching emerges.

Like many other female preachers, Tomlinson survived personal trauma and economic hardship from an early age. Mrs. Tomlinson died when Betsey was still a baby, leaving her children to a father who lacked, among other things, "real religion." "What I have suffered through the loss of my dear Mother," Betsey recorded, "can only be explained in eternity." When she was fourteen, she left her native village of Newbold (Leics.) to become a servant at Derby, and she never returned home. Betsey's curiosity about religion developed during these years; Methodist sermons helped her understand her feelings of alienation from the superficial and worldly lives of her employers. " 'Here we have no continuing city,' " ran one of her favorite texts, " 'but seek one to come.' " Her uprooted state, typical of servants and many laborers, became meaningful when viewed in such terms. "[This] conviction never wore off to the day of my conversion to God," she recalled. As soon as she reached the age of twenty-one, Betsey terminated her employment and moved to Nottingham, where she intended at last to be "at liberty to serve God."[29]

The subsequent steps towards becoming a female preacher were, in effect, stages in renouncing community and family. Through popular evangelicalism, single women could explain the position forced upon them by circumstances. Their solitude thus became the basis for spiritual independence and their deprivation nurtured righteous determination. Conversion became a ritual renunciation of courtship, marriage, and family life. The full implications of conversion emerged clearly in the social behavior of female followers. The intense inner

[29] Taft, *Holy Women*, pp. 146–8.

turmoil that preceded most conversions often led to a denial of typical female concerns including dancing, frilly dress, gossiping, and consorting with "unholy" companions. Such restrictions made participation in ordinary village life impossible and further limited the likelihood of marriage. Despite these sacrifices, female followers celebrated their severance from worldly concerns. "I saw I could make a better use of my time and money," Tomlinson averred, "than to follow the fashions of a vain world." Through the outward signs of conversion, they demonstrated their conscientious objection to a society responsible for injustices and unhappiness.[30]

The rigors of single life only reinforced the female preacher's commitment to a sectarian form of Methodism. Asceticism became a means to greater sanctification; through poverty and celibacy, she achieved proof of her chosen state. Preaching provided the best justification for a life outside marriage, for obligation to God and the religious community took priority over personal wishes and needs. Tomlinson resisted marrying Evans, even though he also preached, for these reasons.

> I saw it my duty to be wholly devoted to God, and to be set apart for the master's use; and after many struggles, thousands of tears, and much prayer, with fastings, I did enter into a glorious liberty.[31]

"Liberty," in this case, meant intensified religious duty: preaching, visiting, leading meetings, and tending the sick occupied most of the preacher's time. Having renounced the wider community for the religious society, the female preacher now devoted herself to serving a new "extended family" of believers. The religious society was in turn interested in keeping the preacher single; members did not hesitate to voice opinions on the marriage—and potential partners—of their women preachers. The special distinction bestowed upon them by their societies recalled the old village custom, still practiced in

[30] Ibid., p. 149.
[31] Ibid., p. 149.

parts of Derbyshire at the time, of honoring unmarried women with special ceremonies at death. Within the intimacy of the religious sect, traditional attitudes mixing private and public concerns still survived.[32]

Homeless and poor, Betsey Tomlinson next found employment taking in lacework in Nottingham, thus maintaining freedom from constraints even in her labor.

> I used to work at my mending of lace until two or three o'clock in the morning, generally that I might be furnished with money and clothes, that I might not be a burden to any one; and this I did with great pleasure. I believe I had one of the best places in the town, I had very good wages and could earn fourteen or fifteen shillings a week, and did not as some may have supposed, go out for loaves and fishes, nor for a husband, as I then believed I never should be married to any one. No, "Christ was all the world to me, and all my heart was love."[33]

Domestic industry enabled her to spend daytime hours visiting the sick, leading prayer meetings, and travelling to and from Derby; but the rigors of such work, unregulated and unsteady in its returns, identified her with the most vulnerable laboring poor. Gradually, Tomlinson surrendered whatever material satisfactions and security she possessed in order to follow her religious calling. When she received an invitation from Staffordshire in 1802, she quit lacemaking altogether and assumed

---

[32] S. Glover, *History, Gazetteer, and Directory of the County of Derby* (Derby, 1829), 1:308. The custom of honoring unmarried women was still carried on at Hathersage and Glossop in northern Derbyshire, as well as in parts of Yorkshire.

Relatively few followers (though very many preachers) *articulated* the extreme position of renouncing marriage and dependence on men, but a considerable number did derive benefits from the female bonding that resulted from joining the religious society. Members often lived and worked together, visited each other, and obtained assistance (medical and material) from local society women. See Kendall, *History*, 1:245–8, on "Village Saints," all of them female. It is no coincidence that Hugh Bourne had "truly a good time" preaching from Ruth to such audiences. (*Journal*, August 16, 1818, quoted in Kendall, *History*, 1:248.)

[33] Taft, *Holy Women*, 1:154.

the life of a mendicant preacher. It was in the course of this mission that she first visited western Derbyshire.[34]

As a modest and humble villager, Betsey Tomlinson must have been amazed by the intense enthusiasm created by her preaching.[35] Her early successes at Derby and Nottingham suggest that many of her listeners recognized something of themselves in the profile of the preacher. Domestic service and needlework employed thousands of women around Derbyshire at the beginning of the century, and Betsey's familiarity with both occupations undoubtedly informed her evangelical message. The only opportunity open to young single women in the Derbyshire area "was some branch of domestic service, either on the farms or in adjacent towns, and the parish as a rule was only too ready to assist them to obtain situations in order to get rid of them, especially if in so doing they achieved a settlement elsewhere."[36] Like Tomlinson, many women entered service at a young age and began to entertain religious ideas often opposed to those of their masters. Though employers often tried to impress their version of piety and virtue upon untutored farm girls, resourceful servants could formulate their own views through Methodism. The upper-class "hypocrisy" so often criticized by Methodist servants helped generate greater enthusiasm for lower-class evangelicalism. "I lived . . . with a family that knew *very* little more about religion than myself," Tomlinson later recalled. "We had plenty of

---

[34] Ibid., pp. 154–5.

[35] "I cannot help seeing the kind hand of a gracious God in these things," Betsey wrote concerning her reception in Derby, "however others may *sneer* at them and call it enthusiasm, or what they please." (Ibid., p. 151.) Betsey Evans had a reputation for "[getting] well into the Power." Her style of preaching was probably more extroverted than that of most other women. Hugh Bourne alluded to her manner when he noted that she "has been very near Ann Cutler's experience." See *Journal* of Hugh Bourne, quoted in Kendall, *History*, 1:142, 144.

[36] Ivy Pinchbeck, *Women Workers and the Industrial Revolution, 1750–1850* (1930; reprint, Totowa, N.J.: Cass, 1977), p. 80; see also Louise A. Tilly and Joan W. Scott, *Women, Work and Family* (New York: Holt, Rinehart and Winston, 1978), pp. 35–6.

prayer books, and saying of prayers, but very little heartfelt religion." Through Methodism, servants sustained a rigorous piety that gave them autonomy—and even a certain superiority—under the constraints of their employment.[37]

Domestic industry offered an alternative means of survival to the same class of women; some, like Betsey Tomlinson, appreciated the comparative freedom of self-employment despite the drawbacks of long hours and uncertain demand. Needlework supplied work for women in their homes throughout the Midlands for generations, and Derbyshire had become a center of hosiery and lacemaking. Up to the Napoleonic Wars, lacemaking could bring a substantial income to women employed full-time, though most chose to use the industry for supplemental earnings. Machinery began to displace both domestic lacemakers and hosiery knitters around 1810, but as in the cotton and woollen industries, many laborers nevertheless continued to rely upon traditional part-time and full-time domestic work. In 1831, Felkin found that around 180,000 women and children still worked in domestic lacemaking, and the Factory Commission of 1833 corroborated his findings. Framework knitting continued to a great extent in eastern and southeastern parts of Derbyshire. The advantages of domestic industry, however elusive, remained important to a significant number of working-class women.[38]

Such material hardship was the breeding ground of popular evangelicalism. The strength of Tomlinson's appeal lay in her identification with poor women with few resources. Through her preaching, she transformed ordinary adversity into the

[37] *Holy Women*, 1:157. For a fuller discussion of the impact of evangelicalism upon domestic servants, see chap. VI. Two other female preachers in Derbyshire worked as domestic servants: Alice Bembridge, (b. 1806) of Brailsford, was also converted while in service; Ann Alexander (b. ca. 1794) worked as a servant at Ellaston (Staffs.) when she encountered Primitive Methodist missionaries and began the preaching career that brought her into Derbyshire. "Memoir of Alice Bembridge," *Primitive Methodist Magazine* (hereafter *PMM*) 1862, pp. 271–2; "Memoir of Ann Alexander," *PMM*, 1831, pp. 381–2.

[38] S. Glover, *The Peak Guide* (Derby, 1830), pp. 14, 21; *VCH*, 2:370; Pinchbeck, *Women Workers*, pp. 203–15.

unfolding of a sacred plan; evangelical religion brought pro-
spective converts into a special relationship with divine power
that would have a direct bearing on their lives. Like Dinah of
Adam Bede, Betsey Tomlinson told simple stories that conveyed
a sense of possibility in the midst of familiar domestic scenes:

> When a poor woman laden with sins went out to the well
> to draw water, she found Thee sitting at the well; she
> knew Thee not; she had not sought Thee; her mind was
> dark; her life was unholy. But thou didst show her that
> her life lay open before Thee, and yet thou wast ready to
> give her that blessing which she had never sought.[39]

Even the unwilling could find her message compelling as she
plied them with numerous accounts of "the Lord's work"
among the sick and poor. Tomlinson's own testimony emphasized the continuous role of divine providence in giving both
spiritual and material assistance to the needy. She attributed
her preaching to "some blessed design" that enabled her "to
know any thing" she desired. "I only had to ask and it was
given, generally in a moment; whether I was in the public
street, or at my work, or in my private room," she claimed.
Her decision to lead a class for the first time sprang from a
revelation that came to her during an illness:

> I did not send for a Doctor. I thought when Christ was
> applied unto in the days of his flesh by any, and for any
> thing, either for body or soul, he did for them whatever
> they had need of; and while I was looking to him, . . . I
> most powerfully felt these words—"And he took her by
> the hand and the fever left her"—was applied to my mind;
> and I felt, in the twinkling of an eye, that all the fever
> was gone, and all my pain had ceased. I was quite restored
> to health.[40]

Such assurance of God's concern, often available through sickness and healing, inspired self-confidence and self-reliance.

[39] Bede, *Seth Bede*, pp. 17–8.
[40] Taft, *Holy Women*, 1:151, 153.

Tomlinson counseled followers to seek personal stability by the same methods.[41]

All these experiences convinced Tomlinson, in the face of Wesleyan opposition, of her right to preach. "Now it may be asked," she pointed out, "would the all wise God have done these things for me and in me, if he had not intended to accomplish some blessed design[?] If the person had been a male instead of a female, would it not have been concluded at once, he is called to preach[?]" For more than a year, Tomlinson was unable to find "a single door open" because of official condemnation of her work, and she temporarily returned to Nottingham and lacemaking. But in witnessing the Taft controversy, which reached a peak at just this time, she must have regrouped her forces. Her marriage to Evans coincided with her return to preaching around 1804. She, like Mary Barritt Taft, was able to find Biblical justification for her continuance in the ministry:

> But it is argued, "I suffer not a woman to speak in the church;" and is the Apostle then alluding to preaching? I believe not[;] if he is, in other places he contradicts himself; which under inspiration he could not do. And does he not sanction women labouring in the Gospel? But is the Apostle alone in this matter? No, search but the old and new testaments, and you will find many daughters that did prophesy, or were prophetesses; and Joel says— in the latter days saith God, "I will pour out my spirit upon my servants and handmaids;" so that you see the dispensation is not ended.[42]

The success of the Evanses' partnership was a sign that cottage religion spoke to the needs of their neighborhood. Preaching in the open air or "in the barn of some friendly farmer," they stimulated revivals at Roston and nearby Snelston. Their work depended heavily upon the hospitality of

---

[41] The expectation of satisfaction through divine intervention occupies a central place in sectarian religion. See Max Weber, *The Sociology of Religion,* Ephraim Fischoff, trans. (Boston: Beacon Press, 1963), pp. 47, 108.

[42] Taft, *Holy Women,* 1:153.

their followers. Class and prayer meetings, as essential as preaching to solidifying membership, took place "at different cottages." In addition to preaching, Betsey Evans acted as counsellor and midwife to women villagers. The couple worked to strengthen ties binding villagers and, in some cases, induced "those who were in good circumstances . . . to take more heed of the necessities of the poor than they had hitherto been accustomed to take."[43] "I believe the whole village had a powerful call," Betsey recorded in her journal,

> We had access to several fresh places, and societies were formed, and we could bear them record that they would have plucked out their eyes and given them to us; we were with them in weariness and in painfulness, in watchings often, in fastings too, of which I am not ashamed to speak.[44]

Together the couple formulated their own kind of Methodism.

Betsey Evans continued to preach until her death in 1849. The Evanses' relationship to Wesleyanism was difficult as a result; they withdrew from the Connexion, according to one account, because officials suggested that Betsey appear on the circuit plan as an asterisk instead of by name. The Evanses then joined the Derby Faith Methodists (also known as the Arminian Methodist Connexion) and from their new home in Wirksworth, an industrial village in Derbyshire, they freely pursued their careers. They eventually returned to Wesleyanism at the end of their lives, though the details of their reconciliation are not known.[45]

Within Wesleyanism, female preachers were of marginal importance; outside Wesleyanism, they achieved more central, strategic status. Their struggle for acceptance and recognition became part of a new movement growing out of Methodism after 1800. Female preaching, as well as cottage preaching and

[43] Bede, *Seth Bede*, p. 21.
[44] Taft, *Holy Women*, 1:157.
[45] Townsend, Workman, Eayrs, *History of Methodism*, 1:413, 427, 520–1; Kendall, *History*, 1:142–4.

revivalism, mobilized working-class leadership and support. Banned by Wesleyanism, women preachers became the focus for a revision of established religion. Demands for a more cottage-based, popular faith emerged during the first decade of the nineteenth century. Fueled by economic and social changes, the revolt against the religious establishment gradually assumed universal significance. In the world of cottagers and laborers, the new movement heralded great things.

FOUR

The Rise of Methodist Sectarianism

COTTAGE EVANGELICALS led a revision of institutional religion that was rooted in popular culture. The incorporation of
local settings and customs, the adoption of characteristics of
the household, and the enlistment of women introduced many
plebeian aspects into the theology set forth by Wesley and
others. Mild Wesleyan precedents, soon well advanced as a
system of evangelism, acquired a more pronounced opposi-
tional character after the leader's death. The political and
social ferment of the 1790s, followed by reaction during the
first decade of the nineteenth century, gave cottage evangelicals an ambiguous status as both Wesleyan and civil authorities
tried to curb their activities. But as sectarians persisted in dis-
tinguishing themselves from followers of more established religions, clearer patterns of practice and belief evolved.
Through activities like camp meetings and female preaching,
Methodist sectarians not only attacked religious authority but
resisted the social conventions of a new era. Their religious
stance preserved plebeian values in a new industrial society.

A controversy over cottage religion provoked the Quaker
Methodists of Warrington to make the first break from Wesleyanism in 1796. Through an adaptation of Wesleyan and
Quaker theology, the society had developed their own method
of worship, and the cottage meeting was "chief among their
agencies." At weekly meetings held in the homes of members,
they conducted "singing, prayer, Scripture reading, testimony,
and meditation." The society relied upon "home [i.e., local]
preachers" most of the time and increasingly felt the visits of
Wesleyan itinerants, however occasional, as intrusive. Not long

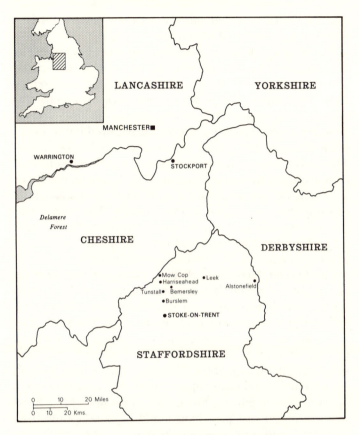

Locations of early Methodist sectarianism

after Wesley's death, conflict erupted. "So self-contained had the Society been," up to 1795, "and so little dependent upon outside help[,] that a meeting was actually held at which it was decided to suggest to Conference that it be left without an itinerant ministry." Not surprisingly, its request met with fierce opposition and reprisals. Conference prohibited further home meetings and placed the society under the supervision of a district itinerant preacher. Viewing these changes as intoler-

75

able, the Warrington Methodists "quietly separated themselves from the main body" of Methodists.[1]

The Warrington sect sought to correct what it perceived as the apostasy of present-day religion. In order to reassert the central importance of the congregation against "conference-made Methodism," the society turned back to seventeenth-century sectarianism. They abolished a paid ministry and established a democratic organization based on the priesthood of all believers. Women, as well as men, acted as preachers. The Quaker belief in the Inner Light supported and enhanced their use of the Methodist testimony. The duty of each follower to express his or her spiritual insights similarly reinstated the power of the congregation over the ministry. Attracting Quakers and Methodists alike, the society reaffirmed the ardent evangelism that once motivated both groups but had diminished in intensity by the late eighteenth century.

The Quaker Methodist rebellion against modern religion also registered an implicit complaint against modern times. With each doctrinal stance, the sect resisted materialist values and the professionalization of the ministry. Outward signs were obvious: rejecting contemporary fashions and manners, Quaker Methodists adopted the plain, outdated dress and speech of the early Quakers. Their deliverance from the cash nexus went beyond quaint appearances. Many members were of lower-class origin; for them, the repudiation of a salaried ministry meant that preaching would offer no escape from hard work and poverty. Peter Phillips (b. 1777), credited as founder of the sect, labored as a chairmaker, while his wife, Hannah Peacock (b. 1780), was a domestic servant and swivel weaver. Phillips became celebrated for his "historic answer" to attacks on Quaker Methodism. "If it could be shown that a man's preaching was better because he was paid for doing it," he challenged their critics, "[we will] admit [our] error."[2] Spir-

---

[1] William Durant, *The Story of Friars' Green Church* (Warrington, 1951), p. 7; Arthur Mounfield, *A Short History of Independent Methodism* (Wigan, 1905), pp. 4–5.

[2] Mounfield, *A Short History*, p. 7.

itual gifts, not position and cash payment, legitimated the work of their preachers. Quaker Methodists adopted the attitude of craftsmen facing redundancy; in the face of modern professionalism, they defined their ministry according to higher principles immune to current values.

All Quaker Methodists, and not only preachers, resisted narrow occupational or gender roles. Religion provided a means of breaking out of the confines of expectation and habit. Hannah Phillips, for example, combined several occupations with her spiritual calling after her marriage to Peter Phillips. She may have continued to work as a part-time servant and swivel weaver; in addition, she acquired the skills of midwifery and medicine and applied them, along with spiritual ministrations, to neighbors and society members alike. More than practical evangelism, her work had a protective function: childbirth and sickness, two commonplace but religiously significant occurrences, remained in the realm of the sacred, safe from the interference of the professional doctor. The spiritual fervor of sectarian Methodism, mixed with elements of popular religion and folklore, infused the material world with antisecular sentiment.[3]

Other societies in the Lancashire and Cheshire area followed a similar path of retreat from institutional Methodism. Like the Quaker Methodists, the Magic Methodists of Delamere Forest (Cheshire) emphasized the importance of free exercise of the spirit. Adopting the epithet coined by their critics, the sect originated around 1800 in monthly meetings held in the home of Wesleyan local preacher James Crawfoot (b. 1758), commonly known as the Old Man of the Forest. The society evolved its own version of the Inner Light: "the trance, or vision state" became the means of engaging the abilities of all members. Sectarians came from distant parts to witness the

[3] Cf. Lois Paul, "Careers of Midwives in a Mayan Community," *Women in Ritual and Symbolic Roles*, Judith Hoch-Smith and Anita Spring, eds. (New York: Plenum Press, 1978), pp. 129–149. For a more extensive treatment of Independent Methodism, see chap. 9 below.

famed gatherings. William Clowes, soon to organize another schismatic society, witnessed one meeting:

> It began always about seven o'clock on a Saturday evening. The house was situated in a very lonely part of the forest, but vast numbers of people attended. The old man began the service by reading some passages out of the Holy Scriptures, then singing and prayer followed; the old man invited any to speak on the things of God that felt liberty. A respectable-looking farmer's wife then arose and gave an exhortation, accompanied with a powerful influence from on high. . . . The meeting was thus carried on with prayer and exhortation until about twelve o'clock, and then it concluded. Some of the people, before they departed, took a little tea; and my friend and I departed about two o'clock in the morning.[4]

As society leader, Crawfoot set a tone of apocalyptic excitement and rebellious agitation. He "specially admired the striking imagery and denunciations of the Hebrew prophets," and when he preached, "the invisible world would appear to open, and all present were made to feel whom he was addressing." Crawfoot flouted one Wesleyan restriction after another. He would "dabble in politics" when he saw fit, he imposed few if any limitations upon the form and length of meetings, and he assumed evangelistic duties without connexional permission. Crawfoot came in frequent contact with Peter Phillips and the American revivalist Lorenzo Dow, who encouraged his instinctive sympathy with Quaker belief and practice. But whatever his debt to others, Crawfoot had developed a form of sectarianism undeniably distinctive and influential. "The broad brimmed hat, and the cut of the coat that he patronised," a contemporary noted, "were kept in vogue by succeeding preachers." Clothing gave simple evidence of more significant differences. His bold departure from conventional Methodism

---

[4] *The Journals of William Clowes* (London, 1844; reprint ed., Glasgow: Wesley Historical Society, 1980), p. 65.

encouraged other popular evangelicals, particularly Primitive Methodists, to fight for their beliefs.[5]

The Primitive Methodist Connexion, largest of all the sects, also aimed towards a more egalitarian form of worship while reinvigorating the teachings of early Methodism. The origins of Primitive Methodism deserve careful note, for its early years reveal aspects of cottage religion essential to an understanding of nineteenth-century popular evangelicalism. Before the formal founding of the Connexion in 1812, the sect consisted of a loose association of cottage societies scattered around Staffordshire and the adjacent counties. Isolated societies heard about the visits of evangelists to neighboring villages by word of mouth, and invited them to preach. The unification of such diverse, dispersed societies was so erratic that Primitive Methodists of later generations disagreed over who the true founders of the Connexion were. Yet there were many similarities among these societies, rooted in the customs of cottage religion. "In the eyes of many," Hugh Bourne admitted, "there was scarcely any visible bond of union." But what Bourne called evangelical "zeal" and the transformation of common laborers into "saints"—in both instances referring to widespread popular practices—proved far stronger than even the members themselves had thought. "Indeed," he added, "such were the peculiar circumstances of the connexion, that no other bond could possibly have kept it together."[6]

The life of Hugh Bourne, the chief founder of Primitive Methodism, sheds light on some of the principal features of the sect. Bourne's birthplace resembled areas historically hospitable to dissent and was typical of Primitive Methodist settlements of subsequent years. He was born in 1772 at Fordhays, "a solitary moorland farm," a typical family establishment, in the parish of Stoke-on-Trent, in Stafford-

[5] George Herod, *Biographical Sketches of Some of Those Preachers of the Primitive Methodist Connexion* (London, n.d.), pp. 241–72; "Our First Travelling Preacher," *PMM*, 1902, pp. 921–4.

[6] Bourne, *History of the Primitive Methodists* (1823), p. 37. See also H. B. Kendall, *History of the Primitive Methodist Church*, 2 vols. (London, n.d.), 1:156–7.

shire. "Our neighbourhood consisted of three rather small farm houses," Bourne recalled; "and there was no other house, and no school nor place of worship within a considerable distance." Another account reported "no road, public or private, not even a foot-road to the house or anywhere near it, and to complete the isolation and loneliness, the only access to the house was over a wide brook upon a plank." Bourne's father, Joseph, worked hard as "a small farmer, a wheel-wright, and a timber-dealer" to support "a numerous family."[7] The county had not yet undergone the phenomenal industrial transformation that characterized it as a major iron and pottery center by the mid-nineteenth century, and Stoke was still relatively sparsely populated and undeveloped. Commenting on the backwardness of its agriculture in the latter part of the eighteenth century, Pitt considered Staffordshire "a county just emerging from a state of barbarism."[8] A visitor to the Bourne homestead remarked years later, "The place . . . had nothing of this world's glory. It was an illustration of God's . . . choosing the weak things of the world, and the things that are despised, to bring to nought the things that are."[9]

In such humble isolation, one wonders how, save by moorland magic, Hugh Bourne developed a body of opinion on religious matters. No doubt the greatest part of his Primitive Methodist theology evolved from solitary study and endless private rumination about religion. "Like Bunyan's Pilgrim," he later recalled, "I had to make my way alone." Nevertheless, Bourne's mother acted as a formative influence. "Notable for industry," she "taught nearly the whole of her . . . family to read," Bourne recorded, "and endeavoured to train them up in the fear of the Lord."[10] Subsequent historians chose to see her in the tradition of Susannah Wesley: Ellen Bourne, according to Kendall, was "a thrifty, long-suffering woman, . . .

[7] Kendall, *History*, 1:7; Rev. T. Baron, "Reminiscences of a Residence at Bemersley," *PMM*, 1900, p. 751.
[8] Quoted in D. M. Palliser, *The Staffordshire Landscape*, p. 127.
[9] Baron, "Reminiscences," p. 751.
[10] Bourne, *History*, p. 3.

the true stay and band of the house," who inculcated sound values and morals in the founder of the church "as she sat busy at the spinning-wheel."[11] Her inclinations were in fact Methodistic, while those of her husband were "much and vigorously opposed" to all forms of dissent, and "especially to Methodism." Described as "dissolute" and temperamental, and yet a staunch churchman, Joseph Bourne provided a counterbalance to Hugh's spiritual training. "When quite a boy," Hugh recorded, "I learned by rote, or committed to memory, the morning and evening prayers of the Church, with the Te Deum, Litany, &c. This was done at my father's instance; . . . We were what are reckoned 'good churchgoers.' "[12] Within the microcosm of the Bourne household, Hugh encountered simple versions of both the speculative, evangelical impulse and the formalistic strictures of eighteenth-century religious thought.

As a carpenter, Bourne travelled freely and determined his own course of work. He cultivated a similar intellectual independence through an autodidactic program based chiefly on religious writings. From neighbors, clients, and acquaintances, he borrowed a smattering of works and contemplated them collectively. Quaker writings, works by Wesley, and tracts by seventeenth-century sectaries went into his meditations, along with solid tomes on eighteenth-century Protestantism. In 1799, though he was not a member or even a regular attender of any religious society, Bourne was converted while reading John Fletcher's "Letters on the Spiritual Manifestation of God." His instincts had led him to a quasi-Methodist position, so he finally joined a Wesleyan society at Ridgeway, not far from the Bournes' new residence at Bemersley. His mother and younger brother soon joined as well, and, like Hugh, saw no need to view their self-styled religion as incompatible with the polity of the Methodist Connexion.

[11] Kendall, *History*, 1:8.
[12] Quoted in "A Sketch of the Life and Labours of the Venerable Hugh Bourne," *PMM*, 1853, p. 516.

It was not long before Bourne's work and friends led him from the narrow path of Wesleyanism. In 1801, Bourne was working "at and near Harrisehead [*sic*], about three miles distant from Bemersley." Perhaps identifying with Wesley's calling among the Kingswood colliers, he set out to "promote religion" at Harriseahead. The place "had no means of grace," he explained in his *History of the Primitive Methodists*, "and the inhabitants, chiefly colliers, appeared to be entirely destitute of religion, and much addicted to ungodliness: it was indeed reckoned a prophane neighbourhood above most others."[13] Bourne's strategy later became customary for Primitive Methodists: their best ventures took place in areas beyond the reach of the Established Church and either shunned or abandoned by the Wesleyan Connexion. Further enhancing the prospects for evangelizing were Bourne's personal connections. By virtue of his occupation, Bourne obtained an *entrée* to the hub of local affairs, the shop of the village blacksmith. Chief among local rogues frequenting the shop, moreover, was Bourne's cousin, Daniel Shubotham. Familial ties probably brought together Bourne and Shubotham at Christmastime, when Bourne finally persuaded the renegade collier "to set out for heaven." Once Shubotham succumbed, others followed "and there was a great reformation in the neighbourhood."[14] Independent of any official appointment, Bourne had started his own revival.

The basis for schism soon appeared, in spite of Bourne's good intentions. Suiting their distinctive tastes in worship, the revivalists established cottage prayer meetings along new lines. Their hostess, Jane Hall, "for long the only Methodist at Harriseahead," had held Wesleyan preaching services "once a fortnight . . . for some years." But the new meetings jettisoned the decorum considered appropriate to country preaching stations. Kendall provided an uncritical description:

> The prayer meetings thus instituted were not of the ordinary kind. Here, again, everybody was expected to take

[13] Bourne, *History*, p. 5.
[14] Ibid., p. 5; Kendall, *History*, 1:24.

part, and liveliness was the characteristic. "The people got
to be, in a great measure, Israelitish," says Hugh Bourne,
which we find, being interpreted, means—noisyish. He
quotes from Ezra iii. 12, 13: " 'And all the people shouted
with a great shout . . . and the noise was heard afar off.' "
This was strictly true of the "Israelitish" prayer meetings
held at Jane Hall's, for Hugh Bourne tells how, the door
of a house on Mow Cop happening to stand open, Elizabeth Baddeley, a miner's wife, who was given to the use
of profane language, distinctly heard the sound of prayer
and praise coming from Harriseahead a mile and a half
off, and was convinced of sin and set out for heaven. . . .
H. B. says drily: "Any one that could distinguish his or
her own voice must have had a pretty good ear!"[15]

The meetings invited loud, spontaneous prayer from all present; the "great shout" of the cottage congregation replaced
the measured tones of the circuit preacher. "Never, perhaps,"
claimed Kendall, "was a revival carried on with less preaching
of a formal pulpit kind." Jane Hall's meetings proved so encouraging that Hugh Bourne, himself, hitherto excessively
shy, realized that "he was fitted to be a public praying labourer." "Conversation-preaching," not sermonizing, made
converts. The cottage evangelists thus abandoned the conventions of institutional religion and instead promoted the
vernacular.[16]
 Loud prayer provoked hot disputes between sectarians and
Wesleyans. Years before, John Wesley had feared that boisterous Methodists, particularly women, would leave bad
impressions upon listeners. "Never scream," he wrote to Sarah
Mallet, a class leader in Yorkshire. "Never speak above the
natural pitch of your voice; it is disgustful to hearers. It gives
them pain, not pleasure."[17] Many biographies testified to Wesleyan intolerance of loud and spontaneous prayer. When the

[15] Ibid., pp. 31–2.
[16] Ibid., p. 31.
[17] John Wesley to Sarah Mallet, 15 Dec. 1789, quoted in Leslie Church, *More About the Early Methodist People* (London: Epworth, 1949), pp. 140–1.

Old Connexion was unable to silence its voluble followers, it hastened their removal to other societies. In Leicester, "an eccentric character" named Andrews "lost his status as a Wesleyan in consequence of breaking out into bursts of praise during the time of service." Such outcasts acquired heroic status among Primitive Methodists. Andrews, for one, was esteemed "a sterling jewel."[18] Sectarians applauded the defiance of chapel etiquette, prompted, they insisted, by spiritual imperatives. Bourne was forever engaging in debates that "turned chiefly on noisy Methodists." When passed, the issue of loudness led to questioning all convention; the "great shout" became a litmus test of true sectarianism.

The challenge to convention extended into the sphere of work. The Harriseahead society soon grappled with a conflict between a free style of worship and the discipline of an industrial age. Fearing the consequences of unbridled revivalism, the society adopted rules of "a very great strictness." ". . . None were willingly allowed to exercise in public who were not correct in their conduct," Bourne recorded, "and diligent in the duties of their callings." Mindful of the pervasive presence of the local mining industry, organizers saw to it that "on week day evenings, the prayer meetings were seldom held very long, that they might not interfere with other duties."[19] Limitations upon time and behavior together operated as a curb against unruliness. When revivalism threatened to destroy regulated time and proper conduct, the rules of the chapel offered a ready antidote. Two competing styles of religion had emerged from the Harriseahead revival.

Bourne soon became cognizant of the conflict between cottage and chapel when, largely at his own expense, he built a chapel at Harriseahead in 1802. At his urging, the cottage society joined the Old Methodist Connexion, and, as a result, "preaching was appointed in [the chapel] for ten and two,

[18] Kendall, *History*, 1:307. See also H. Bourne, *MSS. Journal*, vol. 1, March 20, 1808.
[19] Bourne, *History*, p. 5.

every Sunday." "This," he admitted, "was over-doing it. The work had been raised up chiefly by means of pious conversation and prayer meetings; and so very much preaching at such a place, and under such circumstances, seemed not to have a good effect; it seemed to hinder the exertions of the people." Having chafed at the earlier restrictions, now members openly complained of excessive formalism. Daniel Shubotham, always the instigator, vowed, "You shall have a meeting upon Mow some Sunday, and have a whole day's praying, and then you'll be satisfied." Bourne and Shubotham recognized their error, for it became clear that the mere existence of the chapel suggested a different order of worship. Free and loud prayer did not concur with chapel discipline; nor did plans for "a day's praying upon Mow" agree with the principles of visiting preachers. The cottage-style revival "soon made a pause," checked by the restrictions growing both from within and outside the society.[20]

The Harriseahead revivalists had collided head-on with a mentality increasingly evident within institutional religion in England. Gradually churches and chapels of all denominations recognized their new role in the changing society around them: the growth of cities and towns and the social unrest of the 1790s alerted religious leaders to the need for a forceful, civilizing influence.[21] Wesleyanism shared this vision of the role of the church in the social order; the centralizing, bureaucratic trend within the Connexion gave evidence of this, particularly after 1800. When circuit towns exerted greater control over country stations, the new civilizing impulse travelled from the centers to the margins of the Connexion. As Bourne discov-

[20] Ibid., p. 6.

[21] Ford K. Brown, *Fathers of the Victorians: The Age of Wilberforce* (Cambridge University Press, 1961); Kenneth S. Inglis, *Churches and the Working Classes in Victorian England* (London: Routledge & Kegan Paul, 1963), Intro.; Ernest M. Howse, *Saints in Politics* (Toronto: University of Toronto Press, 1952); Bernard Semmel, *The Methodist Revolution* (New York: Basic Books, 1973), chap. 5; Thomas W. Laqueur, *Religion and Respectability* (New Haven: Yale University Press, 1976), esp. chaps. 2 and 7.

ered, even the humblest chapel became the handmaiden of the larger world if it received appointed preachers from other localities. Preaching at "ten and two" represented a panoply of attitudes and values essential to institutional life but alien to cottage evangelicalism.[22]

Hugh Bourne was not a stranger to "modern" religion. Carpentry, as well as evangelism, had taken him to towns and cities, where he visited churches, chapels, and, in one instance, that queen of institutionalized religion, the Lichfield Cathedral. He recorded a visit to Lichfield in his journal for 1807, and his thoughts on religion—shared no doubt with his close friends Crawfoot and Phillips—reveal the enormous gulf between village evangelists and the Established Church:

> I was at Lichfield, to get a license for Mow Meeting; and I went into the minister [sic]. After the service began, it ran through my mind, "Get thee out of this place, and beware of the woman that has the golden cup in her hand, and those that are with her; their ways are death: sin no more lest a worse thing come upon thee." This startled me, as I had before taken delight in their singing of the service. I saw much lightness and sin among the parsons. It seemed like gross idolatry in them to spend their time in such a manner: but then I thought "The words of the service are good." It then struck me, "These people draweth nigh unto me with their lips," &c. I prayed to God that if the impression to go out [of the church] was from Him, it might increase, if not, that it might go away: it increased till I was quite miserable. I then thought to go out, and a voice came, "Escape for thy life," &c. They were singing the *Te Deum*. I took my hat as soon as they had

[22] W. R. Ward, *Religion and Society in England, 1790–1850* (New York: Schocken Books, 1973), chap. 4, esp. pp. 78–83; James Obelkevich, *Religion and Rural Society* (Oxford: Clarendon Press, 1976), pp. 204–5. Obelkevich concludes that in most exchanges between town and countryside, "the initiating impulse and vigor came from the towns" and that the "flow of preachers was also predominantly from town to village" by the end of the Victorian period.

> done the *Te Deum*, and went out, and the burden was
> removed. It looked as if judgments hung over that place.
> I stopped all afternoon in Lichfield, and such a travail of
> soul came upon me as I never before experienced,—it was
> for the city; . . . I trembled for the place and people; . . .
> I asked James Crawfoot at the Forest about this. He said
> it was the sign of the times. . . . He said something would
> turn up, either the gospel would be introduced, or afflic-
> tions would come upon them.[23]

Frozen in his pew, half by deference, half by revulsion, Bourne
recalled with apocalyptic fervor the lamentations of George
Fox on the city. Clearly the country carpenter inhabited a
mental world totally different from that of the Church minister. Commenting on Bourne's spiritual development, W. R.
Ward has noted that much of "the interest of the journals of
Bourne and Clowes lies in the light they cast upon humble
men for whom adherence to the Establishment was out of the
question and official Wesleyanism offered no way forward."[24]
Confrontations with chapel and Church attitudes slowly forced
Bourne towards reckoning with a new form of sectarian
religion.

Sectarian Methodism promoted an old-fashioned religion
that indeed preserved "primitive" aspects of behavior and belief among laborers. The plebeian mentality of sectarianism
preferred the Old Testament, with its rigorous faith and struggle, to the moralistic evangelicalism of the New Testament.
Religion was an all-encompassing ideology of everyday life for
followers, determining their clothing, speech, and ways of
working. Sectarian Methodism aimed to revise contemporary
evangelicalism with attitudes and values excluded from institutional religion, and in doing so, it launched an attack on the
propriety inherent in modern religion. Nowhere did its quarrel with Victorian convention appear more dramatic than in
sectarian camp meetings and female preaching, where doc-

[23] Kendall, *History*, 1:151.
[24] Ward, *Religion and Society*, p. 78.

trinal conflict finally culminated in the birth of the Primitive
Methodist Connexion.

BY FORCING the break between sectarian Methodists and Wesleyans, camp meetings and female preaching heralded an important new phase of independent religious activity among
the laboring classes. Both represented a challenge to the "order" advocated by institutional religion at the beginning of
the nineteenth century. Camp meetings overthrew standards
of behavior and worship traditionally upheld by churches and
chapels, while female preachers implicitly questioned the
rightfulness of male leadership. The two activities distinguished popular evangelicals from all other religious groups.

Camp meetings were all-day gatherings borrowed from
American revivalism. In form, camp meetings recapitulated
the principles of cottage religion by openly defying restrictions
of time, space, liturgy, and leadership. Camp meetings also
featured a range of activities that engaged the entire congregation instead of assigning a central role to the sermon. The
first in England, held in May of 1807 on Mow Cop, entailed
"singing, prayer, preaching, exhortations, speaking experience, [and] relating anecdotes." Participants also organized
"permanent praying companies," which, unlike prayer under
ordinary circumstances, "did not break up for preaching."
Accounts of the historic day do not include a complete record
of participating preachers, a revealing omission: the camp
meeting discouraged conspicuous preaching performances
and stressed the importance of congregational participation.
The right to speak passed from one person to the next as he
or she—members and non-members alike—volunteered to relate some "christian experience." Any style of presentation was
admissible—one sea captain gave his life history entirely in
verse—and some accounts departed from strictly spiritual matters to include detailed reports of current events. The camp
meeting thus substituted popular speech and traditional folk-
lore for conventional religious rhetoric. Sectarian enthusiasm
for the new ritual signified a convergence of popular religion

and folk tradition, a union that instilled both with new vitality.[25]

The camp meeting meant all things to all people. It soon became "the most distinctive of the means of grace" in Primitive Methodism.[26] To enemies of dissent, however, the massive outdoor event suggested political anarchy and religious heresy. Following the first meeting, Hugh Bourne learned that a local master potter, "a man of standing and influence in the neighbourhood," planned to press charges under the Conventicle Act. By obtaining licenses for the grounds and all participating preachers of the second camp meeting, Bourne avoided prosecution. Primitive Methodism was born during an era when nonconformity was still legally vulnerable to a hostile establishment. Under clauses of the Uniformity Acts, magistrates could prosecute Methodist society members holding meetings in their homes. Itinerant preachers and camp meetings, even more conspicuous, required still more precaution.[27] In most cases, Alan Gilbert has argued, legal confrontations leading up to Lord Sidmouth's bill attempting to check itinerant preachers represented the final surge of Anglican-Tory hostility. After Sidmouth's defeat and the repeal of the Conventicle Act in 1812, the "dependency system" at the root of such antagonism finally ceased to function.[28] But Primitive Methodists continued to encounter harassment at a local level, and defensive measures became standard procedure. The first camp meetings uncovered prejudices that flourished in spite of legal change.

The Wesleyan reaction to camp meetings came quickly and decisively. The Conference of 1807, meeting during the summer, condemned camp meetings without exception:

> Q. What is the judgment of the Conference concerning what are called Camp Meetings?

[25] Reginald Nettel, "Folk Elements in Nineteenth-Century Puritanism," *Folk-Lore* 80 (1969), pp. 272–4.

[26] Obelkevich, *Religion and Rural Society*, p. 227.

[27] Kendall, *History*, 1:72–4.

[28] Gilbert, *Religion and Society*, pp. 78–9.

A. It is our judgment, that even supposing such meetings
to be allowable in America, they are highly improper
in England, and likely to be productive of considerable
mischief: and we disclaim all connexion with them.[29]

For the next five years, the Connexion expelled members for
taking part in camp meetings. The Wesleyan decision to ex-
tirpate popular activism within its own ranks reflected a growing repressiveness throughout English society. The Connexion
allied itself with the government and disowned "mischief" of
the lower classes that threatened its acceptance by the
establishment.

Connexional politics, however, only begin to explain the
significance of camp meetings. A closer examination of the
content of camp meeting revivalism lends a social dimension
to its religious subversiveness. Through its uncensored testi-
monials and open manner of worship, the camp meeting lent
religious legitimacy to the worldly experiences of common
laborers, artisans, and small farmers; indeed, as *volkish* elements came into play, camp meeting narrations focused more
on the crooked, chequered path to heaven than the straight
and narrow. The camp meeting made public the worst private
experiences of lower-class life. Middle-class refinement and
oratorical skill seldom tempered this unembarrassed admission of past degradation. Primitive Methodism thus elevated
the debased to the realm of the sacred and upset the hierarchy
of experience essential to conventional social order.

One picaresque narration met with enthusiastic approval at
the first Mow Cop meeting: William Clowes, later a leader
among Primitive Methodists, must have astounded and delighted listeners with his peregrinations through low life. The
son of a Burslem (Staffs.) potter, Clowes had little formal education or religious training. At ten, he became an apprentice
potter to his uncle, but from an early age, he showed signs of
an intractable and rebellious temperament. Clowes' *Journals*
(1844), a collection of reminiscences, give a remarkably frank

[29] Bourne, *History*, p. 14.

account of these early years. Clowes tells of his early aban-
donment of his wife following a quarrel with his mother-in-
law, his subsequent tramp for work around Warrington and
Hull, numerous nocturnal adventures in wayside public
houses, and even his close escape from a press gang following
a brawl. Noticeably absent is the self-abhorrent and judgmen-
tal tone of most pious memoirs. Clowes instead employed a
narrative, episodic style that sheds a heroic light upon his many
exploits. All this, in fact, survived the revisions of an anony-
mous editor. Popular evangelicalism, in the hands of men like
Clowes, refused to be bowdlerized.[30]

Camp meeting evangelicals quickly promoted Clowes to the
peak of popularity. The renegade potter somehow captured
the spirit of sectarian Methodism: he was a masterless man,
freed from occupational and social constraints and wandering
pariah-like through a hostile world. His refusal to conform
appealed to persons on the margins of a modernizing society.
Clowes championed the loud prayer of cottage evangelism and
camp meetings. The souls of the disorderly had an obligation
to speak out, he argued; "fettering them too much with what
men call system and order" severed their tie to "the order of
God." His objections to orderly behavior in religious services
applied to work time as well. Clowes was notorious for his
inspired outbursts; he prayed and sang with great vigor while
at work, sometimes taking undisguised pleasure in disrupting
the work of others. Clowes promoted a religious unruliness
against the advance of a rational universe and a world which
gave no control to the common laborer.[31]

Like camp meeting revivalism, female preaching subverted

[30] Clowes, *Journals*, pp. 1–21; see also John Davison, *The Life of the Venerable
William Clowes* (London, 1854); John T. Wilkinson, *William Clowes, 1780–1851*
(London: Epworth Press, 1951).

[31] Clowes, *Journals*, pp. 26, 53. When female visionaries described the hierarchy of saints at the Day of Judgment, Clowes ranked just below the highest
of luminaries, Lorenzo Dow; in contrast, James Bourne, brother of Hugh and
the administrative drudge of the Primitive Methodist Connexion in later years,
sat at the bottom of the visionary ladder. Kendall, *History*, 1:153.

Wesleyan attempts to control popular evangelicalism. Though the origins of female preaching lay in the principles of spiritual democracy espoused by early Methodism,[32] the case for female evangelism was never clearly established, and John Wesley's position offered no decisive solution. His lenient policy did not survive his death. Faced with the growing prominence of female preaching during the 1790s, connexional leaders responded with the same disapproval they felt towards cottage evangelism and revivalism. The 1803 Wesleyan Conference finally ruled against women preachers on the grounds that "a vast majority" of Wesleyans were "opposed to it" and, moreover, "their preaching [did] not at all seem necessary, there being a sufficiency of Preachers, whom God has accredited, to supply all the places in our Connexion with regular preaching."[33]

Both points were questionable and only hinted at the real issues in the debate over the value of female preaching. "Unaccredited" preachers created anxiety familiar to Wesleyan Methodists. Charges of ignorance and vulgarity had dogged the Connexion from its start, and in recent years, lower-class preachers ("tailors, pig-drovers, [and] chimney-sweepers") became the focus of attacks by the Established Church.[34] Now unrestrained women, self-appointed and almost exclusively from the laboring classes, threatened to undermine a hard-won image of respectability. Measuring their behavior against polite standards of female etiquette, Wesleyan officials found women preachers wanting. The emotional fervor of revivalist services, the late hours of nighttime meetings, and frequent solitary travel placed women in highly vulnerable situations. Their public display of opinion and emotion suggested a loose-

[32] For a thorough background of female preaching, see Church, *More About the Early Methodist People*, chap. 4, and "The Women Itinerant Preachers of Early Methodism," *Proceedings of the Wesley Historical Society* 28 (1952), pp. 89–90.

[33] Quoted in Ibid., p. 90.

[34] *A Sketch of the History and Proceedings of the Deputies Appointed to Protect the Civil Rights of the Protestant Dissenters* (1813), p. 92 and passim.

ness bordering on licentiousness. They not only appeared improper and indecent; their pretensions to the power of the pulpit overturned the patriarchal assumptions of chapel administration. Female unruliness challenged the prevailing institutional image of masculine reasonableness. The Wesleyan establishment responded with contempt. The funeral sermon for a former Connexional president converted by Mary Barritt gave vent to such feelings. "God often works by strange instruments," his eulogist declared. "Balaam was converted by the braying of an ass, and Peter by the crowing of a cock; and our lamented brother by the preaching of a woman one Good Friday morning."[35]

Exceptions to the prohibitions against female preaching revealed the underlying fear of impropriety haunting Wesleyan authorities. "If any woman among us thinks she has an extraordinary call from God to speak in public," the minutes stated, "we are of the opinion she should, in general, address her *own sex*, and *those only*."[36] In effect, the ruling confined women's work to classes and special functions with restricted audiences. Hence their addresses were not sermons at all, but personal expressions of piety following no standard form of delivery. They could deliver homilies at Sunday School openings and anniversaries, and they continued to win acclaim as leaders of "Dorcas Meetings" (where the Scriptures were read to poor women) and all-female classes. But the increasingly professional Wesleyan ministry closed its doors to women. The roles assigned to women, though essential to institutionalized Wesleyanism, did not include public leadership.[37]

The women of popular evangelicalism rejected the model of female piety promoted by Wesleyanism and established re-

---

[35] Kendall, *History*, 1:195.

[36] Quoted in Swift, "The Women Itinerant Preachers," p. 90.

[37] See, e.g., Annie K. Keeling, *Eminent Methodist Women* (London, 1889); Charles Wesley Buoy, *Representative Women of Methodism* (New York, 1893); for a recent study of women's work in the church, see Frank Prochaska, *Women and Philanthropy in Nineteenth-century England* (Oxford: Oxford University Press, 1980).

ligion. A flow of biographies of eminent Wesleyan women (many of them *wives* of preachers) indicated a mounting pressure to conform to a middle-class prescription of piety. Memoirs and tracts urged the sisterhood to take up unadorned dress ("more plain and simple than that of the lowest servant in the house"), to visit "the abodes of misery and woe," and most important, to protect the "happiness and prosperity" of their own homes.[38] But sectarian women resisted such inappropriate confinement. They wore plain dress by necessity, not choice, and lived in the humble abodes that Wesleyan women were supposed to visit. Sectarian ideals of domesticity rose from different circumstances: the interests of the household and wider community converged. In behalf of that community, women violated conventional codes of piety and privacy, praying loudly, reproving vigorously, and, above all, preaching publicly. The pretenses of polite society, as well as the sins of poorer folk, came under the cudgel of the female evangelist.

Female preaching among sectarian Methodists flourished despite Wesleyan prohibitions. Female visionaries readily controlled Magic Methodist services. Bourne visited Crawfoot's society in 1807 and was favorably impressed by several women. Nancy Foden, the wife of a Delamere Forest bricklayer, spoke at length from her chair "without stopping, or opening her eyes" on a theme recalling Psalm 23. Crawfoot seemed willing to turn over the meeting to the female contingent. After Foden emerged from the visionary state, "several women shook hands with her" in congratulations, and when Bourne tried to question her, another woman put him off. But Foden proved to be "a motherly woman" who "conversed well on religion." Before Bourne left, she gave him sound advice on overcoming his periodic inhibitions in preaching.[39]

[38] Samuel Warren, *Memoirs and Select Letters of Mrs. Anne Warren* (London, 1827), p. 3; *The Influence of Pious Women in Promoting a Revival of Religion* (London: Religious Tract Society [1835]), p. 1; Rev. Joseph Beaumont, *Memoirs of Mrs. Mary Tatham* (London, 1838), p. 55.

[39] Walford, *Memoirs of Hugh Bourne*, pp. 142–3; 154–5.

Women also assumed the full duties of preaching to sectarian Methodist societies. Mrs. Mary Dunnel, a popular preacher from Bemersley, rose to a "pinnacle of fame" for her "volubility of speech and flowery eloquence" among nascent Primitive Methodist societies. She naturally encountered the stiff opposition of Wesleyan authorities, who attempted to prevent her from speaking at the second camp meeting in 1807 by offering her the pulpit of the Tunstall chapel. Her ministry aroused a heated debate when Wesleyans finally denied her the right to preach there and elsewhere. A group of camp meeting sympathizers "said it was enough to make a secession, and they . . . determined to fit up [a member's] kitchen for a place of worship." The progression from chapel to kitchen did not diminish Mrs. Dunnel's usefulness. She continued to preach in homes around northern Staffordshire and Derbyshire, where "she scarcely ever failed" to open "a door for the reception of [Primitive Methodist] gospel."[40]

The debate over female preaching raised issues central to sectarianism. At the urging of Quaker Methodist Peter Phillips, Hugh Bourne collected his thoughts on the subject in "Remarks on the Ministry of Women" published in 1808. Bourne's defense of female preaching showed how far he had departed from connexional authority. "I think [Jesus Christ] authorized Miriam, (Micah vi. 4,) Deborah, Huldah, and perhaps many others not recorded," Bourne pointed out; "and the gospel was preached in those days, (Heb. iv. 2,) and he is the same God now, and acts in the same way." God was immune to the caprice of ecclesiastical fashion, and so, for that matter, was Bourne. His rejection of conventional standards became clear when he enumerated the "women authorized [to preach] by Jesus Christ." The list began with the Virgin Mary and

---

[40] Ibid., pp. 275, 164–5. In 1811, Mrs. Dunnel "made a secession, and set up for herself, as the head of a new community" in Derbyshire. Though Hugh Bourne was very attached to her at one time, by the end of that year he was distressed by her actions and relieved to have lost her. In his journal, he reported that rumor of Mrs. Dunnel's third marriage had reached Staffordshire (pp. 330–3, 346).

other exemplary figures; but then, he continued, "perhaps, you want a personal commission,—very well, then you have Mary Magdalene. She was commissioned by an angel to preach, and then by Jesus Christ himself." Victorian morality never clouded Bourne's perception of Biblical truth; camp meetings and cottage services made room for women like Mary Magdalene.[41]

The separate world of cottage evangelicalism enabled Bourne to maneuver around the most notorious and explicit prohibition, I Corinthians 14:34: "Let your women keep silence in the churches." "I am told," he wrote, "that these [restrictions] speak of church discipline, and of establishing church authority." Bourne invoked a crucial distinction, peculiar to popular evangelicalism, between institutional discipline and preaching. The administrative rules of the chapel had nothing to do with free, divinely inspired preaching; having no churches or chapels, cottage evangelists could ignore laws pertaining to such discipline. "I have heard it stated further," Bourne added,

> that he [i.e., Paul] there says, "If they will learn any thing, let them ask their husbands at home." This they say settles the meaning, for he must be speaking of something that the husbands can inform them of. This well appeals to discipline, but if it extends to preaching also, then all who have ungodly husbands are inevitably bound over to eternal damnation, because they are restricted from learning any thing from any but their husbands.[42]

The right to converse on religious matters gave women the power to override the patriarchal social order. No restriction, Bourne pointed out, should "exclude women from teaching men religion." Their rights extended to domestic life, where worldly circumstances demanded a similar flexibility. Bourne

[41] H. Bourne, "Remarks on the Ministry of Women," reprinted in Walford, *Memoirs*, pp. 174–5.

[42] Ibid., p. 176.

grounded this circumlocutious exegesis upon practical experience. According to the laws of household religion, women had an obligation to speak out.[43]

Bourne's defense of female preaching had broad ramifications as a theology of the oppressed. Like most churchmen, Bourne based his definition of female "prophesy" on passages of Joel and Acts. "We find in Joel 2:28," he argued in his introductory remarks, " 'And your sons and your daughters shall prophesy.' " But unlike spokesmen for established religion, Bourne intended a literal interpretation inadmissible by 1800. His citation of Acts 2:18, "And on my servants and on my handmaidens I will pour out in those days of my Spirit; and they shall prophesy," was highly significant. According to Primitive Methodist authorities, the passage referred to "persons of the lowest condition, such as male and female slaves."[44] Class, as well as gender, identified those qualified to preach. The situation of women, lacking privilege and power, was characteristic of Primitive Methodists, generally. In conclusion, Bourne underscored the importance of this symbolic function of women. "I think all objections that can be brought [against women] may be confined to this, that the woman is the weaker vessel. But this is so far from making against, that it is strongly in favour of it. See 1 Cor. 1. 27." This, as his final citation, carried added weight:

> But God hath chosen the foolish things of the world to confound the wise; and God hath chosen the weak things of the world to confound the things which are mighty.[45]

Women preachers therefore assumed a multifaceted, crucial role in popular evangelicalism. As visionaries and vessels of divine revelation, they perpetuated popular spirituality and fought against secularizing trends in modern religion. A supernatural "extraordinary call" to preach liberated women

[43] Ibid., p. 176.

[44] "On the Ministry of Women," *Primitive Methodist Magazine*, 1821, pp. 180–1.

[45] Bourne, "Remarks," p. 177.

evangelists from the prohibitions of established religions and their direct relationship to divine authority enabled them to defy worldly constraints. As "weak things of the world," women received a special call to represent the claims of the oppressed. Sectarian theology reacted to the powerlessness of the laborer in the face of recent economic and social change; it established a world turned upside down, where women took revenge upon changing rules of social order and etiquette and loudly expressed the miseries of their class.

PART II

RURAL WOMEN AND COTTAGE
RELIGION

FIVE

The Context of Cottage Religion
and Female Preaching

AT THE TURN OF THE CENTURY, the cottage religion of sectarian Methodism entered a new, expansive phase of its existence. As part of the larger history of nonconformity, it
shared in a period of significant growth that added many new
dissenting groups to those active before the 1790s. It also
anticipated a growing evangelical fervor, soon to be associated
with Victorianism, within the Established Church and Dissent.
But the rise of cottage religion demands further analysis in
light of circumstances that were peculiarly its own. Where and
why this domestic form of religion, with its unique female
preachers, found support among the laboring classes can be
explained in part by looking at the new economic and social
relations of industrial England. The history of laboring life in
village communities becomes visible through the experiences
of women preachers, whose careers were inextricably inter-
woven with their domestic circumstances. In examining female
preaching in different regions, the following chapters do not
attempt a study of religious geography, but illustrate rather
the widespread activity of women in relation to general trends
affecting laboring households. The context of cottage religion
cannot be ignored, for such conditions highlight the ability of
followers to construct a religion according to their own unique
history.

Cottage religion was, by definition, a product of rural culture, and it is in the country that we must examine its earliest
social bases. The strength of the Church always played a part
in determining the success of cottage religion; it, too, was based
on a rural prototype, the parish. In the early nineteenth cen-

tury the Church's presence was still felt through rituals and customs, at least in the form of baptism, marriage, and burial, that served every parish dweller. But absenteeism and parochial neglect were rife. The evangelical revival was slow to stir much of the rural clergy, and, until government subsidies of the mid-century, the church fabric itself was in decay. Petitions like the one from Glossop in the 1820s, complaining that "the church is a very ancient structure, . . . so ruinous and in danger of falling down that it is not safe for the parishioners to assemble therein," were typical. In areas such as these, all forms of Methodism made sizable inroads.[1]

Cottage religion flourished in regions free from control by clergy and large landholders. Within the variety of rural localities that gave rise to dissent in the nineteenth century, many were marginal forest, moorland, or waste areas, and "were almost all marked by an unusual degree of freedom" from interference of landlords and clergy. Often these areas were receptive to domestic industries that further freed laboring inhabitants from dependent relationships, and contemporaries sometimes found cottagers there resistant to a rational work ethic and habits of deference. Industrial villages were receptive to cottage religion for similar reasons. Situated near agricultural districts and sometimes functioning as a crossroads or marketplace, the open village was notoriously free from a single influence and the focus for many competing interests. Vast rural slums developed in these villages, as the

[1] David M. Thompson, "The Churches and Society in Nineteenth-century England: A Rural Perspective," *Popular Belief and Practice*, Studies in Church History, vol. 8, G. J. Cuming and Derek Baker, eds. (Cambridge: Cambridge University Press, 1972), pp. 267–76. Examples of such trends are plentiful in Derbyshire records. Rev. J. Charles Cox, *Three Centuries of Derbyshire Annals* (London, 1890), 1:387; S. Glover, *History, Gazetteer, and Directory of the County of Derby* (Derby, 1829), 1:306–8; S. O. Addy, "Derbyshire Folk-Lore," in Rev. J. C. Cox, ed., *Memorials of Old Derbyshire* (London, 1907), pp. 346–70; Clarence Daniel, *Derbyshire Customs* (Dalesman Books, 1976). See also John Farey, *A General View of the Agriculture and Minerals of Derbyshire*, 3 vols. (London, 1811–17). On the Church in rural society, see James Obelkevich, *Religion and Rural Society* (Oxford: Clarendon Press, 1976), chap. III.

promise of shelter and work attracted the rural unemployed and migrant poor. When domestic or small-scale industry formed the basis of the local economy, villagers frequently faced impoverishment because of the sporadic nature of their employment. Such "semi-villages," as Eric Hobsbawm has called them, were noted havens for potential converts to Primitive Methodism. In these pockets of the "masterless" poor, the class basis of Methodist sectarianism gave laborers an ideology and a community.[2]

Popular evangelicalism also flourished, conversely, in the face of an aggressive squirearchy. This trend was not as contradictory as it appeared. Parochial neglect could give way, particularly when land changed hands, to new and subtle attempts to control village life through the Church. Enclosure and commutation of tithes enabled the clergy to accumulate land and power and join forces with village elites. With the substantial increase in the number of clerical magistrates, or "squarsons," in the first part of the nineteenth century, "the bond of church and state was more strongly emphasized than at any time since Laud."[3] Property rights and the desire for social order overshadowed the concerns of laborers and other marginal persons. The Church was no longer so much the locus of village tradition and shared community values as a moralizing, well-circumstanced presence. "The result was that when the Establishment engaged in the conservative social

[2] E. J. Hobsbawm, *Primitive Rebels* (New York: Norton, 1959), pp. 137–8; see also E. J. Hobsbawm and George Rudé, *Captain Swing* (Harmondsworth: Penguin Books, 1973), p. 37; William Jessop, *An Account of Methodism in Rossendale and the Neighbourhood* (Manchester, 1881), p. 190; "Thoughts on Itinerant Preaching," *Evangelical Magazine*, 1810, pp. 468–71; W. R. Ward, "Popular Religion and the Problem of Control, 1790–1830," *Popular Belief and Practice*, Studies in Church History, vol. 8, G. J. Cuming and Derek Baker, eds. (Cambridge: Cambridge University Press, 1972), pp. 240–56.

[3] Eric J. Evans, "Some Reasons for the Growth of English Rural Anti-Clericalism, c. 1750–c. 1830," *Past & Present* 66 (1975), pp. 101–3, 109; *The Contentious Tithe* (London: Routledge & Kegan Paul, 1976); W. R. Ward, "The Tithe Question in England in the Early Nineteenth Century," *Journal of Ecclesiastical History* 16 (1965): 67–81.

functions which once had seemed to buttress the cohesion of a rural community, it did so from the 1790s onwards (in many parts of the country) as an obviously partisan institution."[4] Here sectarian Methodism appeared as a religious rebellion against upper-class moralism and control; in regions where squarsons applied stringent prohibitions, cottage religion was tantamount to a public flouting of the social order itself.

Popular evangelicalism thrived, then, in settings that fostered the growth of independent laboring religious communities, which were posed against local authorities or were attempting to create alliances where local power was diffused. Economic factors contributed still more meaning to plebeian religious affiliation. The isolation and insecurity of small farmers and laborers underscored their need for the autonomous, supportive community of cottage societies. Their beliefs became the basis for a theology of the oppressed. For marginalized small farmers, the new religion reinforced traditional views and status; their defensive identification with laborers, culturally as well as economically, became stronger as the century went on. "So great was the contrast [between large and small farmers] that contemporaries routinely classified cottagers and small farmers with the 'poor' and not with the larger farmers."[5] Cottagers found the cooperative social vision of Methodist sectarianism a validation of their hard-pressed household system of rural industry. For laborers struggling to survive, the sectarian ideals of domestic security and pilgrimage spoke to their sense of daily experience.

Owing to their self-sufficiency and attachment to tradition, small farms became a common locus of sectarian activity. Cottage religion spread into districts of Derbyshire, for example, where homesteads largely depended upon family labor and employed few extra hands, in most cases requiring "no outside help, except in harvest-time." Small farmers showed remarkable ingenuity in sustaining and encouraging independent do-

[4] *Religion and Society*, p. 80; W. R. Ward, "Popular Religion," passim.
[5] See Obelkevich, *Religion and Rural Society*, pp. 46–61.

mestic enterprises. Tenants often treated property as their own, handing down leases from generation to generation, and assumed an attitude of proud independence in relation to local authority. Though such areas were not totally isolated, the inaccessibility of many parts of the Midlands allowed this "old-world state of things" to persist well into the nineteenth century.[6] In northern Staffordshire, where Primitive Methodism was born, homesteads scattered about the central and eastern moorlands provided similar centers of organization. Photographs of these outposts in Kendall's *History* depict the barrenness of the landscape and rough simplicity of its farmhouses even at the end of the century. Recently enclosed and subdivided, many of these farms were small and dependent upon additional sources of income from various trades. The land was suitable for little more than grazing of cattle and sheep; some areas of Staffordshire specialized in dairying, usually on a small scale, as the farms were run by family members and only a few outside laborers. In most cases, these humble farms were hopelessly primitive in the eyes of contemporary improvers. Their occupants lacked a certain drive and commercial acumen, retaining a rustic informality in financial as well as social affairs. Farmers were in constant touch with the moorlands and hardly bothered to distinguish themselves from neighborhood cottagers and laborers. Indeed, relying upon arrangements of part-time employment and local trade, all parties benefited from a spirit of mutuality.[7]

[6] *Victoria History of the County of Derby* (hereafter *VCH*), vol. 2 (London, 1907): 308, 318–9; Glover's assessment supports this view: "The farms in this county are mostly of a moderate extent, there not being more than six or seven that exceed six hundred acres, with the exception of some held by the tenants of the Duke of Devonshire in the Woodlands of Hope . . ." Stephen Glover, *History of the County of Derby* 2 vols. (1829), 1:185.

[7] The household of Hugh Bourne's parents employed "two willing, hard-working, rustic servant-girls from Biddulph Moor" who were "cheerful workers, though not burdened with too much refinement." James Bourne, according to a visiting preacher, "lacked the sharp eye which is attentive to every detail of business, and which watches against all avoidable leakage." Though "honest to the core in intention," Bourne admitted that "some of his friends" saw that

Economic developments at the turn of the century joined two disparate types of settlement and prepared the way for sectarianism. In Staffordshire, where enclosure took place relatively late, change was slow; not until Napoleonic War prices offered the opportunity for expansion into wastes did farmers become fully conscious of the possibilities for improvement. Ambitious farmers then mobilized against perennial squatters around Ipstones, Dilhorne, and other places, driving cottagers into villages nearby. Less prosperous farmers, unable to resist the improvers, were forced to surrender their small holdings. Here, as in other parts of England, many fell under the increasing burden of high taxes and low prices after the war. Some households resorted to a "dual economy" combining agriculture with domestic industry, such as nailmaking around Audley, or tape weaving around Upper Tean. While improving farmers advanced in social status, behavior, and tastes, the state of those who carried on the precarious work of the small household farm grew closer to the world of the cottager. The realignment of the rural community along new class lines contributed to the appeal of sectarian Methodism.[8]

Strongholds of sectarianism also evolved in nearby industrial villages, where more physical, visible signs of recent upheaval were in evidence. Mining villages attracted hundreds of displaced cottagers and laborers from all parts of the county and beyond. Migration of labor to and through Staffordshire had begun in the eighteenth century and increased as the iron and coal industries expanded.[9] The late enclosure of wastes drove

---

"neither his business habits nor experience adapted him for extended and complicated commercial undertakings." Rev. T. Baron, "Reminiscences of a Residence at Bemersley," *Primitive Methodist Magazine* (hereafter *PMM*), 1900, p. 752. On northern Staffordshire, see W. Pitt, *A General View of the Agriculture of the County of Staffordshire* (London, 1796), pp. 12, 170–2; Albert A. Birchenough, "The Topography of Our First Printed Plan," *PMM*, 1901, pp. 52–58; D. M. Palliser, *The Staffordshire Landscape* (London: Hodder & Stoughton, 1976), pp. 115–30, 130.

[8] See Obelkevich, *Religion and Rural Society*, pp. 46–61 and passim.

[9] Arthur Redford, *Labour Migration in England, 1800–1850*, 3rd ed. rev. (1926; Manchester: Manchester University Press, 1976), p. 65.

many more cottagers into local mines. Former squatters crowded into a new village at Wyrley Bank after the enclosure of nearby Cheslyn Common in 1797. The opening of collieries there provided employment for some cottagers, and many also engaged in domestic broom production.[10] The Potteries, too, burgeoned as centers of migration, and villages encircling the moorlands drew other dispossessed cottagers. In the latter settlements, family economies again depended upon domestic industries to make ends meet. Cottagers at Cauldon, Cheddleton, and Leek engaged in silk weaving, and villages around the Six Towns took up subsidiary industries related to pottery making. The slow transformation of both agricultural and industrial production gave rise to an era of cottage industry made possible by the disruption of traditional settlement patterns.[11]

Economic insecurity had a devastating impact on the domestic lives of laborers. "This comparative depression of the lower agricultural class . . . is greater than was ever before known," one surveyor commented in 1816. The diminished demand for labor, particularly in grazing areas, became intolerable for many, and certain districts underwent significant depopulation.[12] The agricultural depression effectively eliminated most employment for laboring women. Some single women endured "the humiliation of being 'on the rounds,' and were sent from one occupier to another in search of employment" of any kind. For most, though, the absence of agricultural work meant total dependence on some form of domestic industry, which was itself becoming increasingly precarious and unremunerative. The trend was apparent in Derbyshire, where the depression contributed to a tremendous

[10] VCH, vol. 5 (1959): 100–2.

[11] VCH, vol. 3 (1970): 129; vol. 8 (1963): 276–7; Palliser, The Staffordshire Landscape, p. 115; on Leek, see pp. 164–6; P.O. Directory of Staffordshire (London, 1854), pp. 285, 290. See also Hobsbawm, Primitive Rebels, pp. 137–8.

[12] VCH, 2:308; J. D. Chambers and G. Mingay, The Agricultural Revolution, 1750–1880 (New York: Schocken Books, 1966), esp. chap. 5; Redford, Labour Migration, pp. 77–8; Farey, General View, 3:499.

expansion in the domestic lacemaking industry. If marriage and maintenance of a family had been difficult in previous years, now the prospects for both nearly vanished. Indigent married women faced the growing likelihood that their households would disintegrate as their children were enlisted as apprentices under local poor laws and their husbands tramped for work. The single female laborer meanwhile became trapped in a self-perpetuating dilemma, for without a steady income, she had little chance of escaping her predicament through marriage.[13]

All these changes solidified the bond between cottage religion and the struggle for survival. By appealing to a lingering sense of the past, cottage religion provided an answer to the loss of domestic security. Women preachers in particular spoke for disrupted rural society with its vanishing social groups and outmoded domestic economy. They represented a coherent set of relations, centered around the household, which grew in importance during hard times. As laboring families experienced impoverishment and dispersal, female preachers became living symbols of solidarity and stability. Like the rituals of local custom, sectarian practices joined household and church, sanctifying and preserving the one through its connection to the other.

[13] Ivy Pinchbeck, *Women Workers and the Industrial Revolution, 1750–1850* (1930; reprint, Totowa, N.J.: Cass, 1977), pp. 81, 238, 78–9; Louise A. Tilly and Joan W. Scott, *Women, Work, and Family* (N.Y.: Holt, Rinehart and Winston, 1978), p. 14.

SIX

Female Preaching and the Collapse
of Domestic Security

WHILE THE WESLEYAN MINISTRY disapproved of female evangelism as it evolved among the laboring classes, sectarian Methodists engaged women preachers in every early mission. Primitive Methodists directly inherited the practices of popular preaching so effectively demonstrated by Ann Cutler and Mary Taft. Extemporaneous and outspoken evangelism, rooted in village traditions and popular customs, became a primary force in spreading the new faith. Against the background of a changing rural society, Primitive Methodist women took up the mantle with a new urgency. The emergence of a large number of female preachers represented more than a rebellion against the prescribed notion of the male pastor; sectarian women also defended a way of life followed by laborers and small farmers. Their role in popular evangelism reflected their involvement in the rural family economy in a period of radical stress.

The rural areas of Wiltshire, Berkshire, and surrounding counties provided fertile ground for the spread of Primitive Methodism during the 1820s. An agricultural depression reached its peak during these years, leading to growing tension between laborers and landowners. A connection existed between rural revolt and the spread of Primitive Methodism, particularly as the sect made its greatest gains in the aftermath of the Swing riots. Were cottage religion and female preaching part of a counterrevolutionary mood described by Eric Hobsbawm and George Rudé in their analysis of the period after 1830? A clear correlation appears in the geography of Primitive Methodism and locations of revolt; Berkshire and Wilt-

Locations of Methodist sectarian activity
in the Southwest

shire, both noted for machine breaking (though not for radical agitation), were focal points for both sectarian Methodism and rural unrest.[1] But sectarianism was more than a despairing reaction to "riot and defeat." Motivated by the same dissatisfactions, sectarians often directly confronted village antagonisms and vigorously joined in the struggle against landed

[1] E. J. Hobsbawm and George Rudé, *Captain Swing* (Harmondsworth: Penguin University Books, 1973), esp. pp. 248–57.

authorities. The prominent and rebellious role of women calls attention to the defiant attitudes underlying this activity. Women preachers were interlopers in a traditionally male preserve who also challenged the authority and power of local elites. At the same time, they demonstrated the powerful impact of economic distress upon social norms. Their ministry was one of many strategies aimed at overturning the status quo.

social subversual

As many as thirty other women preached in the area surrounding the Brinkworth Circuit. Their personal histories reveal conditions affecting poor working families in southwestern England during the 1820s and 1830s. The transformation of rural society disrupted laboring households and set these women on their "earthly pilgrimages." As landholding and methods of agriculture changed, small farmers and laborers encountered hard times. Displacement, unemployment, and insufficient wages created rural poverty on an unprecedented scale, and declining domestic industry made survival increasingly difficult. Migration became inevitable; families were regularly dispersed, making the operation of kinship networks difficult or impossible. In most cases, laboring women and men deferred marriage and faced the prospect of continuing insecurity. The laboring household based upon combined labor and income as well as reproduction was disappearing.

Schooled in creating familial solidarity and security through religion, female preachers could address the collapse of domestic security in the Berkshire and Wiltshire region. Through their efforts, sectarian Methodism established a secure foothold among impoverished laboring families and displaced small farmers. Using the imagery and ideals of cottage religion, they promoted association among the dispossessed and poor, strengthening existing family ties and providing surrogate families for homeless followers.

focus of family unit

The small farmhouse was the mainstay of Primitive Methodism in the Southwest. Throughout Berkshire and Wiltshire, Brinkworth missionaries established "houses of refuge and pilgrim-inns" where humble farmers offered hospitality. Domestic preaching places in the country provided support for societies and aided recruitment. In Hampshire, during the 1830s, over two hundred people were converted in the kitchen of local preacher John Farr and his wife. There the farmer and his family presided with undiminishing magnanimity over a tightly knit community of followers. Not surprisingly, female preachers emerged from these sectarian havens. At least three women in the district circuits came from families providing places for preachers and their services.[2]

The life histories of female preachers in the Southwest raise important questions about the domestic base of rural sectarianism. These women did not offer their own houses as "pilgrim-inns," nor did they project a strong maternal image. Many were daughters of the faith who impressed audiences with their vulnerable and nubile youthfulness. Several even began their careers as celebrated "girl preachers." Elizabeth White (b. 1816) and Martha Green (b. 1825) appeared on preaching plans as fifteen-year-olds; Harriet Randborn (b. 1819) preached when she was sixteen; and Harriet Maslin (b. 1817) began preaching at seventeen, six years after her extraordinarily early conversion. Though these were exceptional, a profile of all twenty-eight women preachers in the district reveals a strikingly young average age (see Table 1). Only four of the twenty-eight women began their careers when they were older than twenty-five. The median age was nineteen and one half, well before most women could expect to establish their own homes and families. If, as James Obelkevich has demonstrated, the majority of early Primitive Methodist congregations were adults over thirty, preaching by women under twenty (and sometimes under eighteen) is indeed sig-

[2] Jane Farr (b. 1807) and Priscilla Lambden (b. 1802) were converted by Ride and Russell in their parents' houses, while Miriam Brown (b. 1815) was influenced by them at a local revival meeting. *Primitive Methodist Magazine* [hereafter *PMM*], 1870, pp. 181–2; *PMM*, 1837, pp. 17–9; *PMM*, 1896, pp. 445–7. Martha Green (b. 1825) also heard preaching in her parents' home in Hampshire (*PMM*, 1843, pp. 81–3). See also H. B. Kendall, *History of the Primitive Methodist Church*, 2 vols. (London, n.d.), 2:335–6, 339–40.

TABLE 1

WOMEN PREACHERS OF THE SOUTHWEST,
1827–1841—AGE PROFILE

Name	Area	Year First Preached	Age	Age at Marriage
Moore	Dorset	1827	17	24
Perham	Dorset	1827	—	—
Parfet	Wiltshire	1827	18	—
Hill	Gloucestershire	1829	ca. 19	28
Herrin	Somerset	1829	24	39
Heath	Wiltshire	1830	ca. 20	—
Young	Wiltshire	ca. 1830	ca. 38	19
Woodward	Wiltshire	1830s	—	—
Gardner	Wiltshire	1832	20	30
White	Wiltshire	1832	15	20
Green, A.	Wiltshire	ca. 1832	—	—
Price	Hampshire	ca. 1832	ca. 25	30
Brown	Berkshire	1833	18	—
Lambden	Hampshire	1833	31	—
Maslin	Wiltshire	1834	17	—
Taphouse	Berkshire	1834	24	—
Randborn	Berkshire	1834	16	—
Wheeler	Berkshire	1834	—	—
Dore	Berkshire	1835	17	—
Maylard	Berkshire	ca. 1835	ca. 18	27
Coling	Berkshire	ca. 1835	—	—
Hambleton	Berkshire	ca. 1835	—	—
Ayliffe	Wiltshire	1836	21	—
Baker	Berkshire	1836	46	33
Ford	Hampshire	ca. 1836	28	—
Haycock	Gloucestershire	ca. 1838	ca. 19	23
Albury	Berkshire	1839	22	27
Green, M.	Hampshire	1841	15	—
Hermon	Berkshire	n.d.		
Scribbans	Berkshire	n.d.		
Wheeldon		n.d.		
Herridge	Berkshire	n.d.		

TABLE 2

WOMEN PREACHERS, 1827–1841—AGE AT
FIRST APPOINTMENT

Age	Number	Percentage
15–19	11	39
20–24	6	21
25–29	2	7
30–34	1	4
35–39	1	4
40–44	0	—
45–49	1	4
Unknown	6	21
Total	28	100

nificant.[3] Why, then, did older adult congregations turn to
young women for direction?

The domestic upheaval experienced by small farmers and
laborers in the Southwest during this time offers some explanation. The small agrarian household was passing through its
final phase. Wartime prices had enabled landowners to con-
solidate their holdings. Hilmarton, for example, comprised
three thousand acres of variously sized farms, all rented, in
1802. Beginning in 1813, the estate changed hands and farms
were gradually combined. Wanborough, too, transformed in
character. Enclosure of the area began in 1780 and continued
until 1815, when its engineer, Ambrose Goddard, acquired

[3] From a profile constructed from Primitive Methodist obituaries, Obelkevich
shows that the average age of conversion for men was 30.3 and for women,
32.5 between 1818 and 1867. In the earlier years (1818–33), women usually
converted in their thirties and forties. Obelkevich also notes instances of early
conversions, pointing out that they revealed a " 'second generation' phenomenon" within Primitive Methodist families in which "evangelism shifted its aim
from outsiders to insiders." *Religion and Rural Society* (Oxford: Clarendon Press,
1976), pp. 235, 242.

The median age of female preachers in the Southwest gives a more accurate
picture than the average age (23.2), which is inflated owing to the three incidences of preachers over thirty.

the lordship. Such engrossment was typical of the age, but in northern Wiltshire the expansion of dairy farming intensified its impact on landless laborers. Because dairy farming required fewer hands (and sometimes only the assistance of family members), unemployment soared in parishes devoted to pasturage. Wootten Bassett became notoriously destitute as a result. By the 1840s, "almost the entire parish was given over to dairy farming." "All but 1,000 acres of the parish belonged to the Clarendon estate," and those thousand acres were divided among only five farms. Hence the majority of the laboring population depended upon occasional and part-time employment handed out by a limited number of farmers.[4]

Young female preachers did not have households of their own, but nevertheless they demonstrated the viability of family ties during times of stress. Elizabeth White, Martha Green, and Harriet Randborn began preaching in small rural villages where listeners certainly would have been familiar with their domestic circumstances. Close relatives of both Martha Green and Elizabeth White were prominent figures in local Primitive Methodist circles: Martha's brother, James, was a local preacher in the Winchester (Hants.) Circuit, while Elizabeth's mother was a class leader at Highworth (Wilts.). Martha's parents held services in their house at Ovington, and Martha no doubt spoke there as well as at other locations in the circuit. Although Harriet Randborn's parents were not Primitive Methodists, she, like Martha and Elizabeth, lived at home and depended upon her family for support and shelter. Girl preachers required protection while still contributing to the household economy. Biographies call attention to their con-

---

[4] *VCH*, 9:195–7, 180–5, 59, 64. Not even Ramsbury was exempt from the encroachment of the consolidating landlord. Cobbett passed through the "large, and, apparently, miserable village" in 1826 and observed, "Burdett owns a great many of the houses in the village . . . and will, if he live many years, *own nearly the whole.*" *Rural Rides* (1830; Harmondsworth: Penguin Books, 1967), p. 412. See also Hobsbawm and Rudé, *Captain Swing*, pp. 37, 152, on the oligarchy of landowners around the village and the "rural slums" created by the resulting lack of employment.

tinuing involvement in their families. Elizabeth White travelled to appointments with her brother, who would "protect her from persecution in the country." Martha Green was always at home, where "she assisted her mother in domestic duties," so that the society at Ovington could rely upon her to speak whenever itinerants failed to appear. The youthfulness of girl preachers enabled them to represent, at least in appearances, an undestroyed household unity.[5]

Their domestic context played an important part in promoting the ministries of girl preachers. Their gospel of "sinners being born again" was charged with a double meaning: salvation came from both lonely individual struggle and the interdependence of household members. They projected this image against a background of harsh reality, for the circumstances of most sectarian families were far from undisturbed. The lives of women preachers as well as girl evangelists reveal economic misfortune. The parents of Elizabeth White held a farm at Stratton St. Margaret's in northern Wiltshire before she was born. Elizabeth's father died when she was still young, and she and the remaining family were forced to move to nearby Hannington. Jane Morse (b. 1812) and her brother Charles, also a noted preacher, came from a family of small farmers at Purton, but neither remained there after reaching adulthood. Lucy Heath (b. 1813) came from Blunsden, not far from Purton, but she too removed to other places. Though she may have begun life as an agricultural laborer, she lived alone and died unemployed. Such displacement was common in the Southwest, and female preachers were often subject to worse hardship. Harriet Randborn grew up in the notoriously impoverished district of Wallingford in Berkshire, where the Primitive Methodist society comprised inhabitants of rural slums. In spite of auspicious beginnings as a girl preacher, Harriet spent the last years of her life in the local workhouse.[6]

[5] "Memoir of Elizabeth Tripp," PMM, 1838, pp. 215–8; "Martha Ann Green," pp. 81–3. Elizabeth White Tripp later preached with her husband in Belper, where she died in 1837.

[6] "Memoir of Harriet Randborn," PMM, 1850, pp. 706–7; see also "Memoir

Female preaching marked an era of diminishing security for laboring women. The marital status of female preachers suggests that the opportunity to establish a household was not readily available. Of the twenty-eight women, only nineteen ever married, and their mean age at marriage, just under twenty-nine, was relatively late for women of their class. Moreover, marriage did not necessarily indicate material security. Ten of the nineteen married other preachers and, in some cases, lived with their husbands only intermittently while one or both partners travelled to preach. Sectarian households were generally very poor; the decision to marry within the Connexion (twelve of the nineteen married women did so) often promised a decline rather than an improvement in economic status. Elizabeth Maylard (b. 1817) clung to humble respectability in her position as a governess before she married preacher John Maylard in 1844. Both she and her husband continued to preach regularly, though they were not always salaried owing to the poverty of their circuit district. Elizabeth gave birth to eight children and died in poverty in a small cottage at Shipley (Berks.).[7] Single women without families or homes epitomized the plight of laborers facing underemployment, emigration, deferred marriage, and, later on, a threatening new poor law. The gospel of female preachers grew out of endemic insecurity within as well as outside marriage.

Emigration and the dispersal of families posed a constant threat to women in the Southwest, and sectarian religion helped render their pilgrimages comprehensible. The unsettled life of her family transformed one young Primitive Meth-

---

of Mrs. Mary Taphouse," *PMM*, 1846, pp. 386–7, for an account of the career of a contemporary from the Wallingford district. One of the largest breweries in the country was located at Wallingford, in the midst of an extensive hop-growing region. Hops, along with sheep grazing, accounted for the high rate of unemployment in the area; both activities required a relatively small and part-time labor force. (Hobsbawm and Rudé, *Captain Swing*, pp. 8, 24.) "Memoir of Lucy Heath," *PMM*, 1852, pp. 711–2; "Memoir of Jane [Morse] Gardner," *PMM*, 1852, pp. 392–3; "Elizabeth Tripp," pp. 215–8.

[7] "Memoir of Elizabeth Maylard," *PMM*, 1862, pp. 325–7.

odist into a seasoned preacher. Jane Ayliffe's family's fortune began to decline at the time of Jane's birth in 1815, when post-war prices and consolidation forced small farmers like her father to search for other holdings. The Ayliffes moved from Rowde, Wiltshire, to the district outside Ramsbury, where Jane spent most of her childhood and first encountered Primitive Methodist missionaries. She joined a society when she was sixteen (her parents did not, though they were sympathizers), and became attached to a close circle of sectarians. In 1833, her parents refused to allow her to join several "sisters" who had decided to move to a distant town to work in a mill. Instead, Jane was apprenticed to a local dressmaker and remained at home. But the Ayliffe household suffered continual decline until the family decided to emigrate to America in 1835. By then, Jane was prepared to assert her independence. She preferred to pursue her own fate among fellow Primitive Methodists and refused to go to America. Shortly after her family's departure, she began to preach. Her solitude soon became true orphanhood when her parents and one of her sisters died in New York the next year. Jane regarded the news as an omen of her calling: by choosing to remain with her society in Ramsbury, she was spared for her work as a preacher. Circumstances now justified a shift of loyalties from family to sect, a shift that had begun when Jane first converted to cottage religion.[8]

Changes in village industries, as well as in agricultural labor, made dislocation common among sectarian families. The Primitive Methodists' earliest circuit in the Southwest was based in Frome in eastern Somerset, once a flourishing woollen center that had suffered a violent and uneasy transition to machine-based industry. Clothiers who survived the Napoleonic wars "obtained varying degrees of success" in adopting new techniques, but competition with Yorkshire effectively destroyed the trade in Frome and Shepton Mallet even before the slump of 1826. The economic crisis of that year took a

---

[8] "Memoir of Jane Ayliffe," *PMM*, 1838, pp. 413–6.

ruthless toll. Inadequate relief schemes could employ only part of the surplus population, and emigration programs, begun in 1819, accelerated during the next decade. When William Cobbett rode through Frome in 1826, he could not fail to notice *"between two and three hundred weavers, men and boys, cracking stones,* moving earth, and doing other sorts of work, towards making a fine road into the town." Half the population of Frome was unemployed that year, giving Cobbett ample opportunity to interview the inhabitants. Startled by the weavers' perspicacity, he commented, "It is curious enough, that they, these common weavers, should tell me, that they thought that the trade *never would come back again to what it was before. . . . This is the impression every where*; that the *puffing is over*."[9]

Women suffered acutely from changes in the textile industry as well as from the depression in trade. The use of machinery in the woollen industry deprived women of the dwindling, but essential domestic work. The transition to machinery had a more severe impact in the south of England than in the north.[10] In southern Wiltshire, where low agricultural wages made the sum of a few pence crucial to the laborer's household economy, the loss of income from spinning forced many to seek relief or emigrate. Town manufactories could hardly absorb increasing numbers of migrant rural women, while the

[9] Cobbett, *Rural Rides*, pp. 339, 341; Julia de Lacy Mann, *The Cloth Industry in the West of England from 1640 to 1880* (Oxford: Oxford University Press, 1971), pp. 160–2; Kenneth G. Ponting, *A History of the West of England Cloth Industry* (London: Macdonald, 1957), pp. 98–101. By the 1820s, it was evident that the factory industry could no longer absorb the unemployed weavers streaming in from the surrounding countryside. Peaceful acceptance of the flying shuttle was "rare" until long after the war; Ponting cites riots occurring as late as 1822. (Mann, *Cloth Industry*, p. 151; Ponting, *History*, pp. 100–1.) On earlier troubles concerning a machine manufacturer in Frome, who "found it more convenient and perhaps safer to remove to Bath," see Mann, *Cloth Industry*, p. 128.

[10] This seems to be the generally accepted view, though in exceptional cases, the introduction of machinery initially increased employment opportunities by creating a new female factory work force. Ponting, *History*, chap. 18; Ivy Pinchbeck, *Women Workers and the Industrial Revolution, 1750–1850* (1930; reprint ed., Totowa, N.J.: Frank Cass, 1977), p. 15.

large number remaining in agricultural areas were unable to obtain wool.[11] Women's work in other domestic industries also underwent a steady decline. Cobbett commented on the "surplus popalashon" of women and girls around Whitney (Wilts.) and the Cotswolds who were left without work in the blanket industry. Small-scale handwork industries continued to provide scanty incomes for women scattered throughout the southwestern counties and particularly Dorset. Around Shaftesbury, Blandford, and Sherborne, the home manufacture of shirt buttons employed large numbers of women and children. Women around Blandford also worked at bone lace, while the borderlands of Dorset and southern Wiltshire supported an extensive domestic silk industry.[12] But during the depression of the late 1820s, domestic industry could supply only a fraction of a subsistence income, while the factory woollen industry declined dramatically after 1826. In Frome, women joined the lines of men drawing coal from the nearby pits for small sums. When recovery came in the 1830s, Frome and Shepton Mallet were not among the surviving centers of the trade.[13]

Migration and the resulting scattering of families affected the pattern of evangelism through Somerset and Dorset. As women preachers gathered converts for Primitive Methodists in industrial towns and villages south of Gloucestershire, the extent of family dispersal became clear. Mary Moore (b. 1809) first heard preacher Ruth Watkins in 1826 when she was visiting her cousin at Nunney, near Frome. After Mary returned to her home in Motcombe, she and her entire family (including several cousins) converted to Primitive Methodism. Mary and

[11] Pinchbeck, *Women Workers*, p. 156; Thomas Davis, *A General View of the Agriculture of Wiltshire* (1813), p. 215; Mann, *Cloth Industry*, pp. 143–4.

[12] Pinchbeck, *Women Workers*, pp. 230–4; Cobbett, *Rural Rides*, p. 406; Davis, *Wiltshire*, p. 220.

[13] Mann, *Cloth Industry*, pp. 173–6, 171, 162. According to Mann, the year 1826 formed "the great dividing line of the period" (p. 168). After severe setbacks during the 1820s, the Stroudwater trade recovered in the 1830s and concentrated around the upper Gloucestershire area (p. 176).

her brother soon became preachers, sometimes sharing appointments and circuit assignments. When Mary travelled in the Salisbury Circuit in Wiltshire in 1829, she found family connections helpful again. Another relative, Cornelius Broadway, had moved several times before settling outside Salisbury. An "old Wesleyan local preacher" himself, he helped Mary "to hammer out her texts" and "visited with her from door to door." Her conversion and her ministry grew out of family networks spreading across the countryside. For Mary and many others like her, Primitive Methodism was a household religion relayed by separated members of extended families.[14]

The religion of the *domus* acquired added significance under such conditions. While helping to preserve a household system of economy and autonomy in work relations, cottage religion also united families threatened or separated by economic change. Primitive Methodism offered a sense of mastery over seemingly uncontrollable events; its domestic theology enabled laborers to resist the dislocation dictated by external forces. Mary Herrin (b. 1805), a Bible Christian preacher, reconstituted a sectarian household after her family was torn apart by rural poverty. As one of eleven children born of agricultural laborers at Norton-Fitzwarren (Somerset), Mary was forced to enter domestic service "very early in life." The demands of "excessive labour" permanently injured her health by the time she was twenty and required her to seek less demanding work. Though silk weaving promised little recompense, it could be carried on at home on a more flexible schedule. Mary and two of her sisters thus settled at Oak Green, where they lived and worked together. At the same time, Mary became involved in

[14] "Memoir of Mrs. Cordingley," *PMM*, 1868, p. 534. See also "Memoir of Mary Snelgrove," *PMM*, 1827, pp. 234–7, for one of numerous biographies of dressmakers involved in Primitive Methodism. Born in 1802 at Hornishaw, Wiltshire, Snelgrove grew up under the care of her uncle and aunt at Nunney, and joined the Primitive Methodists when they first arrived in May of 1824. Like most dressmakers, her conversion followed several dissolute years of apprenticeship. When Mary died in 1825, she was the tenth of her parents' children to suffer an early death.

Bible Christian meetings. Her sisters, a brother, and her mother shared her interest in sectarian religion, and together they travelled around the area to hear preaching. The passionate salvationist theology and the domestic basis of worship of Bible Christianity provided the migrants with an ideology of the family and household. The Herrins converted, and Mary and her sisters began to hold services in their home. Mary's capabilities as a speaker flourished and, in 1829, she was placed on the plan as a local preacher.[15]

Not long after, however, the Herrins' new life was disrupted. The decline of the silk trade forced the three women to move to Wellington, where the large woollen manufacturing firm of Fox Brothers offered the chance of employment. Wellington, like towns in Derbyshire, presented a logical target for village evangelism. The Fox firm drew many women from the surrounding countryside into the town and left them, in the words of one preacher, strangers and pilgrims.[16] Though the Bible Christians had not yet established a society at Wellington, Mary preached to her new friends and acquaintances and eventually founded one herself. The sectarian cottage society re-created family relationships and familiarity left behind in rural villages.[17]

Behind the images projected by female preachers lay the grim reality of laboring life: as daughters and mothers, they

[15] "Memoir of Mary Pennington," *Bible Christian Magazine* [hereafter *BCM*], 1863, pp. 133–5. Although there were several Bible Christian female preachers working in the Somerset and Dorset area, I have included only one in this chapter.

[16] On the Fox Brothers' firm (est. 1783), see K. Ponting, *History*, pp. 95, 107.

[17] "Memoir of Mary Pennington," p. 135. Mary Pennington's obituary credited her with initiating the Bible Christian society that ultimately led to the building of a chapel in Wellington. Before that date, the Bible Christians borrowed the local Independent chapel for occasional sermons by travelling preachers. See "Memoir of Mary Mason," *BCM*, pp. 299–308.

Two other female preachers, Jane Hill (b. 1810) and Elizabeth Haycock (b. 1819), began their careers in similar textile factory villages (Bisley and Stroud, respectively). See their "Memoirs," *PMM*, 1840, pp. 176–7 and *PMM*, 1852, pp. 645–6.

belonged to threatened or dispersed households that had fallen upon recent hard times. Their religious mission aimed to rectify a loss of domestic security, and herein lay the appeal of sectarian Methodism. Through the theology of cottage religion, laboring women could assume control of circumstances that had rendered them powerless. As preachers, they could affirm existing family ties and create a sense of community where such ties were lacking. The continuing dispossession of marginal farmers and laborers in southwestern England not only explained the domestic activity of female preachers but justified their challenge to authority through gender roles and religion.

THE EARLY EXPERIENCES of preacher Elizabeth Smith show the making of a typical sectarian mentality. Schooled in independence and rebelliousness from an early age, Elizabeth was well prepared to challenge authority and convention. Her confrontations with upper-class morality and her search for material security reveal a transformation taking place in the assumptions governing English society. A lack of deference marked her relations with employers; her religious mission demonstrated that the old moral consensus in the countryside was being undermined. Through religion, this female preacher responded to the values of a new order that had penetrated remote corners of laboring life.

Many years passed before Elizabeth Smith heard or recognized an "extraordinary call" beckoning her to preach.[18]

---

[18] Most of the following biographical information was extracted from the six-part "Memoir of Elizabeth Russell, Primitive Methodist Preacher and Missionary, whose maiden name was Elizabeth Smith," which first appeared as a commemorative obituary in the *Primitive Methodist Magazine* for 1837. The biography was written by Elizabeth's husband, Thomas Russell (also a travelling preacher). The veracity of the memoir lies in its copious quotations from Elizabeth's journals and personal correspondence; morever, her assiduous husband did little to camouflage her occasional bouts of less acceptable behavior and thought. Russell later published the memoir as a pamphlet and personally distributed it in his travels. See Thomas Russell, *Autobiography*, rev. ed. (London, n.d.), p. 120.

Her childhood, like that of many female preachers, was remarkable more for the obstacles thrown in her path than for any encouragement. Born in 1805 at Ludlow, Shropshire, Elizabeth entered a troubled household. Her father was a reckless sort who chafed under the responsibility of six children. When he lost everything he owned in a glove business, he enlisted in the navy and never returned home. Elizabeth's mother had a violent temper that only increased with time. Left with a large family and no income, she sent Elizabeth to live with a grandmother in the same village. The move restored order, if not material security, to Elizabeth's life. Her grandmother was "industrious and moral," and Elizabeth soon became "inured to work and to frugality." Added to this domestic regimen was a strong dose of Church of England catechism at a National School. Tossed about by misfortune, Elizabeth had landed upon a woefully rigorous place of refuge.[19]

Careful upbringing, with all its effort aimed at respectability, did not guarantee dutiful passivity. While Elizabeth's grandmother envisioned a genteel future for her young charge, Elizabeth nurtured a natural obstinacy. Her grandmother chose dressmaking as a suitable occupation for Elizabeth, even though the trade could lead a girl to ruin. Working at the needle could offer an acceptable escape from the poverty of spinsterhood, but the dress shop just as often exposed the impressionable apprentice to a world of dangerously stylish living and frivolous gossip. Elizabeth, alas, happily welcomed new adventures. As an apprentice, she worked on costumes for an actress, and she soon began to socialize with a "new circle" of people with highly questionable reputations. "The

[19] "Elizabeth Russell," p. 95. While attending the National School at Ludlow, Elizabeth came under the influence of a thoroughly evangelical Miss Brown, who gave the seven-year-old Elizabeth a distinct picture of Judgment Day that effectively paralysed her until her dressmaking days of "liberation." Certain Scriptures, Elizabeth recalled, "followed me for some time [:] 'Stand in awe and sin not. Commune with thy own heart on thy bed, and be still' " (p. 95). Needless to say, Elizabeth abandoned the latter maxim when she became a Primitive Methodist.

scenes I witnessed, with the company to which I was admitted," Elizabeth recalled, "were so fascinating to me, that I soon became ashamed of everything that was like God." Her grandmother could not have been pleased to see humble piety cast aside. She probably interceded, for Elizabeth abruptly left dressmaking to enter domestic service when she was sixteen.[20]

Servanthood offered no greater promise of reforming Elizabeth's behavior. Obviously, domestic service could lift young women from lowly circumstances into better environments. Homeless girls made ideal candidates for improvement, especially when thrust into the hands of middle-class mistresses intent upon preserving the tranquility of their households. But service also heightened a country girl's awareness of class differences, and some (like Elizabeth) arrived at the job with a willfulness that benevolent mistresses could not always subdue. In the resulting domestic warfare, religion provided a particularly suitable ground for conflict. While masters assumed their preeminence in religious matters, servants armed with their own brand of piety refused to display the expected submissiveness. Elizabeth's four years of domestic service crucially shaped her religious principles, though not, to be sure, in the interests of her employers.[21]

At first, religious ruminations played a minor part in Elizabeth's life with the McDonalds in London. She was dutifully reverent but hardly zealous. Periodically, however, the McDonalds sent her to work for their relative, a vicar of West Stratford in Buckinghamshire, and there her religious devel-

[20] Ibid., p. 95.
[21] At least fourteen other female preachers were at one time in their lives servants, and a cursory examination of any *Primitive Methodist Magazine* reveals a sizable number of female servants among sect followers. Suggestions of conflict occasionally crept into obituaries: "Never ashamed of Jesus, [Ann Preece] preached him to all within her reach and did not quit a single place of service without leaving some one or more the better for her faithful warnings and earnest exhortations." ("Memoir of Ann Preece," *PMM*, 1852, p. 375.) In another case, a servant changed her occupation, like Elizabeth, to dressmaking in order "to be more at liberty." ("Memoir of Mrs. Jane Austin," *PMM*, 1851, pp. 707–9.)

opment took a sharp turn for the worse. "Influence" from above brought about rejection from below. Elizabeth "began to entertain atheistical thoughts," and whenever twinges of conscience troubled her, she sought escape in romances and novels. Upon her return to London, she adopted a different strategy of repudiation. Renewed Bible reading led her to formulate a private ascetic religion that effectively separated her from her employers. An odd ritual appeared in her behavior: every evening she denied herself supper, an act which remained undiscovered, presumably because she dined apart from the family. She was inspired, she recorded, by Matthew 6:16–18: "Moreover, when ye fast, be not, as the hypocrites, of a sad countenance. . . . that thou appear not unto men to fast . . ." She sought spiritual counselling when visiting her grandmother in Ludlow in 1825, but not from any member of the Church of England. Instead, she consulted a local Primitive Methodist woman who put her in touch with a travelling preacher. While continuing to work at the MacDonalds' in London, Elizabeth drew encouragement from correspondence with the Primitives and prayed in solitude until she was converted.[22]

The test of such hard-won piety now lay in its practicality. Assured of her place among the saved, Elizabeth was obliged to aid the damned. The master and mistress did not escape her scrutiny. Elizabeth must have administered frequent proddings, reminding the McDonalds of the Judge who watched both rich and poor, until the time came for a more serious confrontation in the spring of 1826. For exemplary service (Elizabeth had remained dutiful to a fault), the McDonalds chose her to accompany them to the races on Derby Day, "the most noted day" of the social season. Elizabeth refused to obey, and her puritanical stance betrayed—for the last time—religious beliefs intolerable to the McDonalds. "I do not want any Methodists about me," came the testy reply of the mistress. Elizabeth did not intend to stay, but neither she nor Mrs.

[22] "Elizabeth Russell," p. 96.

McDonald wished to lay bare their true feelings. When Elizabeth's health began to fail, Mrs. McDonald hit upon a solution acceptable to all. "Smith," she announced, "I am afraid you are in a consumption." She then dismissed Elizabeth "out of fear lest the children should be . . . injured." This was clearly a fabrication, though no one but the McDonald children appeared to care. Elizabeth promptly returned to Ludlow and to dressmaking, and with greater freedom and miraculously restored health, became a member of the local Primitive Methodist society.[23]

Through the experiences of her childhood, apprenticeship, and domestic service, Elizabeth had achieved a penultimate perception of sectarian sainthood. Not surprisingly, she began to pray in public, and with such success that even the mighty trembled. "The power of God soon came down in such streams," it was recorded, "that a stout man fell, as one shot in battle." Ludlow Primitive Methodists recognized her gifts as well as her worldly triumphs and appointed her local preacher. Elizabeth Smith was "a brand plucked out of the burning," proof of God's judgment in singling out the righteous. "God works by feeble means," wrote Elizabeth to a friend in describing her success as a preacher. When a circuit branch in Radnorshire, South Wales, called for help later in 1826, the

---

[23] Ibid., pp. 96–7. Another dimension of the confrontation emerges from a note addressed to Elizabeth's grandmother from one of the McDonald children:

Dear Mrs. Powell,

I cannot let Betsey go from Bryanstone Square without sending you this little note to tell you that you may depend on us continuing to look (out) [sic] for something that will suit her. For though she will be far away, it will not make us remember her a bit the less; for mamma would on no account have parted with her, had she been able to have stopped here [sic], which mamma very much wanted, as she goes out very much in the spring,
Believe me yours truly,
Julia

Elizabeth's determined resolve probably played a greater part in her dismissal than her biographer (i.e., her husband) cared to admit.

leaders assigned to her the full responsibilities of travelling. Elizabeth thereupon gave up her thriving dressmaking business—"no common sacrifice," according to her biographer— in order to assume her new post.[24]

Innumerable trials now fully transformed Elizabeth into "a stranger and a pilgrim." Her assignment forced her to sever ties with family and friends, who, no doubt, expressed misgivings about her decision to earn her living by preaching. Few assurances of security lay before her. Supplied only with the name of her hosts and a map, Elizabeth was required to raise her own salary (two guineas per quarter) by petitioning her home society. Physical obstacles compounded the risks she faced. Solitary travel on foot promised to threaten her weak constitution as well as her good reputation. Nevertheless, Elizabeth set out for a cottage she had never seen, at a place she had never heard of, thirty miles away.

As sectarian saints always learned, vulnerability and solitude brought forth the hand of God. Elizabeth's journey soon provided her with proof of divine providence. Walking all day until dark, Elizabeth found herself stranded on a pitted, flooded common. She could go no farther, and her path was lost; her only recourse, she decided, was to climb upon a ridge and call for help. From her perch, she sang loudly three verses of "Jesu, lover of my Soul" until "a family residing in a cottage at the edge of the common" heard her mournful lament. The rescue was a sign to both parties, for the cottagers were in fact the hosts sought by the pilgrim preacher. The story of her deliverance gave credence to her mission in Radnorshire. "Being so providentially brought to the family to which she was directed," her biographer reported, "the Lord gave her favour in the sight of the people." Within the few months of

[24] Ibid., pp. 97–8. Elizabeth was not indifferent to concerns related to her profession, despite her observance of the Primitive Methodist "plain dress" rule. At first her appointment to the Wales mission made her wonder, "What shall I do when my clothes are worn out, where shall I go for more?" But the Lord sent a "deliverance" in a dream, revealing to her the true meaning of Luke 22:35: "When I sent you without purse, and scrip, and shoes, lacked ye any thing? And they said, Nothing" (p. 97).

her stay, Elizabeth "opened a number of places, and formed several societies." The poor cottagers of the "thinly inhabited country" responded enthusiastically to her message.[25]

The death of family members also acted as an important rite of passage into sectarian sainthood. Family ties were central to sectarianism, yet the pilgrim necessarily relinquished them in order to assume the obligations of her mission. Elizabeth felt the sharpness of this conflict when her grandmother "was taken with a stroke" during Elizabeth's second quarter in Radnorshire. In correspondence with a fellow Primitive Methodist, she revealed her difficulties in dealing with family obligations. She had returned to Ludlow to care for her grandmother, she wrote, "by a wise Providence." The phrase suggests her reluctance to leave "the work of the Lord" in South Wales; no doubt, too, her grandmother's tenacious commitment to the Established Church made Elizabeth's duty more difficult. "I think she is now seeking pardon through the merits of Jesus," Elizabeth reported, "and I hope my prayers are now answered. The Lord is able to save the hoary-headed." Witnessing death nevertheless provoked deep sorrow and raised questions about attachments to loved ones. "When I am permitted to enter into the work of the Lord again, I trust I shall have received a deeper baptism of the Spirit of God. I hope, my sister," she added, invoking the typical and highly significant sectarian form of address, "I shall be swallowed up of God . . . and only live for him, and to him, speak for him, and by him, and at last, Preach him to all, and cry in death,/Behold, behold the Lamb." Elizabeth's thoughts thus flowed into a familiar sectarian hymn, just as sectarian "sisterhood" took the place of her own family. Elizabeth struggled to free herself from all dependence upon human relationships, elevating instead her commitment to promoting the faith. At such times of stress, hymns provided an epigrammatic language of feelings and values. For Elizabeth, whose literacy appeared limited even after the scrupulous editing of her husband, the verses

[25] Ibid., pp. 98–9.

129

validated an experience expressed only with great difficulty in prose.[26]

Sectarian attitudes towards death and grieving revealed a profound ambivalence about familial relationships and domestic security. The rituals associated with death emphasized the transitory nature of both family and home. "How different Ludlow appears to me now," wrote Elizabeth shortly after the elderly woman's death; "there are not (now) those who were wont to encourage:—there is no grandmother to smile at my approach; I am left a stranger and a pilgrim." Death forced the living to transfer their attention to "invisible" ideals: "Let us live," Elizabeth continued, "as they who are not looking at the things which are seen, but at the things which are not seen. . . . This is not our resting place, our home is above." These other-worldly ideals were abstractions of the family and home drawn from immediate experience. Elizabeth later contemplated her own death as her health declined under the stress of preaching. "I am a stranger in this vale of wo [sic]," she lamented. "I know that there [above] is my house and home

> For me my elder brethren stay
> And sweetly whisper,
> Sister spirit, come away.[27]

In the hymnal language of kinship, Elizabeth described her present deprivation through concrete idealizations. The metaphors of family and domestic security resisted all attempts to etherealize the afterlife. "I do feel," she wrote on another occasion,

> the body is fast sinking towards the grave. But this gives me comfort, because I know I have a building that will stand for ever; it is on a sure foundation.[28]

This cycle of renunciation and re-creation of domestic security and family ties provided sectarians with an important

[26] Ibid., p. 140.
[27] Ibid., p. 141.
[28] Ibid., p. 139.

critique of worldly existence. The metaphors of a holy pilgrimage had literal significance: life experience entailed "travel through [a] howling wilderness"; the battle for survival led "to sure conquest though the warfare is sometimes severe." Elizabeth lavished great attention not upon rewards of the afterlife, but upon vicissitudes of the "tribulation here." "I am yet in search of a better country," she wrote during her stay in Radnorshire. Her search gave cosmic meaning to the loss of her own family and home and contributed to her growing determination.[29]

Sectarian female preachers faced an inordinate number of obstacles. Because of their sex, they endured repeated assaults upon their reputations and right to preach. Elizabeth was far from immune from such attacks and sometimes lost her faith as a result. She described one confrontation with critics of female preaching after she had met their challenge and resolved her self-doubt:

> The cause of my trouble was this: about a fortnight previous to [March, 1828] I was attacked by two clergymen; and their attack was of a nature to discourage me. And when I was alone the enemy of souls harassed me; and my weak faith sunk, and I began to reason on the work of God in preaching the gospel.
>
> These men reprobated the idea of a woman being useful in the work;—the enemy backed their arguments;— and I was sensible of the vast importance of the work; which led me to cry, as I had done many times before, "Who is sufficient for these things? Who among the sons of men? and much less a weak ignorant young woman!"
>
> In a word, such were the effects of this reasoning that I grieved the Spirit. . . . Through this reasoning, the Lord withdrew the light.[30]

"Such severe trials" inspired new determination and resilience. Perhaps more than her male counterparts, Elizabeth was ac-

[29] Ibid., pp. 139, 97, 141.
[30] Ibid., p. 177.

quainted with the ways of the opposition to sectarianism. By the end of her appointment in Wales, clergymen of the Established Church no longer intimidated her.

The independence and rebelliousness essential to female preaching developed in circumstances such as these. Personal misfortune, poverty, and solitary struggle rendered Elizabeth Smith self-reliant; self-reliance rendered her proud and defiant. Class resentment grew as the young woman encountered greater obstacles, in the form of master, mistress, and clergyman, to her self-expression. Elizabeth Smith overcame the limitations set by social class and convention through female preaching. Her experiences, typical of the formative years of other female preachers' lives, would bring her advantages in her assignment in the Brinkworth Circuit later that year.

The struggle to preserve laboring households and village solidarity in northern Wiltshire presented a formidable challenge to Elizabeth Smith and the Primitive Methodists. As working-class dissenters, sectarian Methodists suggested anarchy to the establishment entrenched there. Stiff opposition in the form of hired mobs and angry local authorities led to direct conflict; but female preachers, accustomed to resistance, combatted the hostility of gentry and clergy as they had in more personal contexts. Women brought unforeseen advantages to the Brinkworth Circuit by subtly evading suspicion and arrest. In a tightly controlled region where popular association had been forbidden, they successfully subverted authority.

FORBIDDING COUNTRY HOUSES quietly supervised an area devoid of dissenting chapels in northern Wiltshire. A relatively small middle class and an impoverished laboring class promised little support for Old Dissent. The parish of Lydiard Tregoze, incorporating the Bolingbroke and Midgehall estates, had no dissenters until 1822, when the Primitives licensed a house for worship. At nearby Liddington, the first sign of nonconformity since the seventeenth century appeared in the same year, when Independents licensed a building for meetings. They soon disbanded, however, and left no trace of their activity. Liddington proved even less hospitable to visiting evangelists. Primitive Methodists gathered on the village green when they arrived and continued to meet there for the next twenty years. Not even Swindon, the largest town in the area, tolerated dissenters until the nineteenth century. Wesleyans first sent preachers there on an occasional basis, and Primitive Methodists eventually established regular cottage meetings and a permanent society. Until the sectarian mission arrived in Wiltshire, the Established Church enjoyed a monopoly that few seemed willing to challenge.[31]

When Elizabeth Smith arrived in 1828, the Brinkworth Circuit (established 1826–27) boasted four Wiltshire chapels and a number of cottage societies. The small hamlet of Broad Town, a dairying community far from the parish church, had erected one of the first chapels as early as 1827. Such advancement was uncommon; far more activity took place on a domestic basis, in workshops, barns, and outdoors. Five other preachers (all men) shared over twenty stations. John Ride, a Derbyshire ploughboy turned preacher, and Thomas Russell, a zealous Cheshire convert who would marry Elizabeth, had inaugurated the Wiltshire-Berkshire district mission earlier that year. Determined to strengthen the nascent circuit, the preachers redoubled their efforts and launched into new territories. Their first plan was to hold a massive camp meeting at Wootten Bassett, where a small society of Primitives met regularly in a large room attached to a local public house. Elizabeth spoke to a crowd of four thousand, and invitations to surrounding villages quickly followed. The Primitives thus penetrated the hitherto impenetrable countryside.[32]

H. B. Kendall noted that "persecution was so common" at Brinkworth "as to be the rule rather than the exception."[33]

[31] *Victoria History of the County of Wiltshire* (hereafter *VCH*), vol. 2 (Oxford: Oxford University Press, 1956): 143–4; vol. 9 (1976): 51–2, 74, 85–6.

[32] "Elizabeth Russell," p. 179; Kendall, *History*, 2:310–2, *VCH*, 2:143; 9:41.

[33] Kendall waxed eloquent on the subject of persecution in the Brinkworth district. "You must take your Persecution Map," he intoned, "and with your brush put dabs of colour on the counties of Wilts, Dorset, Berks, Oxon, Surrey; and on Hants it must be darker than anywhere else in England," *History*, 2:330.

The Primitive Methodists arrived at an untimely hour: land-lords and farmers had spent a strenuous decade keeping the peace during a period of intense economic distress. Wage subsidy schemes in the early 1820s had failed to relieve endemic rural poverty, and violence and crime were now mounting steadily. In some parishes, landowners only recently had invested wartime profits in extensive holdings and exercised their new authority uneasily. The Primitives constituted yet another grim annoyance. Street-preaching and cottage meetings brought laborers together in dangerous numbers. In order to check the advance of the new religion, landlords and magistrates refused preachers licenses and evicted cottagers who hosted meetings. Landowners were not above employing clergymen and mobs to help drive away the wandering evangelists with violent attacks.[34]

Village laborers needed little encouragement from landlords to take to the streets and deliver daubings of mud and filth to God-talking strangers. Widespread pluralism and nonresidency, coupled with burdensome tithes, generated anticlerical sentiment in Wiltshire. Crowds welcomed the rare opportunity to vent rage at ministers of the gospel, regardless of their persuasion. Berkshire mobs responded with similar hostility. Villagers at Childrey even attacked neatly bonneted female preachers, whose petitionings probably reminded them of unwelcomed charity sermons. Anticlericalism was a considerable force in the Southwest, and sectarians received the same treatment meted out to their established brethren.[35]

The general outpouring of animosity, however, sometimes

[34] Kendall, *History*, 2, chap. 23, passim; *VCH*, 9:38, 85, on Broad Town and Lydiard Tregoze. When a Primitive Methodist chapel was finally built in 1840 at Hook, Lord Bolingbroke claimed the land and demanded the surrender of the building at valuation. The society then retreated to a cottage until building a second chapel in 1886. (The chapel debt had not been erased in 1907.) Quoted from W. Tonks, *Victory in the Villages* (1907), in *VCH*, 9:90.

[35] Kendall, *History*, 2:331. The Primitives' Berkshire mission grew out of the Wiltshire-Brinkworth base; I have followed Kendall's method of treating the Wiltshire and Berkshire stations before 1832 (when the Shefford Circuit was created from the eastern branch of Brinkworth) as belonging to a single enterprise. See Kendall, *History*, 2:314–6.

brought different results. Primitive Methodist itinerants acted as catalysts in bringing local antagonisms into the open; and when unpopular authorities set out for the intruders, crowds sometimes sided with the preachers. At Chaddleworth, villagers prevented an officious constable from arresting an itinerant preacher. Preacher Samuel Heath so successfully eluded a magistrate at Wootten Bassett that he won the villagers' admiration and hence permission to use a public house as a meeting place.[36] Primitive Methodists discovered that they could capitalize on a readiness to rebel. The interference of the squirearchy drove villagers helter-skelter into the Primitives' camp.

Elizabeth survived the persecution as successfully as her stouter colleagues. Though the novelty of a female preacher always attracted attention, feminine frailty was no guarantee against harassment. At least three other female preachers broke down under the strain of working in the Wiltshire-Berkshire district. But Elizabeth, according to a eulogistic church historian, "moved about amongst the rough crowds as though she had a charmed life." When attacks occurred, she managed to stand firm and repel the onslaughts. At Beenham Green, she remained unflustered when the parson's son fired off a gun "four or five times close to the congregation." Her fearlessness often worked in her favor. When a "Church and King" mob at Ramsbury rushed at Elizabeth and Thomas Russell, Elizabeth sang a hymn "with her usual sweetness and pathos" and subdued the attackers. The ringleader ordered the mob back, and the preachers continued their service. Elizabeth's pilgrimlike pose somehow elevated her above local conflicts and contempt.[37]

[36] Kendall, *History*, 2:310–2; "Elizabeth Russell," p. 181. Thomas Russell reported a rather dubious memorial of one much-persecuted visit to Faringdon: it was "estimated that no less than two sacks of potatoes had been flung at the preacher and his congregation in the streets of that place" and "that some of the thrifty people of Faringdon had picked up and planted the tubers and were calling their produce 'Faringdon-Russells.' " (Kendall, *History*, 2:336–7.)

[37] Kendall, *History*, 2:331; Russell, *Autobiography*, pp. 55–6, 82. Concern for the safety of women was evident in the Minute Books for 1837, which rec-

As a female preacher, Elizabeth brought more important, strategic advantages to the Brinkworth mission. The female sex, at least when clothed in piety, displayed a remarkable immunity from legal persecution. While their male counterparts were badgered for licenses or arrested, female preachers apparently did not merit the attention of constables. Primitive Methodists gladly exploited the oversight. One historian boasted that in Yarmouth, "when the police haled off our preachers to the cells for preaching on the quay, a band of God-fearing women stepped into the breach, and took up the service, carrying it through unmolested. Some of our most useful local preachers in the villages," he added, "have been women."[38] An instance closer to Brinkworth followed the same pattern. The first preacher in the nearby Shrewsbury area, Sarah Spittle, was able to continue her work in 1822 after her "reinforcement," James Bonsor, was thrown in jail.[39] The Wiltshire-Berkshire district was also a bastion of the squirearchy and the Established Church. Thomas Russell accompanied Elizabeth to Chaddleworth, but he ended in jail, while Elizabeth continued to preach. When Russell's replacement arrived, the constable prepared to make another arrest. "But the people made a ring," Elizabeth reported, "and would not suffer him to come near." The constable and clergyman then retreated to the church belfry in an attempt to drown out the preaching, but to no avail. The Primitives revealed the villagers' disregard for local dignitaries and heightened community tensions.[40]

---

ommended that steps "be taken to protect female preachers in going to their appointments." Tonks, *Victory in the Villages*, p. 11.

[38] Arthur Patterson, *From Hayloft to Temple* (London, 1903), p. 45.

[39] Kendall, *History*, 2:278.

[40] "Elizabeth Russell," pp. 179–80; Russell, *Autobiography*, pp. 34ff; Kendall, *History*, 2:332–5. Russell was later "sentenced to three months' hard labour, ostensibly, for selling without a license, but, really, because he would persist in preaching the gospel in the streets of Chaddleworth. . . . It was a 'put-up job' on the part of the clergyman and a magistrate" (p. 332). John Wilks, the secretary of the Society for the Protection of Religious Liberty, learned of Russell's case and worked for his early release. Russell decided to let the case drop. (Russell, *Autobiography*, pp. 55–6.)

Female preachers like Elizabeth Smith offered another advantage: they not only escaped arrest but also exerted a powerful influence upon female listeners. Thus they secured all-important invitations into homes of converted women everywhere in the district, sometimes in the face of landlords' threats.[41] Because women were often less dependent upon local patronage for work, they were free to support new societies in closed parishes. Elizabeth won important allies for the Primitives where landlords, clergy, and mobs had mounted opposition. At Ramsbury, she converted a "female of great respect" who invited Elizabeth to the nearby village where she lived. Primitives established a society there and subsequently expanded into neighboring areas. Another woman at Shefford "had got her husband to build a house with a room large enough for preaching, with lodging rooms above, so that the whole might be occupied by a preacher's family." By 1831, the Shefford district societies had overcome popular (and official) resistance and grown into a separate circuit.[42]

Elizabeth's ministry answered a widespread demand for the services of a woman. As the new religion passed into the hands of rural laborers and small farmers, it mixed easily with folk beliefs in which women played a prominent role.[43] Early in the history of the Brinkworth Circuit, the Primitives noted the high incidence of spontaneous trances among women. Outside camp meetings, such occurrences enabled cottagers to set themselves up as "wise women." At Seagry, in 1827, Margaret Hickson (b. 1805) became "exceedingly ill" and subject to

[41] Elizabeth appeared to be much more skilled at this than Russell. See "Elizabeth Russell," p. 221, on Micheldever. Another preacher in the Brinkworth Circuit rightly wondered "whether [Thomas Russell's] excellent and devoted female colleague, who laboured with him in the gospel, was not still more successful than he" (Kendall, *History*, 2:331). Primitive Methodists have repeatedly attributed their females' successes to their outstanding "modesty" and "good sense," though most biographical evidence contradicts this interpretation.

[42] "Elizabeth Russell," pp. 216, 181.

[43] For an excellent treatment of syncretism and nineteenth-century rural religion, see James Obelkevich, *Religion and Rural Society* (Oxford: Clarendon Press, 1976), chap. 6.

trances, when "the Lord worked powerfully upon her mind." The phenomenon at first appeared "somewhat strange" to one of the officiating preachers. But "since then," he later reported, "many have been affected this way, in almost every part of the circuit." The event, in his view, had practical value: "It drew many, through curiosity, to visit her. And being filled with the Holy Spirit, she spoke much of the goodness of God, and warned all that came to her, to flee from the wrath to come."[44]

Far from condemning folk culture and replacing it with "modern" religion, the missionaries exploited every opportunity it gave to recruit converts. Elizabeth founded a society at Peasemore (Berks.) by responding to an invitation from a woman who wanted her fortune told. "It got circulated that we used the black art, and black books," recalled Russell, "and that Miss Smith was a fortuneteller. This brought many out, and led to their awakening and conversion."[45] More often, Elizabeth answered calls from the sick. Followers attributed powers of healing to the wondrous pilgrimlike figure who travelled across miles of countryside to their cottages.[46] Her services were more often psychological than medical, particularly when spouses disagreed over religion. After hearing Elizabeth speak at Illsley Downs, a woman from Compton (Berks.) became violently ill. Her husband brought forth a string of unhelpful doctors, resorting at last—reluctantly—to Elizabeth. The preacher arrived and witnessed the woman's conversion and quick recovery. It was this many-faceted and flexible aspect of the female preacher's work that enabled her to captivate so many followers and enrich the development of sectarian Methodism.[47]

Female preachers played a crucial part in furthering the spread of popular evangelicalism. Because of their gender and

[44] "Memoir of Mary Hickson," *PMM*, 1829, pp. 315–7.

[45] "Elizabeth Russell," p. 181 (commentary by T. Russell).

[46] E.g. see Ibid., pp. 219–20, and on the cholera epidemic, pp. 258–60.

[47] "Memoir of Mrs. Hannah Baker," *PMM*, 1848, pp. 65–6. Mrs. Baker became a local preacher in 1836—much to her husband's annoyance.

class, they possessed special conviction and talent that enabled them to succeed against withering odds. The career of Elizabeth Smith demonstrates a timely convergence of personal experience and larger social and economic change. She was part of a generation of laborers who faced increasing marginalization in rural society in the Southwest. Poverty, late marriage, and constant migration rendered villagers "strangers and pilgrims" with unformulated grievances and little power to protest recent changes. But female preachers were active rebels; they spoke for a rural underclass and a vanishing culture when they brazenly attacked the establishment, in all its forms of authority, throughout the Southwest.

SEVEN

Female Preaching and
Sectarian Heresy

THE GUIDING PRINCIPLE that legitimated female preaching, "to obey God rather than man," could undermine as well as support the sectarian cause. This antinomian thrust, challenging the foundations of authority within industrial society and institutional religion, led one woman to secede from the Bible Christians. Ann Mason's career illustrates the peculiar fate of sectarian rebellion in nineteenth-century rural Devon and Cornwall. Bible Christians began their work in settings ideally suited to the growth of sectarianism: remote and sometimes hostile districts inspired evangelicals to greater heights of ingenuity and spontaneity. Bible Christians offered the earliest and strongest support for women preachers, and, by 1823, as many as one hundred females were active among them. But the expansion of the sect into southern towns and London led to tension and conflict as leaders sought greater control over country preachers. Self-made women could cause particular trouble when they encountered the formalized religion of the city. In her struggle for ministerial freedom and liberty of conscience, Ann Mason turned the tenets of the sect against the sect itself at a time when Bible Christianity was yielding to the pressures of urban religion and its social constraints.[1]

Ann Mason was born on June 24, 1791, at Horathorne in the parish of Northlew, Devon.[2] Her parents, like the majority

[1] Arthur Warne, *Church and Society in Eighteenth-Century Devon* (Newton Abbot: David & Charles, 1969), chap. 4, 8; F. W. Bourne, *The Bible Christians* (London, 1905).

[2] The following biographical information was drawn primarily from *A Memoir of the Life and Ministry of Ann [Mason] Freeman*, 2nd ed. (London, 1828), by

of the inhabitants of the area, were small farmers. Moorland terrain as well as native temperament defied the march of progress. In 1808, the agricultural surveyor Vancouver noted the small farms in the district, which brought in no more than twenty to fifty pounds per annum. "The farmers," he commented, "though hard-working people, are supposed to remain stationary with regard to the acquisition of property, or the means of enjoyment, beyond that which was known by their great-grandfathers."[3] The parish, however, did boast of a reasonably well-outfitted Anglican Church, indicating, perhaps, that of all Northlew's inhabitants, the tithe-gathering clergyman was the most enterprising.[4] William and Grace Mason brought each of their thirteen children there to be baptized and took the utmost care in raising them properly. "We were early instructed to read, and to say prayers," Ann recalled, "and on First-day evenings we were catechised, and the family [was] called together to prayer, and," she added, "because we did this we were thought to be religious." Though their daughter found life in Northlew singularly dull, the Masons viewed the circumstances of the family, particularly through the war years, as something of a triumph.[5]

According to her memoirs, Ann was depressive and envious as a child. "I could not be a fit companion for the world," she wrote, "though I often desired to." Inclined to ponder "spiritual and eternal things," she "often took much delight in reading religious tracts," particularly those on the experience of children. Ann's parents perceived her ardent, anxious reactions to such pamphlets and eventually banned them from the house, "lest [she] should become melancholy." Likewise, her

---

her husband, Henry Freeman. The memoir was a compilation of her diary and letters, with a lengthy introduction by her husband. Because of her separation from the Bible Christians, little else was published commemorating her career. I am grateful to Dr. Frank Prochaska for bringing this volume of memoirs to my attention.

[3] *General View of the Agriculture of Devon* (London, 1808), p. 107.

[4] Warne, *Church and Society*, p. 57.

[5] Freeman, *Memoir*, p. 1.

first encounter with travelling Methodists when she was fourteen met with no encouragement at home. Thus she "dragged on heavily" through childhood, unable to satisfy inchoate spiritual longings and emotional needs.[6]

Ann Mason's true trials of faith began during her years of apprenticeship. Possibly because the family was experiencing financial difficulties, Ann left home to learn the trade of dressmaking in 1812. As an introspective, sickly fourteen-year-old, she fared poorly during the first year. Signs of consumption soon appeared, and Ann struggled with thoughts of death. She turned to the church for solace, but, failing to resolve her inner conflicts, she then "attempted to get some pleasure from the world." Dressmaking only worsened her plight. Drawn into commercial relations with self-indulgent women, Ann "wandered farther after the vain fashions of a deluded world." Even after completing her apprenticeship, when she left the unfavorable environment of the dress shop to return to the home of her parents, she continued to honor the standards of the marketplace. "When inwardly convinced that it was wrong," she wrote sometime later, "I have pleaded as an excuse, that it was my duty in order to get business." Like other female preachers who had been dressmakers, Ann's experiences silently fueled the conviction that would later emerge as a vehement renunciation of worldliness.[7]

The domestic circumstances of the Mason family also fueled Ann's spiritual awakening. Early in 1814, William Mason took another farm in Northcott in the nearby parish of Sutcombe, and Ann and part of the family moved there in March. It is difficult to determine whether the change marked a rise or fall in the family fortune; given rising prices during the war, and considering the sparse population of Sutcombe, it is likely that the new farm was a more desirable one.[8] In any case, the move appeared to have a decisive impact on Ann's thinking.

[6] Ibid., p. 2.
[7] Ibid., p. 3.
[8] W. G. Hoskins, *Devon* (London: Collins, 1959), p. 98.

Overcoming "various new temptations" in Sutcombe (perhaps related to more affluent surroundings) and "inspite of all opposition," she finally "attended to the inward teachings of the Spirit." She gave up "ungodliness and the ungodly (as companions)" and instead attended a society of Methodists meeting in the village of Northcott. "Now," she wrote, "the day began to dawn on me."[9]

Ann's change of heart soon precipitated family strife. At first her family reproached her "for being, as they said, righteous overmuch." Again spiritual values came into conflict with material success. "I was frequently solicited to be more cheerful," she recalled, "and [was] told that it would be much for my advantage in the world." But parental threats made no impression upon her. While "the black cloud of persecution" gathered on the domestic front, Ann enlisted the support of her sister Mary, and the two young women officially joined the Northcott Methodist society. Finally "the flood broke forth": their parents banished Ann and Mary from the house "to preserve (as they thought) the family from the dreadful delusion." Such open conflict had an obvious beneficial effect upon Ann. "Previous to this," she noted, "I had often doubted of my acceptance with God; but in this time of trial my faith was confirmed. . . . I cheerfully gave up all to be a pilgrim." Their exile, though brief, also made an impression upon their parents. After they returned home, the girls gained the support of their mother and won the freedom to attend preaching services and meetings at their will. Religion became the means by which Ann and her sister established their autonomy within an isolated custom-bound family.[10]

Meanwhile, the earliest group of Bible Christians was gathering strength in nearby Shebbear. The new religious association sprang from sources similar to those that created the other Methodist sects: parochial neglect by the Church of England, anticlericalism, geographical isolation, impatience with

9 Freeman, *Memoir*, p. 4.
10 Ibid., pp. 5–6.

the conventions of established religion (including Wesleyanism), and a popular impulse to revitalize belief and practice. The Bible Christian movement also displayed characteristics unique to the West Country. In many areas, chapels opposed to the church were unheard of. Bible Christians were pioneer dissenters encouraging rebellion through religion. Poor roads and impassable moorlands preserved a wealth of regional customs and belief. The world of Joanna Southcott, filled with portents, prophecies, and dreams, was part of this Devonshire milieu. Stimulated by Bible Christian missioning, indigenous popular religion flourished as it rendered the new brand of faith its own.[11]

The first Bible Christian society, organized by William O'Bryan and James Thorne, met in Shebbear, Devon, in October of 1815. The organization proclaimed its independence from Wesleyanism only after protracted struggles over ministerial freedom. The new popular evangelicalism adopted a distinctly antiestablishment tone. The name "Bible Christians" pointed to the contrast between "those who in church use Bible and Prayer Book and these who on village green, in farm shed, and everywhere used only or chiefly one book and appealed to it for everything."[12] Bible Christianity gradually infiltrated the kitchens and barns of small farmers throughout northern Devon, capturing outposts that Wesleyan Methodism and the Established Church had failed to win. Poor villagers, as well as farmers, adopted the religion in defiance of warnings and threats of landlords and clergy.

In the south and west, as in the north of England, cottage religion gave voice to dissatisfaction and distress in the countryside. The timing of the rise of Bible Christianity was more than fortuitous. Before 1815, Devonshire rural society enjoyed prosperity and expansion; wartime demand and freedom from competitive imports kept prices high and enabled some farmers to acquire new land. With a fall in prices after the

---

[11] Warne, *Church and Society*, chaps. 4, 8; W. J. Townsend, H. B. Workman, and G. Eayrs, *A New History of Methodism* (London: Hodder and Stoughton, 1909), 1:502–3, 510–1.

[12] Ibid., p. 511.

war, massive reorganization took place. "All farmers had a bad time, but the big men had the capital reserves to weather the crisis of the 1820s while the smaller men had not." Many families gave up their land and moved to nearby towns, while others separated to find work as laborers. The consolidation of capitalist agriculture spelled hard times for laborers, too. Throughout this period, the laboring class underwent steady immiseration as their swollen numbers pushed wages down and often forced them to offer the work of wives and children in bargaining for positions. Opportunities for female laborers were diminishing in the countryside. An abrupt decline in the number of women in many rural parishes suggests that male laborers had displaced them. No longer able to find work in the country, women migrated to the towns.[13]

For Ann Mason, these changes generated uncertainty and brought injustice close to home. Bible Christianity, more than Wesleyan Methodism, became a weapon in a struggle to defy parsons, magistrates, and well-to-do farmers. As popular evangelicalism swept through the Devonshire countryside around her, Mason witnessed the magnetic power of the movement. Women figured prominently in the emerging ministry as specially inspired advocates of the household and vessels of the oppressed. It was only a matter of time before she identified her cause with theirs and offered her help.

"In consequence of many things I had heard against the [Bible Christians], I had formed an uncharitable opinion of them," Ann Mason admitted. But the power of their preachers nevertheless greatly moved her. During the autumn of 1816, she walked long distances to hear various evangelists and chanced upon a service by James Thorne, one of the sect founders. Under his influence, Mason resolved to pray for "a new heart" and soon was converted. The Bible Christians by

---

[13] Ernest W. Martin, *The Shearers and the Shorn: A Study of Life in a Devon Community* (London: Routledge & Kegan Paul, 1965), pp. 216–7, 76–7; Hoskins, *Devon*, pp. 98-9. Hoskins cites the example of his own ancestor, George Hoskins (1773–1839), who lost a sizable tenancy after 1814 and sank to the status of laborer by 1827. Townsend, Workman and Eayrs, *History of Methodism*, p. 508.

this time must have made considerable inroads into West Devon, for a few months later, Ann attended their Quarterly Meeting held in a barn belonging to her aunt in Alsworthy. The meeting convinced Ann and her sister to continue "among the Bryanites," as they were called, though many friends disapproved. Ironically, Ann viewed opposition to the Bible Christians as the "sectarian" error; rejection of the new evangelical religion represented a deliberate separation from the true church. "The love of Christ in me was not limited," she wrote. "I found my safety was in obeying the truth; for I must obey God rather than man. . . . I now saw that the best men were liable to err, and therefore the only safe way was to follow Christ." Such was the reasoning that would remain central to her preaching career. Early in 1817, she and her sister broke from the Methodists and joined the Bible Christians, who then numbered about one thousand.

Within a month, Ann was promoted to the position of class leader and, soon after, to that of preacher. Though she became the target of "much censure and reproach," she felt compelled to accept "the commission from Heaven." "I felt it was 'woe unto me if I preached not the gospel,'" she reported in her journal. She regularly filled local appointments while living at home throughout 1817; then in March of the following year, she gave up dressmaking and began travelling. Setting out on foot with Em Cottle, a fellow female preacher, she made her way through the countryside into South Devon. Battered by the weather as well as by threats from hostile natives, she continued alone after Em returned home. Though sickly, she accepted an assignment to the inhospitable Brentor moorlands. "The parsons and parish officers have searched for me, as though I was come to destroy the land," she wrote in June, 1818. By the time she reached Cornwall in August, the strain had taxed her health considerably. With her thoughts again fixed on death, she returned to her parents' house in Northcott in the latter part of 1818.[14]

[14] Freeman, *Memoir*, pp. 10–14.

Through her preaching experiences and especially during
her illness, Ann Mason's position on doctrinal questions and
matters of church government became increasingly radical.
She prided herself on an instinctual free style of preaching
that never failed to see results. "An old man asked me if I
took a text," she once recorded, "or only exhorted. I told him,
just as I feel liberty."[15] Her words had almost magical effect
upon her audiences, and particularly upon women, whose
testimonies bolstered her cause.

Actual records of testimonies are nearly nonexistent; only
one Bible Christian narrative remains extant, and though it
no doubt was edited, it provides plain evidence of typical concerns. Mrs. Hopper of Chatham, Kent, might have been one
of Ann Mason's advocates:

> If any one here has reason to bless God I am sure I
> have, for before our brothers came up here to preach my
> husband and I lived a shocking life. On Saturday nights,
> when he received his wages, he would set off after supper
> to the publichouse; when it was ten or eleven o'clock I
> should go off after him, and should have to hunt him up
> from one publichouse to another; and when I scolded
> him he would curse and swear at me. If he came away
> with me we should quarrel again, and curse and swear at
> each other; for the devil was in me as well as in him; and
> the children had learned to curse and swear as badly as
> ourselves, till our house was like a little hell. [Here she
> burst into a flood of tears, and was stopped in her
> narrative.]

Whether apocryphal or not, the confession included predict-
able family problems: financial difficulties, marital discord,
immoral behavior, and unhappiness were pulling apart the
Hopper household before their conversion. While Mr. Hopper
belonged to the society of the pub, his wife evidently fre-
quented that of the chapel. The appearance of a female

[15] *Ibid.*, p. 16.

preacher tipped the balance of the household in favor of the latter:

> [After a pause she continued.] One Saturday he had been out late drinking, and I was much distressed; but the next day I asked him to go over on the Brook where a woman was going to preach; he consented, and we both came into this room. When I looked at the woman I fancied I had never seen such a woman in my life. She had not been preaching long before I thought it was all to me. She spoke of sinful practices such as we had followed, and I thought surely some person had been telling her all about us. . . . When she went on to show what would be the consequences, I began to cry like rain. I wet both corners of my shawl wiping away my tears. . . . All at once I thought, I wonder where Hopper is! The room was packed full of people, but on looking around I saw him, and he was weeping too, which made me weep the more, though all the bitterness went out of my heart from that moment! [After describing how they both sought and found mercy, she added,] And now, bless the Lord, we are both as happy as we used to be miserable. My husband brings home the money on Saturday nights; I tidy up the house, then we go and get our marketing, and come home and sing a hymn, and have prayer. On Sundays we attend the services here throughout the day, and close with singing and prayer in our home, and the children sing with us, and we are all happy together.[16]

The testimony described the conversion of a household, rather than that of an individual. Bible Christianity, like other forms of cottage religion, enabled women to effect change within the family. During times of economic distress, this kind of conversion gave women leverage in a struggle that pitted the household against competing social ties. Female preachers

[16] F. W. Bourne, *The Centenary Life of James Bourne, of Shebbear* (London, 1895), pp. 66–7.

148

might attract listeners by virtue of their novelty; they changed listeners' lives by reformulating the dictates of necessity.

Similar experiences motivated many women to preach, and sometimes they consulted Ann Mason on their right to speak in public. Having faced frequent attacks upon her own legitimacy as a preacher, Ann had mounted formidable defenses against such aspersions. In Cornwall, for example, where the practices of the Bible Christians still startled some audiences, she found one woman the victim of scripture-waving oppressors:

> In this neighbourhood I visited a young woman who I believe was called to preach; but being oppos'd by man she omitted her duty, and the distress of her mind had almost destroyed her body. It appears, an old preacher was the chief instrument of her misery: she seemed to feel some relief in telling her sad tale to me. Many females are kept in bondage by those who say, 'we suffer not a woman to teach;' thus quoting Paul's words, and not rightly applying them. Man's opinion on this subject is nothing to me; for it is woe unto me if I preach not the gospel.[17]

Her advice to women, as years passed, revealed an acute awareness of the obstacles confronting them. " 'Hold that fast which thou hast, that no man take thy crown' " she intoned to another female preacher. "If we withhold more than is meet, it will tend to poverty, and through scattering we may increase. Yet in this respect," she added, "take not me for an example. I have too often been guilty of putting the candle under a bushel."[18]

Bible Christians wholeheartedly supported female preaching, and Ann Mason's sentiments only echoed those of other women in the sect. The wife of William O'Bryan, also a

[17] Journal entry dated 1 Sept. 1818, Freeman, *Memoir*, p. 16.
[18] Mason to Sarah Cory, Plint, April 17, 1823, Ibid., pp. 51–4.

preacher, had written original verse on the subject, entitled "The Female Preachers' Plea":

> By sweet experience now I know,
>   That those who knock shall enter in;
> God doth his gifts and grace bestow,
>   On Women too, as well as men.

> The sacred fire doth burn within
>   The breasts of either sex the same;
> The holy soul that's freed from sin,
>   Desires that all may catch the flame.

> If we had fear'd the frowns of men,
>   Or thought their observations just,
> Long since we had believ'd it vain,
>   And hid our talent in the dust.

> While men with eloquence and fame,
>   The silver trumpet manly blow,
> A plainer trump we humbly claim,
>   The saving power of God to show.

Bible Christian women nurtured a definite sense of self-assurance and equality which the Connexion promoted through preaching appointments. The Plan of 1819, for example, assigned both women and men to ten out of twelve stations. But Ann Mason's notion of spiritual freedom was moving beyond equality to a more privileged position. In a letter to another preacher, she exhorted her in what would become a familiar fashion to follow the Holy Spirit rather than mortal man. "Let all thy movements be the perfect will of God," she wrote. The special dispensation of the female preacher, based on a direct relationship with divine power, was leading to an ultimate repudiation of any form of control.[19]

The evolution of Ann Mason's personal ideology, shaped

---

[19] Mason to Mary Cottle, Wolwich, April 17, 1824, Ibid., p. 187; Swift, "The Women Itinerant Preachers of Early Methodism," *Proceedings of the Wesley Historical Society* 29 (1953): 76; *Primitive Methodist Magazine*, 1821, pp. 190–2, verses 7, 10, 12, 18.

by her struggles as a woman, ran headlong into the emerging doctrine of the Bible Christian Connexion. As Mason worked to free herself from hierarchical control, the Bible Christians became increasingly interested in imposing such constraints upon their growing network of societies and preachers. Following Methodist protocol, the new Connexion held its first Conference in August, 1819, to discuss administrative and doctrinal issues. Like other Methodist connexions, Bible Christians organized districts, circuits, and societies, presided over by superintendents, pastors, and elders (or leaders). The latter two titles were new names for familiar positions, and the change indicated a deeper transformation. "The polity developed along Presbyterian lines, and to these the body adhered faithfully," explained their historian, "at some cost." More power accrued to one man, William O'Bryan, than in other Methodist sects. As General Superintendent of the Conference of 1819, O'Bryan presided over twelve (male) itinerant preachers and exerted considerable personal influence in the matters at hand.[20]

Ann Mason sensed these developments; though motivated by illness and divine inspiration, her actions betrayed a determination that was neither impaired nor spiritually possessed. When she returned to Northcott at the end of her itinerary in 1819, the frequency of her communications with the Holy Spirit increased and convinced her that she must carry out a specially designated mission at once. She took the liberty of sending a circular letter to the Bible Christian Conference at Baddash that summer. The letter itself expressed no particularly unorthodox ideas. In the tone of a last will and testament, Ann Mason urged her "brethren" and "fathers" to "use every effort in [their] power to pull down Satan's kingdom." But the assumption of so much authority by a woman, directed at the seat of power occupied by men, represented a challenge to the new Bible Christian polity.[21]

[20] Townsend, Workman, Eayrs, *History of Methodism*, 1:512.
[21] Freeman, *Memoir*, p. 29.

Mason's letter aroused immediate concern, for O'Bryan soon after appeared at Northcott to discuss theology with the ailing female itinerant. Ann recorded their extraordinary exchange in her journal. O'Bryan, "expecting it would be the last time" he would talk with her, spoke "in a manner he was not accustomed." Ann, whether assuming the poetic license of the dying or simply taking advantage of a good opportunity, soundly put O'Bryan in his place:

> In our conversation, he said, ... "Ann, do you believe there is any greater blessing to be attained to here than sanctification? (meaning the being cleansed from all sin.) I answered, *I do*; and that moment my soul did so partake of the powers of the world to come, that I could desire no greater confirmation than the Lord gave me, that I had testified the truth. I sat at the Saviour's feet, and He spoke. W. O'B. then said, "I, some time since, was of the same opinion; but one day I conversed with J. Thorne on the subject, and we read John Wesley's thoughts on it, and we concluded it could not be." I said, "Did you and J. T. find out the Almighty to perfection?" adding, "I know I have a blessing far superior to the being only cleansed from all sin; this I call being sealed to the day of redemption, or wholly restored to the image of God, which all that enter heaven must receive here; and if it is our privilege to enjoy it one moment, why not all our remaining days?" I told him; I knew his soul was not thus saved, and begged he would expect it; and he answered, "Well, Ann, if it be attainable, pray that I may receive it." He left me with the same request.[22]

Ann Mason's position on the question of entire sanctification, a well-worn issue in sectarian circles, indicated that her views had progressed beyond those of most believers. But "perfectionism" alone did not threaten the basis of the Bible Christian Church. Her audacity in correcting a church father, however,

[22] Ibid., pp. 29–30.

portended a more serious divergence of opinion over the question of ministerial rights.

While convalescing during 1819 and 1820, Ann continued to receive "impressions" from divine authority concerning matters ranging from the personal to the ecclesiastical. When she finally returned to itinerancy in the latter part of 1820, her willingness to comply with the dictates of the Bible Christian Conference had greatly diminished. Thus she "yielded" to appointments with slow reluctance, convinced that the assignments were "not of the Lord." Speaking of her work in the Canworthy-water Circuit, she wrote, "I came to this circuit not in [sic] my own will, but in obedience to the elders."[23] Ann's mounting irritation with "the elders" became more apparent in her journal entries throughout 1821. "I feel as if there is too much preaching in Shebbear for real profit," she wrote in an obvious reference to the home base of leaders O'Bryan and Thorne.[24] She longed to "deviate from the old, or regular way of holding meetings" under the watchful jurisdiction of the Conference. Her dissatisfaction grew more serious when she began to question the importance of the sacraments. "Water-baptism," she suspected, was "the work of the devil." Her attitude towards baptism echoed the heresies of seventeenth-century sectaries.[25] With these objections slowly eroding her commitment to institutionalized religion, Ann continued to travel throughout Devon and Cornwall until receiving an assignment to London in 1823.

A wealth of new experiences in the city prompted Ann Mason to give expression to smoldering dissatisfactions. Upon her arrival, she found a sympathetic listener in Henry Freeman, a fellow preacher also from Devon. When she first met

[23] Ibid., pp. 38–9.
[24] Ibid., p. 42.
[25] Ibid., pp. 43–4. In spite of these feelings, Ann evidently associated with the Baptists, for on June 24, 1822 (almost a year later), she recorded having "blessed liberty among the Baptists" (p. 45). It is likely that her critique was aimed at infant baptism and that her position now resembled that of anabaptism or even antinomianism.

Freeman back in Baddash in 1820, she had recognized in him a kindred spirit. " 'Tis primitive Christian simplicity I long to see revived," she had recorded, "and through H. F. it seems to dawn with a pleasing prospect."[26] In London, the two preachers resumed their critical exchange of ideas. Together they discussed the potentially subversive question of a "believer's privilege" and the need for a mission to Ireland, as well as their daily encounters with formidable obstacles in London. City magistrates and clergymen goaded them into angry frustration. Freeman's difficulties culminated in imprisonment after he was arrested for holding a meeting in the street. Meanwhile, Ann Mason's hitherto restrained tongue came gradually unleashed. At dinner with friends, she soliloquized passionately on the subject of the Irish ("It was as giving vent to a vessel ready to burst," she recalled), and enjoying a certain immunity from arrest on account of her sex, she continued to "pull down [Satan's] strong holds" among the masses in the streets.[27]

Protected by the anonymity of the city, Mason's penchant for reproving her superiors became more pronounced. While visiting a dying woman in East London, Ann confronted an officious clergyman whose method of saving souls seemed woefully inadequate.

. . . I found [the woman] without a knowledge of God. I was directly drawn to speak of the fall of man, and of salvation by Christ, and the way to attain it. As I had thus spoken, the parson came in, who had also been sent for. He first inquired what place of worship she attended; being answered, the church, he asked if she had attended the Sacraments. I was then moved with indignation against such daubings, which constrained me, as it was on life and death, without delay to break silence, and interrupt the conversation, saying "What she wants is the Holy Spirit, to bear witness with her spirit, that she is a child

[26] Ibid., p. 36.
[27] Ibid., pp. 57–60.

of God." He then turned to me, and began to apologize for introducing shadows; and readily consented to all I said with respect to real Christianity, which is not composed of shadows, in whole or in part.[28]

The parson, so wedded to the letter of church law, proved to be "a yielding teachable man." The two ministers therefore parted from the sickroom in peace, though not before Ann had bested the clergyman by praying extemporaneously following his rather tedious reading from the Prayer Book. The deathbed setting gave the cottage preacher the license to contradict church authority, and, in an instant, a series of oppositions became evident: salvation through faith challenged salvation through sacraments; cottage candor challenged urban church protocol; and female preachers challenged male clergymen. As the bearer of "real Christianity," Ann Mason emerged from the confrontation in triumph.[29]

Growing confidence undermined still further Ann Mason's allegiance to the Bible Christian mission in London, and personal considerations added to her wish for autonomy. As her involvement with Henry Freeman became more serious, Ann ruminated over the "degree of bondage" entailed in marriage. Slowly, she and Freeman deliberated over questions of commitment and independence, and, once assured that the two concerns were not mutually exclusive, Ann agreed to marry that spring. The decision seemed to unlock her last bit of reserve in religious matters; having clarified her thoughts on the subject of personal "bondage," she now reconsidered her position in the church. "For several years," she wrote to a friend,

> my soul hath been kept in a degree of bondage through too much looking at, and expecting from books and preachers, and thereby I have been suppressing the power within; but of late, praise the Lord, He hath brought me

[28] Ibid., p. 62.
[29] Ibid., p. 63.

out of that bondage, by showing me the vanity of all that is not of God wherever it is . . .³⁰

Her disillusionment with the Bible Christians, and indeed all churches, became increasingly apparent. She repeatedly advised others to rely upon "the inward whisper" and "the assurance within." "These weapons," she pointed out, "are mighty to the pulling down of strong holds." Then she added, "The glory is departed from most professed churches. I am expecting to see a tremendous shaking of the kingdom of antichrist, and Babylon's strong walls and tower to come down."³¹ Her position on doctrinal matters, as she acknowledged, was moving closer to Quakerism. Personal spiritual illumination and equality of believers superseded the paraphernalia of worship offered by modern churches.³²

Together Mason and Freeman finally rejected the Bible Christian Church. In June, 1824, they notified the Conference of their intention to marry and their mutual dissatisfaction with their place in the church. Freeman outlined three reasons for their disaffection: he and Ann no longer believed in the scriptural validity of the sacraments; both preachers wished to "go abroad," meaning to Ireland; and they intended to marry and work together, regardless of the opinion of church elders. The couple recognized that their position on the question of ministerial control as well as on the sacraments effectively estranged them from the Bible Christians.³³ But to their dismay, James Thorne and the Conference chose to interpret their declaration of separation as an indirect plea for reacceptance into the church. "In consideration of your former

³⁰ Ibid., p. 72. Mason to Paul Robins, Nov. 13, 1824.

³¹ Mason to William Lawry, April 15, 1824, Ibid., pp. 80–1; see also Mason to Paul Robins, Op. cit.

³² In April of 1824, she recorded meeting with Methodists to discuss Quakerism, and she felt "convinced that thereto the Holy Spirit would lead all, if submitted to." (Ibid., p. 83) She expressed her position to William O'Bryan in a letter on June 21, 1824, explaining that she agreed with Quakers on questions concerning the sacraments (pp. 97–100).

³³ Ibid., pp. xxv–xxvii, 104–5.

zeal, piety, and diligence," wrote Thorne, "and from a persuasion that you still intend to promote the glory of God, the
Brethren assembled in Conference are agreeable that you
should try some time longer." He added, "They therefore
propose to bear with you one year longer, and to appoint you
here at Devonport, to labour under the direction of the general
superintendent."[34] In one sense, the leaders could be credited
with a faithfulness to the founding principles of the Bible
Christians, which grew from similar disputes within Devonshire Methodism. But beneath the extended offer lurked intensified supervision and an authoritarian attitude that did
not allow even a voluntary severance from church rule.
Though Freeman never published the content of his final
letter to Thorne and the Conference, he did reveal that he
had simply reiterated his original declaration. "I could not but
act in obedience," he explained, "to what I apprehended to
be my religious duty: and that I must 'obey God rather than
man;' and could not acknowledge myself after that time a
member of their society." Though he wrote without the assistance of Ann Mason (who was then staying in Brighton), he
supported his statement with the precept of female preachers.
The Conference thus removed the names of both Freeman
and Mason from the Plan, and the couple finally set about
making arrangements for their independent evangelism.[35]

The last year and a half of Ann Mason's life, though fraught
with hardship, nevertheless brought fulfillment of her desire
to work on her own. Her journal provides only a rough sketch
of her movements. She and Freeman were married on August
9, 1824, and after a brief stay among relatives and friends in
Devon, they embarked for Dublin in October. There they began their difficult migration from meetinghouse to chapel,
consorting with Quakers, Methodists, and Catholics, in an attempt to evangelize wherever possible. Fierce persecution followed them throughout the city of Dublin; in one instance,

[34] Ibid., pp. xxvii–xxviii.
[35] Ibid., p. xxviii.

even Methodists angrily attacked them. Country people proved more hospitable to the English travellers, but by the summer of 1825, Ann's health was seriously in question. The couple returned to England in October of that year. While Henry resumed preaching in London and then Liverpool, Ann remained at her father's house in Northcott, where she died on March 7, 1826.[36]

So thoroughly had Ann Mason rejected obedience to religious and social law that she finally jettisoned all affiliation with sectarian societies. Her position evolved from her experiences as a rural preacher and her eventual clash with the institutional and secularized world of the city. Mason and Freeman never attempted to form their own sect; they demonstrated an absolute disagreement with organized religion by reverting to extemporaneous, informal evangelizing. Bible Christianity was, in fact, moving in the opposite direction. The departure of Ann Mason and Henry Freeman foreshadowed the eventual incompatibility of the rural evangelist, true to her grassroots principles, with modern evangelicalism.

[36] Ibid., pp. 106–7, 116–7, 134, 138, 158.

EIGHT

Female Preaching and
Village Industry

NEVER ISOLATED from modern urban influences, cottage religion indeed thrived on resisting changes that emanated from such centers. The conflict between old and new, stability and change, provoked diverse and sometimes contradictory responses; in industrial villages where rural tradition gave way to rapid population growth and factory discipline, cottage religion provided an important means of preserving continuity and insulating laborers from new forms of authority. The interaction between popular culture and new forces was particularly noticeable in areas like Derbyshire, where rural districts and industrial villages were in close proximity. An exceptionally large number of active female preachers calls attention to the receptiveness of the region to cottage religion and all it stood for. As the county underwent a classic shift from dependency upon agriculture to reliance upon industry, female preachers supplied an essential component of popular religion to laborers grappling with dislocating changes. As carriers of rural customs, they resuscitated traditions and spoke for threatened, lost, or idealized values. In new industrial settings, women evangelists continued to help laborers shape a domestic ideology of their own.

New village factories offered employment to sectarian "pilgrims and strangers" who abandoned agricultural labor or cottage industry and left their native villages searching for work. In the midst of rural areas, industry was expanding with remarkable speed. Farey commented on the early transformation of the northern part of Derbyshire:

*Selected locations of Methodist sectarian
activity in Derbyshire*

It is surprising with what rapidity the different manufacturing Establishments were accumulated, in some places,
in the parish of Glossop, at the northwest extremity . . .
I was told, that about 25 years before I visited it, in 1809
[i.e., ca. 1784], only one old Mill existed, appropriated to
the making of Oatmeal for its few Agricultural Inhabitants; yet at the time of collecting my Notes, out of the
112 *Cotton Mills* of the County, . . . 56, or just half of these,
were found in this Parish![1]

In addition to mills in the industrial north of the county, many
villages scattered throughout the central and bordering regions of Derbyshire became sites for relatively small factories.
Since the eighteenth century, Derbyshire rivers provided
choice settings for entrepreneurial ventures; the Arkwrights
and Strutts, among others, created industrial centers that
brought fame to the county. Cotton- and silk-spinning mills
sprang up in bucolic outposts, changing remote crossroads
into bustling centers of trade. In central Derbyshire, Belper
and Darley Abbey more than doubled in size between 1788
and 1811, and textile factories at Wirksworth, Chesterfield,
and Cromford constantly absorbed laborers from the surrounding countryside.[2]

The problems of the industrial village became the concern
of female preachers. Textile factories, particularly during the
early decades of the nineteenth century, relied heavily upon
female labor and, before the passage of the Factory Acts, child
labor as well. Farey noted the numerical predominance of
women in the population of Derbyshire as a whole; he also
remarked on the importation of women and children to supply
expanding industries with labor. "Children are not only sought
for thro' the adjoining districts, but in many instances have
been imported by scores at a time, and by hundreds in a year,
from London, Bristol, and other great Towns," he pointed

[1] John Farey, *A General View of the Agriculture and Minerals of Derbyshire*, 3
vols. (London, 1811–17), 3:498.
[2] Ibid., pp. 481–5.

out. Long before factory commissions uncovered the worst evils of the industrial age, Farey found the problems attending this mass migration (mostly of women) overwhelming:

> A considerable majority of the Cotton-Mill Apprentices appear, I think, to be Girls, particularly of those born in distant places; . . . [many of whom] are retained on Wages, at particular Mills . . . but too often, such truly unfortunate young Women, disperse themselves over the Country, and for want of friends or employ, prematurely and inconsiderately get married to, or more improperly associate themselves with Soldiers, or other loose and unstationary Men, and at no distant periods, are . . . passed home to the Parishes they were apprenticed in, for want of any other settlement . . . with several children, to remain a burthen thereon.[3]

If economic necessity did not drive female preachers there, their identification with displaced and distressed women eventually incited them to visit or to move to the growing industrial areas. Sectarian "mothers in Israel" found new demands for their services; their message of domestic security, maternal strength, and solidarity took on added meaning among factory workers in unfamiliar surroundings. "I never felt quite at home," Betsey Evans contended, "until we came to Millhouses, near Wirksworth . . . I believe we are just where the Lord would have us to be."[4]

FEMALE PREACHERS from farming backgrounds projected a double image when they confronted the industrial village: their connection to the farming homestead suggested both a tradition-bound, stable past and a turbulent present. The unpretentious clothing of rural preachers marked them as ordinary country folk; it was often more suited to work than

---

[3] Ibid., p. 502. On the predominance of females throughout the county, see pp. 586–7.

[4] Z. Taft, *Holy Women* (London, 1825), 1: 156.

"church," and in some cases, it betrayed everyday occupations. Female preachers also cultivated a plain and humble image that identified them with country customs. In rejecting fashionable frills for plain poke bonnets, they opted for the attire of rural laboring women over "modern" dress imported from distant cities. Speech identified preachers with their native districts as well as their social class. With their rudimentary education, usually in local dialect, these women did not develop oratorical skills that would soften harsh sentiments and disguise social origins. Adjectives like "original" and "natural," used to describe the preaching of Sarah Kirkland, probably referred to unembellished Derbyshire "conversation-preaching." The "rustic" image of Primitive preachers was the key to their acceptance in some places where anticlericalism had defeated the best efforts of better educated clergymen.[5]

No matter how traditional or familiar the style of a female preacher, she nevertheless was a woman removed from the domestic setting, travelling about alone and on foot. Her arrival in a factory locality naturally invited speculation and often genuine concern, for the texts of the preacher supplied an accompanying note of pervasive dangers; her own apparent homelessness and, in some cases, destitution underscored the message. She rarely experienced difficulty in securing a place to stay or hold meetings. Through private conversation that followed public appearances, the preacher's personal history— essential testimony of her call to preach—circulated among neighbors. Her experiences were themselves news of current events as well as the acts of God. During the years of agrarian hardship after 1815, such news was seldom heartening.

Perhaps no place in Derbyshire witnessed a more dramatic transformation than Belper; within a half-century, the village grew from "the insignificant residence of a few uncivilised nailers" to the second largest town in the county. For centuries, the village served as a marketplace for farms around central

[5] *Primitive Methodist Magazine* (hereafter *PMM*), 1881, p. 422; Rev. John Barfoot, *A Diamond in the Rough* (London, 1874), p. 75.

Derbyshire while supporting a number of small local industries. By far the most important activity was nailmaking. The
"peculiar qualities of the iron and coal in this area" made
Belper a leading supplier of horsenails through all of England
during the first half of the eighteenth century. The nailers
themselves were notoriously lawless and tough, committed to
their cottage-based shops and the secrecy of their handicraft.
Other industries in the village included spinning, weaving, and
framework knitting, also organized on a domestic basis, along
with some pottery manufacturing. Yet Belper remained "as
low in population as it was backward in civility," in spite of so
much activity, well into the final years of the eighteenth
century.[6]

The fate of the small village changed decisively in 1776,
when Jedediah Strutt and partners decided to build a cotton
mill on the banks of the Derwent at Belper.[7] Three additional
establishments soon followed the first, and besides their cotton
works, the Strutts became proprietors of coalfields at Dally Pit,
an iron foundry at Milford, and extensive gritstone quarries
outside Belper. The Strutts irreversibly altered the village
landscape. Jedediah's mansion, situated in the center of town,
gradually expanded to subsume even the ancient market site.
(The market subsequently moved to its present location at
Marketplace.) By 1830, the family, "own[ed] several hundred
houses, and a valuable tract of land on the banks of the Derwent, extending nearly three miles, in the townships of Belper
and Makeney."[8]

[6] D. P. Davies, *A New Historical and Descriptive View of Derbyshire* (Belper, 1811),
p. 344; D. Wilson, "Belper Nailers," *Derbyshire Countryside* 50 (1943), pp. 21–
2, 26; R. J. Millward, *Belper in Bygone Years* (Belper, 1977), p. 3; *P.O. Directory
of Derbyshire*, 1855, p. 20.

[7] For an exhaustive examination of the Strutt and Arkwright families, see
R. S. Fitton and A. P. Wadsworth, *The Strutts and the Arkwrights, 1758–1830*
(Manchester: Manchester University Press, 1958). The work, however, includes
very little on Belper.

[8] S. Glover, *History, Gazetteer, and Directory of the County of Derby*, 2 vols. (Derby,
1829), pp. 6–9; Davies, *View of Derbyshire*, pp. 243, 340, 356; Fitton and Wadsworth, *Strutts*, pp. 78–9.

The Strutt empire brought thousands of laborers to Belper. The population of the town increased by 25 percent between 1801 and 1809, from 4,500 to 5,635. "Between 1,200 and 1,300 persons [found] daily employment" at the Strutt factories. Town growth continued at the same rate between 1811 and 1821. The number of residents increased from 5,778 to 7,235, and by 1821, a third of the town worked for the Strutts. Out of 1,418 families in Belper, only 65 were employed in agriculture while 1,309 were listed under trade or handicraft.[9] The Strutts acted as beneficent patrons of this enormous enterprise. In order to "fix their [workers'] residence at Belper," the factory owners built terraces of gritstone cottages and back-to-back houses. They also undertook a number of philanthropic ventures, including Sunday Schools (650 children attended their school by 1817), Lancastrian day schools, and new almshouses. Not surprisingly, members of the family rose to positions of political power. Jedediah's son, George Benson Strutt, assumed the office of Justice of the Peace in Belper, and later became Deputy Lieutenant of the County of Derbyshire. Of the following generation, Edward Strutt (1801–1880) was created first Baron of Belper in 1856, and made Lord Lieutenant of Nottinghamshire in 1864.[10]

Religion always found a place in the expansive scenario created by the Strutts. Jedediah himself was a committed Unitarian, and in his early years of financial success, he provided most of the funds for a chapel at Belper. Established religion, meanwhile, seemed to suffer from neglect. A decaying church, with a bare capacity for three hundred persons, held services every other Sunday and referred marriages to other parishes. Thus the climate proved favorable to the growth of Wesleyan Methodism, a faith which neither threatened nor supported the dissenting spirit of the Strutts. Methodism arrived in Belper around the same time as the Strutt industries; a society

9 Glover, op. cit., p. 101.

10 Ibid., pp. 101–5; Fitton and Wadsworth, Strutts, chaps. 8 and 9; Marion Johnson, Derbyshire Village Schools in the 19th Century (Newton Abbot: David & Charles, 1970), p. 42.

began meeting in 1770, and for the next decade, occupied a humble place beside the growing industrial enterprise.[11]

In its meeting places and the status of its members, the Wesleyan society exhibited all the characteristics of sectarian cottage religion. The active agent behind the organization of the first society was Thomas Slater, a farmer from nearby Shottle. While Slater's brother Samuel allied himself with local industrial interests (and later became famous for his reconstruction of the Arkwright frame in America), Thomas helped to unite representatives of "old Belper." Factory workers, perhaps, joined the Wesleyan society in small numbers, but the core of the group undoubtedly belonged to the class of tradesmen and domestic knitters outside the Strutt establishment. The Wesleyans sometimes convened outdoors in the marketplace, and at other times at Slater's farm, in a cottage in Chapel Street, or in a butcher's shop in Wellington Court. The society continued to operate out of private and domestic quarters until 1781, when Slater donated land for the erection of a chapel.[12]

During the 1790s, the obscure rural society rapidly transformed into a leading town congregation. More than tripling its membership within the decade to a total of 164 in 1799, Belper became the largest society in the Derby Circuit. Its metamorphosis was complete in 1803, when the Wesleyan Conference created a new circuit with Belper at the head of eighteen other places. The society replaced its old chapel with a much larger one in 1807. "Exactly 53 feet square and [holding] 630 people," the building is still considered "a good ex-

[11] Fitton and Wadsworth, *Strutts*, p. 102. The Rev. D. P. Davies, author of histories of Derbyshire and Belper, was the minister of the Belper Unitarian Chapel in the 1830s. Glover, *History and Gazetteer*, p. 103.

[12] G. Arthur Fletcher, *Records of Wesleyan Methodism in the Belper Circuit, 1760–1903* (Belper, 1903), pp. 31, 26–7; Millward, *Belper*, p. 4; Fitton and Wadsworth, *Strutts*, p. 103n; Glover, *History and Gazetteer*, 102–3. Fletcher listed the first chapel trustees: "Thomas Slater, farmer, Shottle; James Chritie, framework knitter, Belper; William Bourne, potter, Belper; Daniel Street, Jr., framework knitter, Belper; John Jillett, farmer; Joseph Statham, framework knitter, Belper; John Rice, malter, Kilburn; Thomas Pedley, malter, Belper; Samuel Robinson, shopkeeper, Belper" (p. 27).

ample of a small urban chapel." Though unmistakably domestic in style, the Wesleyan structure represented the
achievement of institutional status in the midst of a growing
factory town.[13]

Despite this wealth of Wesleyan activity—or perhaps because
of it—there was still room for cottage religion in Belper. When
a Primitive Methodist itinerant wandered into town in 1814
and gave out a sermon in the marketplace, he found a ready
audience. (Ironically, he chose to stand in front of a butcher's
shop, no doubt a competitor of the Wesleyan butcher in Wellington Court.) The Primitives soon established a following,
and in spite of ritualized heckling by the local mob, the "Ranters" shared in a village-wide Methodist revival during the year
1815–16.[14] Wesleyans occupied two chapels by then, but they
too held cottage meetings every night of the week for nearly
a year and, like the Primitives, engaged the help of neighboring farmers in holding prayer meetings. Cottage evangelism became the popular religion of the town, and followers
often disregarded the distinction between Primitives and Wesleyans in order to pass freely from one meeting to another.
Eventually the Primitive Methodist society outgrew the house
of local preacher Thomas Jackson and moved to a large rented
room in the village. Finally, in 1817, the society purchased
land from the Strutts at a reduced rate of one shilling per
yard and began building a chapel. Thus the Primitives passed
from cottage to chapel standing in a short period of time; but
like the Wesleyans, they erected a building that only enlarged
upon the domestic meeting places they had occupied before.[15]

These years of "high evangelistic fervour" clouded differences that profoundly divided religious groups in Belper.
Primitive Methodism, more than other local denominations,
succeeded in mobilizing migrant and local factory workers.

[13] David Barton, *Discovering Chapels and Meeting Houses* (Shire Publications,
1975), pp. 24–5; Fletcher, *Records*, p. 29; Charles Willott, *Historical Records of
Belper* (Belper, 1885), p. 5.
[14] H. B. Kendall, *History of the Primitive Methodist Church* (London, n.d.), 1:192.
[15] Fletcher, *Records*, p. 29.

Strutt recognized "the influence for good which the labours of [the Primitives] had exerted upon many of his work-people"; his aid to the group showed a shrewd awareness of the power of the plebeian preachers and their advantage over local Wesleyans.[16] In spite of such paternalistic generosity, however, the Strutts apparently felt the air of competition for souls that pervaded the town. Methodism had made a remarkable and unsettling sweep through Belper between 1815 and 1820, and the factory owners were not about to surrender their dominion to the groundswell of popular evangelicalism. Around 1821, the Strutts took a supremely calculated step into the fray of religious activity. Even though the family remained dissenters after Jedediah's death in 1797, George Benson and William Strutt decided to act in the interest of the Established Church. "Anxious that their workpeople, tenants, and neighbours should be adequately provided with . . . religious instruction and discipline," the brothers "opened and greatly promoted" a subscription for the erection of a new Established Church in Belper.[17]

The undertaking provided an ideal opportunity to arouse public spirit. The festivities, moreover, underscored cultural differences between Church and chapel. In high paternalistic fashion, the Strutts presided over a series of events that upstaged solemn Methodist processionals and overwhelmed dissenting sobriety. Their campaign began in October, 1822, when "the first stone [of the new church] . . . was laid, amid an immense concourse of people":

It was on the day of a great annual fair, and the day was uncommonly fine. The Duke of Devonshire, who had announced his intention to officiate at the ceremony of laying the first stone, was met by the delighted multitude at an early hour: his travelling equipage was stopped by the crowd, the horses were taken from the carriage, and his

---

[16] Kendall, *History*, 1:193; *The Journals of William Clowes* (London, 1844), p. 117.
[17] Glover, *History and Gazetteer*, 2:103.

Grace was drawn by the shouting populace to Bridge Hill, the residence of G. B. Strutt, esq. where he breakfasted. At about half past one, the noble Duke proceeded in his carriage to Long-row [the location of workers' cottages built by the Strutts], from which place to the spot on which the new church was to be erected, the procession was on foot; his Grace being supported on the right and left by W. Strutt, esq., and G. B. Strutt, esq. After the ceremony, the Rev. Mr. Barber, vicar of Duffield, delivered an address upon the occasion, and the noble Duke declared the satisfaction which he felt in such an opportunity for visiting a town, situate in the heart of a county to which he was warmly and deeply attached.

A monumental structure, the completed church towered over the seven dissenting chapels of the village. The opening ceremony took place in September, 1824, after over £11,000 had been spent in construction. Two-thirds of the 1,800 sittings were free. Situated "on a bold elevation" overlooking the town, the new church stood as a testimonial to the renewed importance of religion in local affairs.[18]

Wesleyans, meanwhile, did not remain unaffected by the growing importance of prosperity and polish in the town. Despite their doctrinal kinship with Primitive Methodists, the Old Connexion began to show decided differences of opinion and status. Both groups brought together sympathetic farmers and town dwellers; but, unlike Primitive Methodist alliances that remained outside the mainstream of local power and prestige, Wesleyan farmers joined forces with "a large proportion of the principal tradesmen" of the town. The "large and respectable body" of Belper Wesleyans included Mr. John C. Topham, a noted linen and woollen draper "who commenced business in Belper in 1819." Another leading figure was the Reverend B. Gregory; his clerical title, in spite of his humble home address "on the 'Common Side,' " gave reliable evidence of cur-

<hr/>

[18] Ibid., p. 103. See also Patrick Joyce, *Work, Society and Politics* (New Brunswick, N.J.: Rutgers University Press, 1980), chap. 7.

rent Wesleyan attitudes towards the ministry.[19] A plan adopted
for Wesleyan Sunday Schools proved that the Connexion had
abandoned its early democratic tendencies for a more conventional, class-based social order. The schools offered two
different curriculums, depending upon ability to pay: three
pence a week could purchase reading instruction, while ten
pence bought both reading and writing. The system thus
sorted out most factory children from the rest in a manner
unknown to other schools in Derbyshire.[20]

Just as telling was the growing formalization of Wesleyan
administration. The Wesleyan Conference became increasingly wary of popular insurgency after 1790, and a more solid
church hierarchy crystallized during the early part of the nineteenth century in order to ensure direction from above. As a
result, local leadership did not often reflect the social composition or attitudes of society membership.[21] The peculiarities
of the Belper district—its growing class of factory operatives
and its high proportion of women—appeared to have little
effect upon connexional administration. At the pottery outside
Belper, for example, a class of twenty women was led by a
man. Belper Wesleyans also observed Conference rules banning female preaching, even though women had spontaneously assumed a prominent part in cottage societies around
the factory town. Prosperity also meant respectability in Belper, and Wesleyans gradually shed their heritage of country-
style revivalism.[22]

As common laborers themselves, Primitive Methodists maintained practices and beliefs that still appealed to Belper audiences. Their initial attempts to mission the area aroused
suspicion and concern; it was at Belper, in fact, that the Primitives acquired the controversial epithet "Ranters," suggestive

[19] Fletcher, op. cit., p. 31; *P.O. Directory of Derbyshire*, 1855, p. 23.

[20] Johnson, *Derbyshire Village Schools*, pp. 35–6.

[21] For changes within the Wesleyan Connexion, see chap. 1.

[22] Fletcher, *Records*, p. 54. See also "Memoir of Rebecca Potter," *PMM*, 1825,
pp. 85–9.

of political radicalism and religious heresy.[23] But what some townspeople condemned, others saw as only too late in coming. Charges of disturbing the peace, satanism, and conjuring came from unfriendly observers, while the same activities stimulated interest in others. Primitives legitimated belief that no other association (religious or otherwise) formally recognized.[24] It seemed to some that the hand of God had played a special part in introducing an early missionary. A prophetic dream helped to convince Belperites that the Primitive Methodists were indeed emissaries from above.

> A good man had dreamt that a person preached in a particular part of the village, in the open air, and on a certain text; and the dream was told to several of the inhabitants. In a short time afterwards, J. Branfoot, now deceased, missioned that village; and his text, preaching place, and person, corresponded exactly with the representation of them as given by the dreamer.

This "concurrence of events made a deep impression on the minds of the people, and had some influence in the early formation of a [Primitive Methodist] society in the place." The Primitives did not fail to exploit the incident. The easy communication between preacher and audience promised a religious organization more democratic than the Wesleyan church, and one which would admit greater doctrinal latitude.[25]

Primitives also mobilized a native interest in ceremony and custom. While remnants still survived in many nearby villages, local customs in Belper were fast disappearing with the growth

[23] Kendall, *History*, 1:185–7.

[24] "Memoir of Joseph Brindley," *PMM*, 1862, pp. 9–11, recounts how a Hulland farm servant attended preaching services at Belper, despite protestations from his father; the older Brindley had heard that William Clowes, Primitive preacher and one of the founders of the Connexion, "was possessed of the devil" and that conjuring went on at meetings. Joseph Brindley later became a preacher in the Belper Circuit.

[25] "Memoir of Elizabeth, Wife of Ormond Leavers," *PMM*, 1843, p. 13.

of the town and its burgeoning factory industry. The Strutts
attempted to re-create a similar community spirit through the
pageantry of paternalism, and they probably met with occasional success. Primitive Methodists, meanwhile, offered yet
another alternative. Organized by country preachers uncon-
nected with the factory culture, Primitive pageantry enabled
followers to separate themselves from Strutt and adopt a new,
composite popular culture. As recent immigrants from villages
nearby, many town laborers identified the rituals of Primitive
Methodism as rural custom. The new religion and the old
calendar of customs had much in common; annual camp meetings, seasonal lovefeasts, and holiday services performed similar social functions and conserved remnants of Derbyshire
traditions.[26] The public display that usually accompanied
Primitive missioning made this syncretism of popular culture
and religion unavoidable. Even when Belper Primitives began
the simple operation of building their new chapel, they
aroused local interest. "To save expense," Kendall relates, "the
wood was drawn on trucks from Mr. Strutt's timber-yard to
the site by willing hands. This . . . brought many to their doors,
and others . . . belaboured the human teams with bladders tied
to the end of sticks!"[27]

The rural roots of the religion provided a good deal of the
impetus behind the Primitive Methodist mission. In clear contrast to Wesleyan strategy, Primitives regarded their town missions as simple extensions of their country circuits. This
worked to their advantage in Belper, where the first foray into
the town owed its success to the help of outlying societies.

---

[26] Folklorists have noted several incidences of Primitive Methodist ritual becoming incorporated into local calendars of customs. At Bradwell, for example,
Primitive Methodists celebrated their own "tharcake supper" on "the Saturday
which is nearest to the Fifth of November." S. O. Addy, "Derbyshire Folk-
Lore," in J. C. Cox, ed., *Memorials of Old Derbyshire* (London, 1907), pp. 166–
7. And at Alport Castles Farm, love feasts are still celebrated each year on the
first Sunday in July according to a long-standing tradition in the area. Clarence
Daniel, *Derbyshire Customs* (Dalesman Books, 1976), p. 12. See also A. D. Gilbert,
Religion and Society in Industrial England (London: Longmans, 1976), pp. 90–1.

[27] Kendall, *History*, 2:193.

Country wanderings came naturally to John Benton, credited as founder of the first Belper society; earlier that year, he had helped in missioning Hulland, Mercaston, and other rural places south of Belper. The factory town, however, held a mysterious, forbidding challenge to the maverick preacher. For support, Benton mustered a boisterous collection of country Primitives from Mercaston, Turnditch, and Weston-Underwood before entering Belper. "Singing as it went," the group crossed "the bridge over the Derwent" and "moved on to the market-place, where . . . Benton took his stand and began a service." The odd invasion attracted an audience and found local support (probably raised by the dream incident) for future meetings. As soon as a society was formally established, Belper Primitives received preachers from the surrounding countryside and held camp meetings that drew participants from villages nearby. On a regular basis, Primitive Methodism offered country "society" to town dwellers.[28]

Besides organizing literal contact between country and town, Primitive Methodists re-created the close familiarity of village life among their town following. Benton himself was an expert cottage evangelist. Using hymns and verses of his own composition, he accosted Belperites with specific accusations designed for missioning "at close quarters."[29] A straightforward, blunt style became the trademark of Primitive Methodists. Moreover, "a more united society has seldom been met with," one account of Belper Primitive Methodism claimed:

> so closely were its members knit together in christian love, that they took the liveliest interest in each other's prosperity; and when distant from each other in the street, so as to be unable to speak, reciprocated their christian experience by signs, the meaning of which was known only to themselves.[30]

[28] Ibid., p. 184.
[29] Ibid., pp. 182–3.
[30] "Leavers," p. 13.

The language of Methodist sectarianism was thus rendered exclusive through signs, serving a new purpose in the town environment. As the factory town grew in population and institutional sophistication, cottage religion provided a refuge of antithetical values.

In the factory town, the domestic imagery of cottage religion and the leading role of women became strategically important. Many Belper workers were migrants from nearby rural villages whose lives were transformed by their move to the factory town. Others entered the factory having lived in Belper for all or part of their lives, perhaps working previously in cottage industry or domestic service. Though factory wages (for the male worker) promised a higher standard of living than earnings from rural labor or cottage industry, working conditions and domestic arrangements demanded difficult adjustments to a new way of life. The possibility of carrying on an "economy of expedients" narrowed considerably; when factory employment fluctuated or terminated, there were few alternative sources of income for the propertyless wage earner in the town. Cottage industry continued to struggle alongside factories in Belper, but the majority of working-class people relinquished their ties to a domestic-based economy and turned to the new working environment of the factory. The effects of this change upon laborers (documented in an extensive historical literature) were obvious: the factory exercised both overt and subliminal control over matters concerning personal discipline, social behavior, and work time.[31]

Obviously, not all Belper laborers perceived a direct conflict between cottage and factory production. For many, the route from domestic industry to factory work was a circuitous one; Anderson and other scholars have pointed out the wide variety of experiences that ultimately brought laborers to the

[31] See, for example, Michael Anderson, *Family Structure in Nineteenth-century Lancashire* (Cambridge: Cambridge University Press, 1971); E. P. Thompson, "Time, Work-Discipline, and Industrial Capitalism," *Past and Present* 38 (1967), pp. 56–97.

factory town.[32] And yet Belper topography provided plentiful reminders of predecessors of factory work. The old part of town stood in sharp contrast to the new carefully planned factory area. Around the ancient marketplace, a number of "stone built cottages irregularly arranged" housed the remaining domestic industry in the town. The "association of home with place of work influenced the building styles and arrangement of buildings": in the case of framework knitting, a second floor, usually sided almost entirely with windows, enabled cottagers to maintain frames under their own roofs; nailers required separate shops located in their yards. Domestic industry thus "resulted in a disorderly clustering of buildings, with only a rudimentary plan form"—a labyrinth of constant activity compared with the neat streets and regular cottages constructed by the Strutts.[33]

Amidst confusion and steadily increasing destitution, Belper nailers reigned supreme. Always praised for their unfaltering independence, the nailers possessed an unusually acute awareness of the latent conflict between the old world of domestic industry and the new factory. One Derbyshire local historian recalled observing survivors of the trade and recounted their characteristics:

There never was a freer, more independent set of men. Their hours were regulated by no factory "blower"; they owned often the shop in which they worked; they worked when they liked, they played when they liked; they struck when they like, and that was often. They made obeisance to no man. . . . They had a complete disregard for time; they honoured no master. As masters of their craft they considered themselves equal to the best, and they were

[32] Anderson, *Family Structure*, part 3; Joan W. Scott and Louise A. Tilly, "Women's Work and the Family in Nineteenth-century Europe," *Comparative Studies in Society and History* 17 (1975), pp. 36-64; Arthur Redford, *Labor Migration in England 1800–1850*, 3rd ed. rev. (Manchester: Manchester University Press, 1976), passim.

[33] J.R.G. Jennings, *Belper: a study based on visual evidence* (Belper Historical Society, n.d.), p. 14.

ready at any time to maintain that equality in strikes against their "masters" (who after all were only factors) or in bouts of fisticuffs amongst themselves, or against any intruding stranger.

Admittedly, the writer exaggerated and romanticized the "freedom" of Belper nailers. He conceded that "they seemed to have established complete freedom in all things, except economic freedom": owing to their tireless refusal to recognize the introduction of machinery to the nailmaking process, the old craftsmen of Belper suffered the same demise as so many other artisans of the nineteenth century. The portrait nevertheless highlights the nailers' conscious resistance to the factory system and all it represented. In Belper, the factory constituted an unavoidable psychological presence.[34]

In this context, cottage religion came to represent the autonomy, whether real or idealized, that laborers ascribed to former times. Though religious discipline arguably reinforced the authority of factory whistle and master, the mode of worship that prevailed in cottage religion, as well as many doctrines, pointed to a different state of affairs. Primitive Methodism re-created the world of cottage industry, village familiarity, and household unity. For factory employees, many of whom were women, these values could exert a powerful attraction. External forces may have torn asunder their families and households; but whatever fell prey to circumstances could be overcome by extra effort and divine grace. The Primitive Methodist faith and the religious community could supply a substitute for family and village.

The first Belper Primitives shared early experiences of dislocation and insecurity that probably enhanced their vulnerability to cottage religion. For older women, the religious society reconstituted a distant past. One founding member, Ann Hatfield (b. ca. 1779), had moved to Belper as a girl, probably in order to work at the Strutt factory. By the time Primitive Methodists missioned the town in 1814, she was widowed with

---

[34] Wilson, "Belper Nailers," p. 22.

*1. Mary Barritt Taft (1772–1851), Wesleyan Methodist preacher.
Courtesy Methodist Archives of the John Rylands University Library
of Manchester*

*2. Hugh Bourne (1772–1852), principal founder of the Primitive
Methodist Connexion. Courtesy Methodist Archives of the John
Rylands University Library of Manchester*

3. *William Clowes (1780–1851), one of the founders of the Primitive Methodist Connexion. Courtesy Methodist Archives of the John Rylands University Library of Manchester*

4. *Sarah Kirkland (b. 1794), Primitive Methodist preacher, in about 1870. From* The Origin and History of the Primitive Methodist Church *by H. B. Kendall (London, n.d.)*

5. *Elizabeth Smith (1805–1836), Primitive Methodist preacher. Courtesy Methodist Archives of the John Rylands University Library of Manchester*

6. *Ruth Watkins (b. 1802), Primitive Methodist preacher and missionary to America. Courtesy Methodist Archives of the John Rylands University Library of Manchester*

7. *Filey "flither lasses" posing for the hand-camera. Courtesy of John Crimlisk*

four children. She remained an active member until her death at age seventy-two. Another mother of a large family supported the first Primitive missionaries at Milford, where the Strutts ran another textile factory. Hannah Woolley (b. ca. 1770) invited preachers into her home shortly after she and her family had moved to Milford from the village of Kelstige. Regarded as a "pious old pilgrim" of the milltown society, she eventually selected and paid for a prized seat in the new chapel, which she held until her death in 1857.[35]

More commonly, young unmarried women converted to Primitive Methodism in Belper. Women between the ages of sixteen and twenty-one made up the bulk of female factory workers in most parts of England and Europe during early industrialization, while married women with children represented a small part of the work force.[36] Perhaps an especially great predominance of younger women in Belper explains the relatively low rate of participation in female friendly societies there, in comparison to other Derbyshire factory towns. Only three percent of the women in Belper joined female friendly societies, while the figures for Chinley, Cromford, and Wirksworth were forty-two, fifteen, and seventeen percent, respectively. The friendly societies admitted women between the ages eighteen and twenty-five "without an entrance fine," though they requested regular contributions. But obviously the benefits of such societies, mainly "support ... [when] rendered incapable of work, by means of Sickness, Lameness, Old Age, or Casualties, and for the Interment of deceased Members, their Husbands and Widowers," appealed less to young women who considered factory work a temporary expedient. Further limiting enrollment was a rule that excluded women "eloping from their Husbands, and cohabiting with other Men, or having a Bastard by a Married Man, or three Bastards by any

[35] "Obituary of Hannah Woolley," *PMM*, 1857, p. 574; "Obituary of Ann Hatfield, of Belper," *PMM*, 1852, pp. 191–2.

[36] Anderson, *Family Structure*, pp. 39–40; Louise A. Tilly and Joan W. Scott, *Women, Work, and Family* (New York: Holt, Rinehart and Winston, 1978), pp. 87–8.

persons" and fined those who had "a second Bastard by single Men." These factors probably influenced membership in the Belper society.[37]

Primitive Methodist circuit reports for Belper support such indications of the numerical stength of young persons. "The work is chiefly among young people," a visiting preacher recorded in 1819. An account of a lovefeast in 1821 conveyed a similar impression and underscored the prominence of women. At a gathering of five hundred people, a young woman delivered an emotional testimony in which she confessed that "she was come to Belper love feast to have all her sins pardoned." "Many began to weep all around," and before the evening was over, twenty-nine people were converted.[38] Children also attended Primitive Methodist revivals and experienced conversion. Ann Atfield (b. 1810), the daughter of a society member, was converted at age eleven; Mary Hunt (b. 1799), a native of Belper, was converted at fourteen. Martha Munks could not have been much older when she became active during the early years of the society. She served as a class leader until 1825, when she married a preacher and emigrated to America.[39] For such young women, religion provided a rite of passage into a new world of uncertainties. Primitive Methodism offered a carefully worked-out code of behavior for young and unmarried women; and unlike the friendly society, the sect gave help to unmarried mothers and the chronically unemployed. The village values of cottage religion had a special significance even for girls who had never known the rural past, for, in many cases, the religion re-created the world of their mothers.

It is not surprising, then, that female preachers played a prominent part in Belper Primitive Methodism. At least six women preached in the circuit during the 1820s, not including notable travelling preachers, such as Sarah Kirkland and Bet-

[37] Farey, *General View*, 3:566–8.

[38] "Extract of T. Jackson's Journal," *PMM*, 1821, p. 133; Report of the Tunstall Circuit, *PMM*, 1820, p. 248.

[39] "Memoir of Mary Hunt," *PMM*, 1821, pp. 30–1; "Memoir of Ann Atfield, of Belper," *PMM*, 1833, pp. 261–2.

sey Evans, who occasionally visited the town. Significantly, all of them came from small villages organized around rural or household economies. Only one preacher, Elizabeth Leavers (n.d.; ca. 1798?), was born in Belper village itself, and she, too, came from a rural background. Part of "old" Belper rather than the new industrial Belper, her parents were local farmers who had achieved relative prosperity. According to her obituary, Elizabeth spent her childhood in apparent conviviality and security. Her parents supervised a "liberal education," including "alas! . . . the practice of dancing," and Elizabeth happily adorned herself in girlish finery. But at the age of fifteen, after an illness, she stopped to reevaluate her surroundings and behavior. As Belper grew and as local industry altered relations within the village, Elizabeth decided upon a personal reformation: she "threw away all her bunches, frills, and other things of the kind" and withdrew from customary social life of the village. During her years of soul-searching, Elizabeth deliberated over the various social options before her. "Many whom she knew" had joined the Wesleyans, but Elizabeth remained unaffiliated with any religious group, even after her conversion. Separated from both factory culture and a Wesleyan alternative, she finally found a comfortable place in the first Primitive Methodist society formed in Belper. Abandoning all reserve, she began to preach before she was twenty, "and for many years laboured with great acceptability and usefulness" around Belper. Like many other female preachers, Elizabeth remained unmarried for some time; her commitment to Primitive Methodism, both spiritually and socially, severely decreased the likelihood of meeting a suitable partner. Yet in 1828, she found a spiritual match within the close circle of the Belper society in the person of another preacher, Ormond Leavers. Having performed the role of celibate, committed ascetic, Elizabeth made a swift transition to the alternative Primitive archetype: she became a model of maternal and domestic virtue, bearing five children and continuing to preach as often as physically possible until her death in 1840.[40]

[40] "Leavers," pp. 12–15.

The life of Elizabeth Leavers spanned a period of gradual transition in Belper history: her early years belonged to rural, remote Belper, colored by cottage industry and domestic self-sufficiency, while her adulthood took place in a highly developed industrial environment. Against this background, signs of her rural origins stood out as identifiable symbols of continuity. But few other female preachers in the Belper Circuit spent their entire lives in the places where they were born, and hence they present more complex images. More often, the coming of the industrial age had a disruptive and deleterious effect upon their families. Lydia Murfin (b. 1809), of nearby Turnditch, enjoyed considerably less security than Elizabeth Leavers. She grew up in rural Windley, raised not by her parents but by her uncle and aunt. Though she, too, became religious around the age of fourteen, her passage into womanhood signaled not just the formulation of her spiritual and social identity; as a member of the laboring classes, Lydia also assumed greater economic responsibility, intensified further by her early marriage. Her obligations as a preacher required solitary travel around the Belper Circuit, and she also continued to work for a living after her marriage and even after the birth of several children. Her portrayal of maternal and domestic virtue conjures up a far grimmer image than that projected by Elizabeth Leavers. Lydia Murfin's self-sacrifice ended in her early death at the age of twenty-four. "Venturing out to labour for her family too soon" after the birth of her last child, "she took cold, from which she never recovered. . . . She was always," concluded her obituary with significant emphasis, "a mother in Israel."[41]

The economic distress of the 1840s laid waste to any illusory claims to security among laboring preachers around Derbyshire. Members of the Belper Circuit witnessed the worst effects of the downturn when the Strutt empire faltered and sent shock waves throughout the area. At Heage, two miles northeast of Belper, the tightly knit society typical of mining

[41] "Memoir of Lydia Murfin," *PMM*, 1835, pp. 185–6.

villages underwent similar trials. Necessity forced preacher Mary Sims (b. 1808) and her husband, Samuel, to move to the Vulcan Iron Foundry near Warrington in search of work. Their cottage religion, however, survived one upheaval after another. At their new home, "they opened their house for preaching; and Vulcan was put on the plan of . . . the Warrington Circuit." When "through the fluctuations of trade the Vulcan Iron Foundry closed," the couple again moved, this time to Manchester, where they again "pursued the Christian course" and joined a neighborhood Primitive Methodist class. Finally, "they returned to Vulcan, and joined [the Primitive Methodist] society at Earlestown, St. Helen's Circuit." Economic reality had transformed totally the conditions surrounding Mary Sims; and yet, from the time of her conversion at Heage to her death at Vulcan, "Sister Sims set the Lord always before her, so that she should not be moved."[42]

In later years, female preachers in the Belper Circuit diminished in numbers, while in the mining community of Bradwell, in contrast, they remained prominent until the end of the century. The reasons for their decline around the industrial town remain obscure and complex. Obviously, the overall decline in female preaching throughout England was related to changing social mores as well as the growth and sophistication of the Primitive Methodist Church.[43] Nevertheless, the case of Belper offers useful material for speculation. The last documented instance of female preaching in the circuit concerned a domestic servant, Miss Alice Bembridge (b. 1806), of Brailsford. Her obituary, the only known evidence of her career, revealed little personal information. Her birthplace was not mentioned; her conversion took place at age fifteen, "while [she was] in service, whither the influence of her mother's piety followed her." The most noteworthy aspect of Alice Bembridge's work was its duration: of her forty years as a society member, she acted as a local preacher for thirty, from around

[42] "Memoir of Mrs. Mary Sims," *PMM*, 1883, pp. 54–5.
[43] See chap. 3.

1831 until her death in 1861. A career of such constancy, particularly in the Belper Circuit, was possible only in an agricultural area like Brailsford. Though just seven miles northwest of Derby and about ten miles from Belper, Brailsford remained a serene agricultural village through the 1850s. Alice's position as a servant must have afforded her considerable security, for she possessed sufficient financial means to care for her aging parents and two nieces towards the end of her life.[44]

Alice's status as a servant, coupled with the proximity of traditional landed wealth in Brailsford, made female preaching an attractive and realistic form of expression for her. Domestic service often, as pointed out above, inspired covert religious "rebellion" in the form of female preaching; and upper-class charity worked to provoke strong competitive action from Primitive Methodists. Just as in Belper earlier in the century, paternalism colored class relations in Brailsford. The Lord of the Manor from the 1820s was William Evans, Esq., the son of the pioneering industrialist of Darley Abbey, Thomas Evans. At Darley Abbey, the younger Evans took it upon himself to create "an industrial community on the pattern laid down by Strutt"; assisting him in his venture was his wife, the former Elizabeth Strutt, daughter of Jedediah Strutt of Belper. The philanthropic couple extended their efforts to Brailsford, where they eventually established a school "on a large scale, [modeled] upon the National System," around 1840. The Evans family supplied numerous examples of feminine piety. Alice Bembridge must have known of the "beautiful marble monument," dedicated to the wife of Walter Evans, that stood in the church at Darley Abbey. The Primitive preacher nevertheless maintained a separate faith. She provided theology and services of another sort and trusted her followers to recognize the difference.[45]

[44] "Memoir of Alice Bembridge," *PMM*, 1862, pp. 271–2.

[45] Johnson, *Derbyshire Village Schools*, p. 42; *Directory of Derbyshire*, 1855, pp. 28, 50–1.

Upper-class philanthropy eventually overshadowed figures like Alice Bembridge; such village evangelists had little to say to the new industrial working classes that were coming of age.[46] The relationship between village and town, even in relatively isolated parts of Derbyshire, had changed by mid-century. The North Midland Railway, completed by 1840, soon proved "as significant in its impact on Belper as had been the coming of Strutt."[47] Small villages became satellites of the factory town, and the factory town in turn spread its influence in ways that would never be reversed. As champions of village virtue, Primitive Methodists found themselves increasingly out of tune with mid-Victorian Belper. Their determined display of plain dress and poke bonnets, their dogged resistance to railway travel, and their hatred of the modern city gave them—probably to their own dismay—a rather quaint, archaic look. Few Belperites fully understood local preacher Billy Hickingbotham when he railed against the new "fashion . . . of wearing cap-borders" in the 1850s. "The women wear'n something called caps, but they arn'na caps," he complained; "and some folks have something like religion, but it in'na religion." Sarah Kirkland no doubt shared his dissatisfaction when, shortly before her death, she donned her poke bonnet and sat for a full-length photographic portrait. Her silent demonstration appeared in the definitive history of the Primitive Methodist Church.[48]

[46] When female preaching did occur later in the century, it appeared in different circumstances under the direction of very different women; for a description of the genteel and learned discourses of later women preachers, see Olive Anderson, "Women Preachers in Mid-Victorian Britain," *Historical Journal* 12 (1969): 467–84.

[47] Millward, *Belper*, pp. 7–8.

[48] Barfoot, *Diamond in the Rough*, p. 78. Sarah Kirkland's portrait appears in Kendall, *History*, 1:177.

PART III

FROM THE COUNTRY
TO THE TOWN

NINE

Women and the Industrial Town: Ann Carr and the Female Revivalists of Leeds

COTTAGE RELIGION found a new home in the industrial town. In the North, the massive expansion of the textile industry promised employment to laborers affected by changes in the countryside. The woollen and commercial center of Leeds attracted hundreds of villagers and preachers from nearby districts; the small-scale, domestic-based woollen industry offered a setting conducive to the autonomous activity of rural religion. Leeds, like Belper, employed a large number of female laborers who presented an important challenge to cottage evangelists. Uprooted, homeless, and sometimes without kin or acquaintance, women in the town were truly pilgrims and strangers. While Leeds still had much in common with the village, the sheer scale of the place distinguished it from its historical precedents. Leeds accommodated the world of cottage religion while creating an awareness of something new: its anonymity threatened the sense of family and home that were central to village life. In this new setting, female preachers endeavored to establish a unique religious community led by women and incorporating the poorest sectors of the Leeds population. Rural religion penetrated Leeds at the very moment when it stood poised between its village past and the emerging urban future. The faith of Ann Carr and the Female Revivalists flourished on the eve of the transformation of the industrial town into the modern Victorian city.

Ann Carr was a "Methodist minister of the old stamp." Her early experiences lay in village life and cottage revivalism; like

Ann Cutler and Mary Barritt, she worked within the early Wesleyan traditions of female preaching and, in fact, received her first society ticket from Zachariah Taft.[1] Born in 1783 at Market Rasen, Lincolnshire, Ann Carr was the youngest of twelve children of a "humble" builder and his wife. Her mother died when she was five, and henceforth Ann received a pious upbringing from a Congregationalist aunt who came to live with the family. Her "gay" but "volatile" temperament turned to somberness when a fiancé died, causing her complete breakdown at the age of eighteen. Through personal trauma came religious vision. When Ann recovered in 1801 through the aid of Taft's cottage prayer meetings, she recognized her calling to tell others "what the Lord had done for her soul."[2]

Ann Carr soon showed extraordinary talent in cottage evangelism. Visiting neighbors and friends around Market Rasen, she organized and led two classes in the Grimsby Circuit of the Wesleyan Connexion. Her reputation spread, and she soon received more "invitations and appointments" to speak than she could accept. "This was contrary to her design," argued Taft, somewhat apologetically. ". . . But being persuaded that necessity was laid upon her, to publish salvation by Jesus Christ, she so far obeyed as to do this occasionally, and in the neighbourhood where she lived."[3] Just as the issue of female preaching reached a high pitch of dissension among Wesleyans, Ann Carr embarked on an ambitious independent ministry. "If God be for me, no matter who is against me," she vowed, ". . . it is better to obey God rather than man." When

---

[1] Most of the following biographical information concerning Ann Carr was obtained from Martha Williams, *Memoirs of the Life and Character of Ann Carr* (Leeds, 1841) and Zachariah Taft, *Holy Women* (Leeds, 1828), 2:287–91. I am also greatly indebted to Mr. D. Colin Dews of Leeds, who is working on a comprehensive history of religion in the Leeds area and has shared a great deal of information with me. Mr. Dews has significantly enhanced my research on the Female Revivalists.

[2] Williams, *Memoirs*, pp. 19, 13; *Leeds Mercury*, Jan. 30, 1841; Taft, *Holy Women*, 2:288.

[3] Taft, *Holy Women*, 2:289–90.

the Connexion issued its ban against women preachers in 1803, Carr ignored it. The disciplinary arm of the Connexion was not nearly so evident as the arm of the Lord around Grimsby.[4]

"Stout and broad in person," Ann Carr was as unavoidable as divine will itself. "Some thought her too obtrusive [*sic*], talkative, and zealous," Taft confessed. She boasted "a spirit of singular energy," a "powerful voice," and an "unfeminine degree of boldness."[5] In short, Ann Carr was loud and aggressive. Descriptions fall short of calling her offensive, but every account (including those by admirers) allowed for more than one interpretation. "The preacheress was an indefatigable labourer," a Hull woman (also a female preacher) pointed out, "and was never prevented publishing her thoughts by the absence of a pulpit." In this case, "indefatigable" meant pushy. She continued: "Indoors and out were all the same to her, and it was as great a pleasure to her to preach on a stool in a court as it was to preach in a place of worship." Ann Carr was not to be stopped by her exclusion from chapels, nor by the lack of them.

"During a service I have noticed that she preferred the method of individual attention to collective exhortation ..." The preacher liked to point a finger at each sinner, one by one, "and excellent results were generally obtained by her plan. Her zeal seemed never to flag, and the possession of a powerful voice truthfully indicative of courage and command enabled her to attract large audiences." Carr's voice carried far and was truly intimidating. "She interspersed her deliveries with singing, which though not accomplished in anything like the scientific manner that is required at the present day, was nevertheless felt by all." Her singing, like her preaching, was loud and strong and not always pleasing to the ear.[6]

[4] Williams, *Memoirs*, p. 21.

[5] Leeds Methodist, "Recollections of Methodism at Leeds, during the past fifty or sixty years," *United Methodist Free Churches Magazine*, 1863 (extract in Leeds Public Library); Taft, *Holy Women*, 2:289.

[6] Jane Garbutt, *Reminiscences of Primitive Methodism in Hull* (Hull, 1886), p. 7.

Ann Carr's idiosyncratic movements and style provoked conflict with Wesleyan officials, and the creation of a Market Rasen Circuit in 1814, which brought superintendents and ministers closer to home, perhaps hastened her decision to leave. While the Old Connexion had no room for women like Carr, Primitive Methodists provided models of encouragement. Sarah Kirkland made a successful tour of Nottingham in 1818, and other women were travelling around Derby and Hull. Between 1818 and 1820, Carr extended her work to Nottingham and Hull. She and several other women, all without denominational sanction, organized a group that later became the first Primitive Methodist society in Hull. At Nottingham, she preached in millrooms, courtyards, and at a camp meeting that attracted "many thousands." In the industrial towns, "the field opened wider and wider" to the village evangelist.[7]

The flamboyant preacher took her cue from her audiences. Ann Carr's startling success called attention to equally startling circumstances: masses of poor laborers, many of them women, were uprooted and distressed and willing to match the preacher's aggressiveness with their own "overpowering loudness and immense fervour."[8] Unemployment in agriculture and distress in trade had brought migrants from the countryside into the Midlands and northern towns. In Nottingham, the lacemaking and hosiery industries attracted large numbers of men and women in search of employment. Hull became a center of migration following recent enclosures and improvements in the East Riding of Yorkshire. Technological changes also affected villagers outside the towns, as mechanized factory production outstripped domestic industries that provided essen-

[7] Taft, *Holy Women*, 2:289; Williams, *Memoirs*, pp. 27–9; J. Ritson, *The Romance of Primitive Methodism* (London, 1909), pp. 142–3; H. B. Kendall, *History of the Primitive Methodist Church* (London, n.d.), 1:245, 364, 366, 373; Garbutt, *Reminiscences*, p. 7; James Obelkevich, *Religion and Rural Society* (Oxford: Oxford University Press, 1976), p. 184.

[8] *Leeds Times*, Jan. 23, 1841.

tial income for laboring families.[9] Ann Carr's travels convinced her that "the last days" were at hand; though "retirement" was "woman's proper sphere," exigencies recalled the scriptural justification for female preaching. Carr soon found evidence of troubled times in the person of a young female preacher, Martha Williams (b. ca. 1790), whose personal experiences gave proof to the hardship of Nottingham laboring life. Adopting Williams and Sarah Healand (b. ca. 1788) as assistants, Carr systematically missioned the Nottingham area and "travelled through six or seven of the largest counties" in the Midlands and in the north of England.[10]

The inevitable destination of Ann Carr, as well as of many of her village followers, was the town of Leeds. The Yorkshire textile centers attracted many laborers from the Nottingham area; Ann Carr sensed the flow of humanity and decided "to yield to the voice of entreaty." In 1821, she and her companions entered the town and settled in the east end, where the expansion of the woollen industry had given birth to a conglomeration of cheap cottages and ramshackle workshops. While the setting was new, the character of the place was in one way familiar. The woolen industry of the West Riding, and notably in Leeds, depended upon "household and other smaller-scale production units." Village migrants found work not in factories, but in domestic industry carried out on a massive scale.[11] Leeds' textile industry employed large numbers of women, who frequently worked in the worsted trade where they could compete with men more easily than in woollen weaving.[12] Textile firms multiplied at a fast rate after the

[9] Arthur Redford, *Labour Migration in England 1800–1850*, 3rd ed. (Manchester: Manchester Univ. Press, 1976), pp. 47, 52; E. P. Thompson, *The Making of the English Working Class* (New York: Vintage Books, 1963), pp. 521–52.

[10] Taft, *Holy Women* (London, 1825), 1:172–4 (on Martha Williams); 194–201 (on Sarah Eland [*sic*]); Williams, *Memoirs*, p. 21.

[11] W. G. Rimmer, "The Industrial Profile of Leeds, 1740–1840," *Publications of the Thoresby Society* 50 (1967): 147; see also Redford, *Labour Migration*, chap. 4.

[12] Ivy Pinchbeck, *Women Workers and the Industrial Revolution* (1930; reprint, Totowa, N.J.: Frank Cass, 1977), pp. 119–20, 157.

Napoleonic wars and offered employment to those who could crowd into the cottages and houses spreading thickly towards the eastern boundary of the town. After 1815, population increases began to press upon available housing. During the next decade, the northeastern ward, where the Revivalists lived, became one of the "nauseating black spots of Leeds."[13]

Once situated in Leeds, Ann Carr encountered the unavoidable presence of chapel religion. Nottingham had been unusually receptive to interdenominational evangelicalism, and Primitive Methodists had accepted her work in Hull without restricting her. But Leeds posed new problems for the "free lance" female preacher. Carr now found that Primitive Methodist leaders objected to her method of free evangelism; independent and unpaid, she and her associates assumed the license to preach when and where they were called. Their "irregular" movements and "officious" manner provoked the ire of the local circuit and finally ignited a full-scale controversy:

> For these things they were called to account by the Circuit authorities, and they took offence. Ann Carr, especially, was very popular in Leeds, and she, together with her friends, made known their grievances amongst the society. What their status was does not appear; for their names do not stand upon the plan as preacher, or even helpers. Yet they seem to have had a place in the Quarterly Meetings, for Mr. G. Allen relates that "their presence at those meetings led to business becoming complicated." Some societies were anxious to have women preachers when men were appointed, and these women were ready to go and were there when the men appointed came. When this was complained of and the women were unwilling to be

[13] W. G. Rimmer, "Working Men's Cottages in Leeds, 1770–1840," *Publications of the Thoresby Society* 46 (1960): 178, 188; Charles M. Elliott, "The Social and Economic History of the Principal Protestant Denominations in Leeds, 1760–1844," (Oxford D. Phil., 1963), chap. 1.

planned as were the men and take work regularly, a disastrous division ensued.[14]

Rejecting the directives of Primitive Methodist authorities, whose actions recalled the restrictions of Wesleyans only two decades before, Ann Carr founded a separate society. She and her followers officially became known as the Female Revivalists.

The strength of the Female Revivalists grew rapidly, and, in 1825, the society decided to build a chapel. Through small donations collected from door-to-door and one substantial contribution from a "gentleman" of Boston (Lincs.), Carr managed to obtain a mortgage.[15] The society chose a site in Regent Street in the Leylands, a destitute part of Leeds, "where the cottages, dyehouses, weaving sheds and press shops were jumbled together in a confusion that shocked visitors to the town."[16] Though Leeds was a town of socially mixed neighborhoods, the Leylands was classified as nearly entirely working class; in some parts, the density of population rose as high

[14] William Beckworth, *A Book of Remembrance being Records of Leeds Primitive Methodism* (London, 1910), p. 50. Kendall's comments are less restrained: "There was a good deal of the masculine in Ann Carr's composition, and neither she nor her colleague took very kindly to the yoke imposed by a regularly organised Connexion. They preferred a roving commission and to take an erratic course, letting fancy or circumstances determine their direction and procedure. It is intimated by Mr. George Allen that they had no predilection for the plan, but were quite willing on invitation to take the pulpits of those who *were* planned, and that misunderstanding and collisions were the natural result." *History*, 1:69–70.

[15] Parson and White's *Directory of Leeds*, 1830, p. 201. Ann Carr obtained a mortgage of £650, with a provision for anything more she might need, from a Mr. William Taite, a gentleman of Boston, Lincs., later of York, on October 11, 1825. Presumably she had collected funds sufficient to purchase the land for the chapel, which cost £216 15s. Mr. Taite later lent her an additional £350, probably for her other building ventures. I owe thanks to Mr. D. Colin Dews for this information; he somehow retrieved the deed to the chapel from county records now in the Terrier Section of the County Land Unit, Wakefield. Deed Ref. No. 3452.

[16] R. G. Wilson, *Gentlemen Merchants: The Merchant Community of Leeds 1700–1830* (Manchester: Manchester University Press, 1971), p. 197.

as four times that of a more affluent suburb.[17] Neither Wesleyans nor Primitive Methodists had penetrated the Leylands to plant chapels. The Female Revivalists settled in with ease and established a complex of buildings (the chapel itself was in fact a series of shops and cottages with a common meeting room one floor above) that quickly became part of the social landscape. Not without a certain effrontery, they positioned themselves within sight of the monumental Wesleyan Brunswick Chapel: the notorious symbol of rising Wesleyan prosperity looked down on the Leylands from a distant northwestern hill.[18]

Female Revivalism contradicted the conventional notion of institutional religion in the Victorian town. While Wesleyans moved into loftier chapels, the women of the Leylands remained tied to a humble, hybrid chapel and domestic bases. Even those few buildings represented "a most injudicious step," in Williams' opinion, forcing Carr "to secularize her mind," "paralyse her exertions, and . . . impair her usefulness."[19] The Female Revivalists maintained close ties to cottage societies in neighboring villages. Their fissiparous ideology, advocating autonomy in evangelism and freedom in worship, appealed to women of industrial villages, but ran headlong into the path of Primitive Methodist officials. At Morley, a textile village southwest of Leeds, another Primitive Methodist society suffered a "disastrous division" as a result. As part of the Leeds Circuit, the society at Morley began meeting in a house at Morley Hole in 1819 and later moved to a nearby barn. A chapel had just been built in 1826 when "dissension" broke out, "caused by the female part of the congregation imbibing the notions of Ann Carr." The women of Morley evidently demanded the services of the Female Revivalists,

[17] Rimmer, "Working Men's Cottages," pp. 173–4.

[18] The first stone of the chapel was laid on March 7, 1825. Ann Carr and Martha Williams officiated, "assisted by 8 female and 12 male local preachers." White's *Directory of Leeds* (1830), p. 201. I am grateful to Mr. Michael Collinge for bringing this reference to my attention.

[19] Williams, *Memoirs*, p. 74.

while Primitive Methodist leaders refused to associate with their former "free lance" rivals. Angered by the intractableness of their superiors, the women decided to exercise their influence and overturn the entire society. The community was "rent to pieces," the chapel "had to be sold, and the society was broken up—some uniting with the Wesleyans and others becoming adherents of Ann Carr."[20]

The dispute revealed a more important rift: between the cottage evangelism of the Female Revivalists and the chapel religion of town Primitives lay the difference between a migratory and stable community. The autonomous evangelism of Ann Carr in many ways mirrored the condition of her followers. The Female Revivalists used the tenets of cottage religion to administer to laborers, and particularly women, who were "pilgrims and strangers" in the factory town. Sanctifying domestic security and uprootedness, their religion heightened the tensions between the world of the cottager and institutionalized religion. "And were we to go among the Churches themselves," Carr claimed in a sermon, "even there how many should we find who had not only not departed from evil, but whose lives and conduct give lie to their profession [?]" Rejecting the formulas and moralisms of Victorian religion, the Female Revivalists rendered meaningful the experiences of the most destitute poor.[21]

THE HYMNALS of the Female Revivalists, by far the most durable remains of the group, express these central experiences of displacement, uprootedness, and solitary wandering.[22] The collections included original works by members of the society

---

[20] Beckworth, *Book of Remembrance*, p. 50; William Smith, *History of Morley* (Morley, 1876), p. 194.

[21] "Anathema Maranatha," reprinted in Williams, *Memoirs*, appendix 5.

[22] The British Library holds three editions of the Female Revivalist hymnals: Martha Williams, Ann Carr, Sarah Eland, *A Selection of Hymns, For the Use of the Female Revivalists* (Dewsbury, 1824); another edition (Leeds, 1828); A. Carr and M. Williams, *A Selection of Hymns for the Use of the Female Revivalists, A New Edition with Additional Hymns* (Leeds, 1838).

and popular selections from Issac Watts and various Methodist hymnals. By drawing upon a body of traditional hymnology, the volume legitimated th———————————————————————— a chapel (the first hymnal appeared in 1824), the need for recognition and respect was especially great. Despite such borrowings, however, the Revivalist hymnals retained a distinctly partisan flavor. Emblazoned upon the title page of the first edition was the indomitable quote from Joel: "Fear not, O land; be glad and rejoice: for the Lord will do great things. —And your sons and your daughters shall prophesy." Several hymns, obviously adapted or composed by members, addressed women exclusively and sometimes spoke to specific groups—"young virgins," fallen women, or widows. Only the Female Revivalists could have conjured up felicitous images like the following:

> Happy Magdalen, to whom
>   Christ the Lord vouchsaf'd t'appear?
> Newly risen from the tomb,
>   Would he first be seen by her?
> Her by seven devils possest,
>   Til his word the fiends expell'd;
> Quench'd the hell within her breast,
>   All her sins and sickness heal'd.[23]

Through careful and deliberate selection, the hymnal displayed an independent spirit and a wealth of significant images pertinent to the experiences of sect members.

Female Revivalists generally avoided references to submission and restraint in their hymns. Though sometimes unremittingly grim in their depiction of earthy struggles, the works never condescended to contrived images of pastoral peace common to evangelical hymns of other denominations.[24] A

[23] *Hymns* (1824), no. 321. See also *Hymns* (1828), no. 7, for a unique rendition of "Is there any body here like weeping Mary," which includes "Mary Magdalen" as one of the verse substitutions.

[24] Cf. "How happy are the little flock," quoted in George Shaw, *Life of Parkinson Milson* (London, 1893), p. 13.

vivid instance of editing altered a rendition of the Primitive Methodist hymn "Where shall my soul begin to sing." Verses one and two remained intact, but verse three, beginning with

> My feeble voice I cannot raise
> As angels do above,

vanished from the Revivalist version.[25] The hymns were not meant to inculcate standards of propriety, but instead vigorously encouraged loud complaint. Through no accidental arrangement, Hymn Number 1 in the first edition was "Shout, for the blessed Jesus reigns."

The Female Revivalists borrowed several other hymns from the early collections of the Primitive Methodists. All of these selections, however, disappeared from subsequent Primitive Methodist hymnals and became part of a mystery that puzzled connexional hymnologists in later years. "We look in vain among the original hymns . . . for one that has survived the test of three-quarters of a century's wear," lamented one collector.[26] By calling attention to these "lost" works, the Revivalist hymns suggest an explanation. Hymns of early Methodist sectarianism often demonstrated a specificity of time and place; they sometimes arose spontaneously from congregations that preferred the literal to the figurative. Vivid depictions of houses, ships, parenthood, pain, poverty, and bloodshed often had real-life counterparts that governed the popularity of the hymns.[27] An overwhelming literalism replaced an "etherial

---

[25] *Hymns* (1828), pp. 176–7; Hugh Bourne, ed., *A Collection of Hymns, for Camp Meetings, Revivals, Etc.*, 6th ed. (London, 1848), no. 101. See also I. Dorricott and T. Collins, *Lyric Studies* (London, 1891), p. 140.

[26] J. O. Gledstone, "P.M. Hymn Books," *The Puritan* (n.d.) quoted in Kendall, *History*, 2:10-11. Jane Garbutt noted a similar instance of disappearance when she recalled hearing Ann Carr sing "with strong energy and powerful voice": Haste again ye days of grace,/When assembled in one place,/Signs and wonders mark'd the hour,/All were filled and spoke with power./Hands uplifted, eyes o'erflowed,/Hearts enlarged, self destroyed:/All things common now we prove,/ All our common stock be love. (*Reminiscences*, p. 8.)

[27] See, e.g., Dorricott and Collins, *Lyric Studies*, pp. 177–8, on the popular Cowper hymn "There is a fountain filled with blood." A factory manager once

[*sic*] quality" that might have made them immortal.[28] The Revivalist hymns convey an immediate sense of the material world of their followers. Female Revivalist hymns directly ad dressed the transient poor. The works repeatedly attempted to explain, in more than simply a spiritual sense, a migratory existence:

> Tell us, O Women! we would know
> > Wither so fast ye move?
> We, call'd to leave the world below,
> > Are seeking one above.

> Whence come ye, say—and what the place
> > That ye are trav'ling from?
> From tribulation, we thro' grace,
> > Are now returning home.[29]

"O Women! wither travel ye?" embarked on a similar search for identity through a sense of family:

> What is your stock, and what your birth?
> > Strangers ye seem to be:
> Our stock is Christ, (scarce known on earth)
> > Our birth is heavenly.[30]

Through questions and answers, the hymns affirmed the salvation of the disinherited in religious symbolism. The form of these hymns, more than their content, revealed their significance. The dialogue hymn was actually a contest between the voice of convention and the outcast. The "symbolic" response of the Revivalist served as a thinly disguised rejection

---

witnessed his "entire premises resound[ing] with the strains," and the editors agreed that the hymn was indeed "everybody's song," naming soldiers, miners, laborers, and mechanics among its greatest admirers. The editors also gave an example of a man whose arm had been recently amputated after an accident, who, upon hearing the hymn, came to the "Saviour's . . . glorious service" (p. 178). Numerous similar instances in deathbed revelations indicate the same kind of literal interpretation.

[28] Kendall, *History*, 2:11.

[29] *Hymns* (1824), no. 330.

[30] Ibid., no 331.

of the question itself. "Stock" and "birth" were concerns of respectable, established society; but Female Revivalists jettisoned both and even retorted that their standard—free from hypocrisy—was "scarce known on earth." Questions like "Is not your native country here/ the place of your abode?" invited the singer's denial. On an important subliminal level, the hymn castigated reality through its stubborn refusal to accept any of its terms.

The pilgrim imagery of Female Revivalist hymnology similarly led to a rejection of the "here and now." Heightening an awareness of loneliness through hymns was crucial to the recruitment of followers; yet in the context of a hymn (which created a community of singers), this process often ended in a reaffirmation of togetherness. The imagery of "the bride of Christ," for example, singled out the believer before reuniting her with "the bridegroom."[31] Pilgrim hymns presented an opportunity for greater variation. Primitive Methodists called attention to isolation and, at the same time, depicted the pilgrim joined in union with the sectarian society on earth:

I am a Christian pilgrim, a sinner saved by grace,
I travel to Mount Zion, my final resting-place;
Through many a storm and trial by Help divine I'm come,
And soon shall rest for ever in heaven, my happy home.

Sing glory, hallelujah, the Lord is with us still,
The little cloud increases that arose upon Mow Hill.[32]

But Female Revivalists painted a much less sanguine picture. Their hymn stressed solitude throughout and subjected every aspect of this world to criticism:

[31] See Margaret W. Masson, "The Typology of the Female as a Model for the Regenerate: Puritan Preaching, 1690–1730," *Signs* 2 (1976): 304–15. For a general but less useful treatment of imagery in hymns, see Susan Tamke, *Make a Joyful Noise Unto the Lord* (Athens, Ohio: Ohio University Press, 1978). On American hymnology during a later period, see Sandra S. Sizer, *Gospel Hymns and Social Religion* (Philadelphia: Temple University Press, 1978).

[32] Quoted in Arthur H. Patterson, *From Hayloft to Temple* (London, 1903), x–xi.

I am a Pilgrim here below,
   A stranger wand'ring to and fro:
The world's a wilderness to me,
   There's nothing here but vanity.
Here then no longer will I stay,
   Resolv'd I am, without delay,
To take my Pilgrim's staff, and move,
   To seek a better world above.

Though the pilgrimage pointed to a "better world above," the hymn dwelt more upon the "here below." Not even the final verse (which Primitive Methodists used to reaffirm membership in their "happy band") admitted any respite in a lashing censure:

But, that I may my Canaan gain,
   I'll suffer hardship, grief, and pain;
Through cold and nakedness I'll go,
   A pilgrim, through this vale of woe.[33]

The Female Revivalist hymnal was, in effect, a collection of grievances. The rate of literacy within the society probably was low; this suggests that the hymnal did in fact intend to publicize views to those outside the sect rather than simply providing written verses for those within. While publication may have attracted persons to the group, its purpose was not only evangelical. The long list of complaints in verse performed the same function as sectarian processionals: the characteristics and condition of followers were made public, and, in the case of such utterly downtrodden women, their visible and vocal presence was a rebuke to more fortunate onlookers. When "multitudes" of Revivalists followed Ann Carr's coffin from the chapel to the cemetery (a route stretching several miles across town), singing hymns "all the way," the spectacle was sufficiently startling to warrant comments from local newspapers.[34]

[33] *Hymns* (1828), no. 54.
[34] *Leeds Mercury*, January 23, 1841.

Little is known about the poor migrant women who joined
the Female Revivalists. Two brief biographies of Primitive
Methodist women once associated with the sect corroborate
the impression that most followers came from the enormous
number of female laborers migrating to and through the textile town. Sarah Hales was born in 1800 at Leek, Staffordshire,
nearly seventy-five miles away from Leeds. Sarah grew up "in
ignorance of religion and in oppressive labour." She probably
worked at silk weaving, a major cottage industry that had
survived for centuries in the ancient market town. Some time
during her adolescence, Sarah attended a Wesleyan Sunday
School, where she learned to read and became interested in
religion. Far from encouraging domestic harmony, Methodism at its evangelical best was a notoriously divisive force. Religion and literacy undoubtedly changed Sarah's behavior, and
her family, displeased by what was happening, persecuted her
until she finally left home. As a single young girl with weaving
experience, her natural destination was Yorkshire. Eventually
she found refuge with the Female Revivalists and remained
with them (probably in the Leylands) for several years. After
her conversion, Sarah bravely returned to Leek, where she
was among the first to join a newly formed Primitive Methodist
society. Her conversation and prayer soon gave "irresistible
evidence" of a budding talent in the ministry. An appointment
as preacher "was forced upon her," and in 1827 her name
appeared on the Ramsor Circuit plan. Not surprisingly, Sarah's reputation reflected her difficult past: "One leading characteristic which ever distinguished her . . . was a spirit of fer-
vent, struggling, resolute, Christ-honoring prayer" that
"defeated the purposes of her spiritual adversaries." Sarah
travelled until she married at the age of thirty-seven. She subsequently gave birth to five children but did not stop preaching
until she died in 1856 from an ulceration of the throat.[35]

[35] "Memoir of Mrs. Sarah Hales Birchenough," *PMM*, 1857, pp. 66–7. See
also "Memoir of Harriet Hainley of Leek," *PMM*, 1827, pp. 227–30. On Leek,
see D. M. Palliser, *The Staffordshire Landscape* (London, 1976), pp. 164-6.

Mrs. Caroline Wordsworth led a less distinguished life, but she was nonetheless representative of the influence of the Female Revivalists upon working-class girls. Unlike Sarah Hales, Caroline Wordsworth was a native of Leeds. She was born in 1820, and though responsive to education during her childhood, "the way of salvation she learned more fully while attending the religious services conducted by Ann Carr." She probably lived near the Female Revivalists in East Leeds during that time, but a move to the more prosperous west side of town must have preceded her admission into the Primitive Methodist society at Park Lane in 1839. All evidence suggests that Caroline Wordsworth passed through the personal and social transformation of a servant; next to work in textiles, domestic service counted for the employment of the largest number of women in Leeds, and such employment would have offered Wordsworth a way out of the Leylands. Thus she began a modest social ascent. For some time, she taught Sunday School at the Primitive Methodist Rehoboth Chapel (an eminently respectable calling for a Primitive Methodist servant), and, in 1842, she moved to Huddersfield "to occupy an important situation," probably as a governess. Caroline joined the Primitive Methodists there and met Mr. R. Wordsworth, a local preacher and a Barnsley Town missionary. The couple married in 1846, and Mrs. Wordsworth continued as an active member of the chapel until her death in 1868.[36]

The Female Revivalists provided a way-station, if not a home, for many such women. Sarah Hales and Caroline Wordsworth illustrate the temporary nature of followers' affiliation with the Leylands organization. Ann Carr's proto-institution flourished during a period of intensified immigration into Leeds, when geographical mobility was a common feature of laborers' lives. The Female Revivalists also belonged to a specific era of industrial development: while the textile industry lingered in its final stages of domestic production, the improvised offerings of revivalist theology and community

---

[36] "Obituary of Mrs. Caroline Wordsworth," *PMM*, 1870, pp. 428–9.

enabled women to construct new strategies of survival using familiar tools. Neither woman advanced greatly in conventional economic or social ways; both may have weakened their chances for improvement by publicly aligning themselves with lower-class religion. Female Revivalism provided them with a more conscious lower-class identity but with few assurances of success. Their rise out of the anonymity of the manufacturing town testified to the sense of individuality that they gained through religion rather than to any world of opportunity open to them.

The Female Revivalists captured the spirit of the times and transformed it into a colorful, albeit impermanent, religious organization. By 1840, the women ran a second chapel and two schoolrooms in Brewery Fields, "a prosperous adult school" in the Leylands, a Sunday School at Holbeck, and another schoolroom at Hunslet. Administering over all these neighborhoods, which included several collieries, glassworks, potteries, and a number of small factories, was a Female Revivalists' Friendly Society.[37] The success of their ventures depended heavily upon the charismatic powers of Ann Carr. She continued to pursue an energetic ministry, travelling extensively and speaking for a full range of worthy causes, throughout this time. And yet a certain quality and style distinguished her work from conventional female philanthropy of the Victorian age. Her forthright manner, her passion, and her unbridled *ressentiment* were signs of empathy, not charity.[38] After Ann Carr's death in 1841, the Female Revivalists foundered and Martha Williams finally sold the Regent Street chapel to

[37] Elliott, "Social and Economic History," chap. 4.

[38] Ann Carr's speech at the Home Mission of the Hull Female Temperance Society in May, 1838, gives some sense of her distinctive approach to giving moral advice: "I have often thought a woman can do anything with a man, only go the right way about him. Every innocent means is right to be used, to bring him over to our cause. When he is angry, his wife must be affectionate, (laughter). Never mind a black eye! It never broke a bone. (Here Miss Carr's manner was more expressive than her language)." (Recorded by Martha Williams, *Memoirs*, p. 85.)

Wesleyan Methodists three years later. Under the less robust Wesleyans, a sardonic observer noted, "the cause soon began to droop," showing the loss of "the peculiar circumstance of female government and administration." Successive attempts by other denominations (including Primitive Methodists, Congregationalists, and Roman Catholics) failed to revive religion in the Leylands. With the influx of Jewish immigrants at the end of the century, the chapel was converted to a synagogue. The Leeds Corporation finally purchased the building in order to demolish it in widening Regent Street in 1927.[39] The last reminder of the Female Revivalists now stands in the Leeds cemetery in the form of a carefully worded tombstone:

In Memory

of

ANN CARR,

Foundress of the sect of Female Revivalists and for 23 years one of its most devoted preachers. Her naturally strong intellect and ardent spirit were early sanctified by the grace, and consecrated to the glory of God, and she became, by her holy zeal and untired efforts, an instrument of extensively making known the gospel of Jesus Christ.

She died on the 18th of January, 1841, Aged 57 Years.

"I know thy works and thy labour, and thy patience, and for my names' [sic] sake hast laboured and hast not fainted."

This tablet is erected in grateful remembrance of her worth & labours, by the members of the Female Revivalists' Friendly Society, of which she was presidentress.

[39] D. Colin Dews, unpublished material and papers on Ann Carr; Will and Codicil of Ann Carr, Leeds. Ainsty D. June 1841; Borthwick Institute of Historical Research, York; "Recollections of Methodism at Leeds," pp. 356–7; *Leeds Mercury*, January 30, 1841.

TEN

The New Mendicant Preachers: Independent Methodism in Industrial England

INDEPENDENT METHODISM originated in the town of Warrington in Lancashire around 1796. Unlike neighboring Manchester and Liverpool, Warrington retained a village-like character into the nineteenth century. Perhaps because of its proximity to two major population centers, Warrington grew slowly: by 1801, its population was a relatively small 10,000. The town was a crossroad of commerce from "north and south, and east and west" and the center of a village network. Warrington's economic activity in fact more closely resembled that of an open village than a burgeoning industrial town. A large number of industries and crafts, carried out in cottages or workshops, made the dimensions of the town seem more an accident than a design. "Her shops, warehouses, and places of business, and her traders, wholesale and retail, were packed so close together that there was little room for them to quarrel," commented a contemporary, "and there was a good understanding in the place." The small scale of industry perpetuated the familiarity of earlier times.[1]

Such diversity also encouraged freedom in religion. Warrington's industries and commerce promoted a strong tradition of dissent—the town had been the seat of a famous eighteenth-century dissenting academy—and no single religious or

---

[1] William Beamont, *Walks About Warrington* (1887), p. 111; Pigot and Dean's *Commercial Directory for Lancashire*, 1816, 1818; J. Corry, *History of Lancashire* (1825), II: 682; Arthur Bennett, *Warrington* (Warrington Chamber of Commerce, 1929) pp. 13–28.

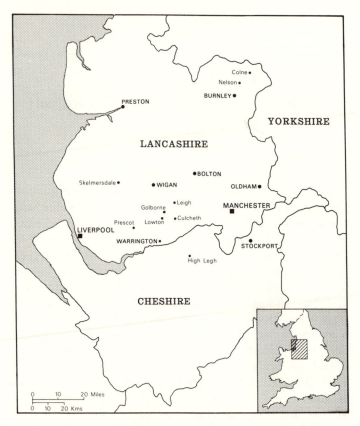

Independent Methodism in Lancashire and environs

social influence controlled local life. The autonomy of certain occupational groups contributed to the social independence of artisans and laborers. Potters, for example, "formed a separate colony" in Warrington, and tanners, pinmakers, and weavers retained freedom by working at home. Appealing to the humbler classes, Wesleyan Methodists easily established a society in the town in the 1770s. Village closeness, combined with a religious tolerance, made Warrington a likely setting for early cottage evangelism.

The same factors brought about a rebellion against Wesley-anism. Wedded to locally run cottage meetings, the Warrington society resented the occasional visits of itinerant ministers and tried to eliminate such intrusion some time during the 1790s. Connexional authorities reacted with characteristic sternness in the aftermath of Wesley's death: they assumed control of the Warrington chapel and outlawed cottage meetings. Secession soon followed, arising from the "closing of the home meetings."

> There were men of independent spirit serving in the local ministry. They had been accustomed to simplicity in Church life and to the free exercise of gifts; they had enjoyed the Methodism of the days of its founder. A Conference-made Methodism which demanded obedience to an itinerancy they could not accept.

The Warrington society formally recognized the affinity between two theologies: they identified themselves as Quaker Methodists and proceeded to practice cottage religion without interference. Engaging the help of several local Quakers, the founders laid the basis for an ingenious blend of doctrines. Their stance against Wesleyanism, moreover, represented a triumph of popular village religion over the institutional religion of growing towns.[2]

The Warrington Quaker Methodists set a pattern for other cottage evangelicals contemplating secession. One by one, societies in nearby villages followed them in breaking away from Wesleyanism and proclaiming "independence," and Warrington became the head of a new connexion of secessionists. A society at High Legh, an agricultural village just over the Cheshire border, had begun meeting in 1783, when Betty Okell organized Wesleyan preaching services in her dairy. Her initiative was all the more admirable for its frontal assault upon

---

[2] Beamont, *Walks About Warrington*, p. 62; William Durant, *The Story of Friars' Green Church* (Warrington: The Guardian Press, 1951), pp. 1–2; Arthur Mounfield, *A Short History of Independent Methodism* (Wigan, 1905), pp. 4–6.

the Established religion of nearby High Legh Hall. By 1800, Wesleyanism proved too restricting and perhaps too prestigious for the modest society. The High Legh sectarians joined Warrington and henceforth stood as the "oldest meeting" associated with the Independent Methodist Connexion.[3]

The wave of cottage revivalism that produced the Primitive Methodist Connexion also gave birth to Independent Methodist societies. Services at Stockton Heath began when the American revivalist Lorenzo Dow "took a whim that he would like to preach in a certain wayside barn" in 1806. At Risley, a society of Quaker-styled revivalists began meeting in a member's house in the same year. When Hugh Bourne visited them, he recorded favorable impressions. "I received new light on the ministry," he wrote in his journal. "Here each one does that which is right in his own eyes. They stand, sit, kneel, pray, exhort, etc., as they are moved." A tenant farmer at Culcheth hosted Independent Methodist meetings in his kitchen, and at Lowton, an industrial village near Warrington, a society based at a local farm also sought membership. The Connexion thus gathered a variety of associations under its umbrella and allowed them, by virtue of its unique polity, to retain their distinctive identities.[4]

The government of Independent Methodism, a typical blueprint of sectarian polity, ensured a popular, village-based organization. By eliminating all hierarchical administration and declaiming all payment for preaching, the Connexion preserved the autonomy of local societies and the hegemony of local preachers. In effect, their rules strove towards egalitar-

---

[3] Mounfield, *History*, pp. 24–6. The High Legh society is also famous for the encouragement it gave to Robert Moffat, the Victorian missionary, who attended its cottage services and was converted there in 1816. An Independent Methodist society still meets in a cottage at the same site; Miss J. Okel (b. 1889), a direct descendant of the society founders, continues to attend services.

[4] Bourne cited in *Ibid.*, p. 20. The first annual meeting of the Independent Methodist Connexion took place in 1806. Records date from 1808, "when at the Annual Meeting, held at Macclesfield, 16 Churches were represented, with a membership of 1,199" (p. 34).

ianism and local democracy. "They were quite sure," their historian pointed out,

> that they were moulding their new society on the pattern of the New Testament Church. They believed in the Scriptures in their entirety, and read and expounded them with every opportunity. They refused to acknowledge external authority; they believed that their society should be self-governed; they believed in the freedom of religious expression and in the priesthood of all believers, in accordance with the teaching of George Fox, who had emphasised "that we must all minister according to our light, but not for hire."[5]

Their declaration combined the anticlericalism, antiauthoritarianism, and resistance to prescriptive codes of behavior that had characterized popular dissent since the seventeenth century. The changing mood of established religion warranted an appeal to the ancient authority of the Scriptures and the founders of Quakerism and Methodism to support their controversial stance.

Like other Methodist sectarians, Independent Methodists created a religion of the *domus*: the household and family, intertwined with village life, provided the material as well as the organizational basis for the religion. For many Independent Methodists, the home was the center of economic activity such as domestic industry or craft production. Through female preaching, regular visiting, and schooling for society children, the sect engaged the entire household in religion and thus in another form of familial cooperation. The home was also the center of informal networks binding together the religious community at large. The Warrington founders laid the basis for Independent Methodist practice. Peter Phillips (b. 1778) used his chair-making shop as a meeting place for members and friends, and his adjacent home as a way-station for travelling evangelists. Hannah Phillips (b. 1780), a former ser-

5 Durant, *Friars' Green*, p. 8.

vant, combined her work as nurse and midwife with popular evangelism: it "took her into the homes of the people" and provided opportunities to discuss domestic and social matters with potential converts and followers. The close connection between physical and spiritual states made medicine an essential part of popular religion. Hannah Phillips was really a preacher in disguise: "She made it her practice to carry about with her her Bible, so that after performing her duties as nurse or midwife, she could become [her patients'] spiritual advisor as well."[6] Village familiarity and mutuality characterized the ideal relations of sectarian religion.

Preserving the quality of village relations became a primary goal of Independent Methodism in later years. The earliest sites of the Connexion, including Warrington, transformed with the growth of population and industry during the first third of the century. While linen and sailcloth production for military use declined, Warrington adopted new industries, such as iron wire and soapmaking, of major importance to Victorian society. The size of new firms increased, and the population of Warrington grew with them.[7] Industrial cities generated demand that revolutionized agricultural areas, and factory industry moved into many villages and altered them beyond recognition. Especially after 1826, the transition to factory textile production in some places was rapid; in other areas, the factory engaged in a slow and tortuous competition with handloom weaving.[8]

Against the background of these developments, Independent Methodists poured new life into the household ideology of cottage religion. Faced with visible and often violent changes, preachers formulated a more strident salvationism depicting the home as their last refuge. Telling selections of scriptural domestic imagery appeared in their sermons. In

[6] Ibid., pp. 16, 13.

[7] *Commercial Directory*, 1828; Bennett, *Warrington*, pp. 13–4; Beamont, *Walks About Warrington*, pp. 114, 132.

[8] Duncan Bythell, *The Handloom Weavers* (Cambridge; Cambridge University Press, 1969), pp. 75–91.

Psalm 27:4, they found a typical idealization of both the home
and place of worship:

> One thing have I desired of the Lord, that will I seek
> after; that I may dwell in the house of the Lord all the
> days of my life, to behold the beauty of the Lord, and to
> enquire in his temple.

Context was significant, for in the Psalms, such peace existed
only in the midst of warfare. The initiated listener would recognize the importance of the preceding and following verses:

> Though an host should encamp against me, my heart shall
> not fear: though war should rise against me, in this will
> I be confident.

> For in the time of trouble he shall hide me in his pavilion:
> in the secret of his tabernacle shall he hide me; he shall
> set me up upon a rock.

While idealizing the home, preachers depicted the struggle
for existence through violent metaphors of war. Reflecting
industrial society, home and work became separate, even an-
tagonistic, spheres of life, no longer under a common roof.
As the world of sectarianism grew more fragmented, the
household acquired a more isolated, symbolic importance.[9]
   Frequent use of the Psalms betrayed the residual *ressentiment*
of Independent Methodists. Unlike the New Testament theology of established Evangelicalism, their faith was full of
vengefulness and self-righteous anger aimed at those who enjoyed material comfort in the face of the humble poor.[10] Dis-

[9] See "Memoir of Jepheth Thompson," *Free Gospel Advocate* (hereafter *FGA*),
1852, pp. 87–8.
[10] Max Weber discusses this aspect of the "religion of the non-privileged
classes" at greater length. "The religion of the Psalms is full of the need for
vengeance," he pointed out, "and the same motif occurs in the priestly re-
workings of ancient Israelite traditions. The majority of the Psalms are quite
obviously replete with the moralistic legitimation and satisfaction of an open
and hardly concealed need for vengeance on the part of a pariah people. . . .
In the Psalms the quest for vengeance may take the form of remonstrating

satisfaction with pervasive social inequities percolated just beneath the surface of their sermons and prayers and, on occasion, erupted into public demonstration. When death exacerbated financial difficulty, funerals became an occasion for vigorous denunciation of earthly oppressors. Survivors exhaustively assessed the life of the deceased and complained of the unwarranted suffering endured by the righteous. Instead of calling attention to future rewards, preachers ranted against past injustices. Retribution, not heavenly peace, was the keynote of their addresses.[11] Psalm 58:11, rendered more powerful in conjunction with its preceding verse, was a favorite text of funeral orators:

> The righteous shall rejoice when he seeth the vengeance: he shall wash his feet in the blood of the wicked.
>
> So that a man shall say, Verily there is a reward for the righteous: verily he is a God that judgeth in the earth.

Even when they urged patience, preachers called down harsh judgments upon their oppressors. One preacher chose to read Psalm 37 at the bedside of a dying member, conveying an immediacy and energy belonging to this world rather than the next:

---

with God because misfortune has overtaken the righteous individual, notwithstanding his obedience to God's commandments, whereas the godless conduct of the heathen, despite their mockery of God's predictions, commandments and authority, has brought them happiness and left them proud." *The Sociology of Religion*, Ephraim Fischoff, trans. (1922; Boston: Beacon Paperback ed., 1964), p. 111.

[11] Working-class attitudes towards death were notably different from those of elites. "The relation of age-specific mortality rates to the dominant social relations of production and family organization gave to death a far greater significance to the living than it has in our own time. . . . When death strikes young, while men and women are fully engaged in family life and when the family as such performs a critical role in the social division of labour, a social vacuum is created whose effect was not one of sentimental loss only, but of deep moral and material consequence." Peter Linebaugh, "The Tyburn Riot Against the Surgeons," *Albion's Fatal Tree: Crime and Society in Eighteenth-Century England* (New York: Pantheon Books, 1975), p. 116.

Fret not thyself because of evildoers, neither be thou
envious against the workers of inequity.

For they shall soon be cut down like the grass, and
wither as the green herb.:

Trust in the Lord, and do good; so shalt thou dwell in
the land, and verily thou shalt be fed.

The alternating images of violence and serenity depicted a
world divided between evil and good, rich and poor:

The wicked have drawn out the sword, and have bent
their bow, to cast down the poor and needy, and to slay
such as be of upright conversation.

Their sword shall enter into their own heart, and their
bows shall be broken.

A little that a righteous man hath is better than the
riches of many wicked.[12]

Independent Methodism was a religion of the dispossessed.
Its angry fulminations were the grievances of uprooted laborers in search of work and domestic security. The sanctification of the family and household was a reply to the uncertainties of new circumstances in industrial towns. That
sermons dwelt upon images of shelter, clothing, and food was
no accident. Religious demands reflected the deprivation of
laboring life, and thus material comfort occupied a central

---

[12] "Memoir of Ann Hill," *Free Gospel Magazine* (hereafter *FGM*), 1871, p. 45;
"[Memoir of] James Longworth," *FGA*, 1852, p. 86. Again Weber clarifies the
concept of vengeance: "Resentment is a concomitant of that particular religious
ethic of the disprivileged which, in the sense expounded by Nietzsche and in
direct inversion of the ancient belief, teaches that the unequal distribution of
mundane goods is caused by the sinfulness and the illegality of the privileged,
and that sooner or later God's wrath will overtake them. In this theodicy of
the disprivileged, the moralistic quest serves as a device for compensating a
conscious or unconscious desire for vengeance." (*Sociology of Religion*, p. 110.)
See also Eric J. Hobsbawm, *Primitive Rebels* (New York: Norton, 1959), p. 133.
Although Hobsbawm describes the religious drive as "etherealized revenge,"
his depiction of the vengeance sought by plebeian social bandits suggests a
close resemblance between rebels and saints.

place in apocalyptic visions. After the introduction of the five kingdoms of Daniel, one preacher described the rewards finally presented to the righteous poor:

> The privileges of this kingdom [of the righteous] come next to be considered; and the first I shall name is, a rich and plenteous provision for all our wants. The King, who reigns in righteousness, is not only a hiding place from the storm, and a covert from the tempest, but as rivers of water in a dry place, and as the shadow of a great rock in a weary land. He liberally supplies all our needs according to his riches in glory. The garments of salvation, and the robe of righteousness are provided for those who are made sensible of their spiritual nakedness. A large and splendid table is spread, and richly furnished with delicious and substantial food, to which the hungry are graciously invited.[13]

The prospect of the last days gave preachers the opportunity to catalogue, in lavish detail, the needs of a working-class congregation.

Through the demands of sectarian discipline, Independent Methodist preachers found meaning in deprivation. Discipline transformed need into virtue, providing a defense against destructive temptations. Identifying with the apostles, preachers saw themselves as "utterly destitute of learning, wealth, or power" and dedicated to exposing "the blinded judgment, deep-rooted prejudices, and long-standing customs of the people." Teetotalism, fasting, and plain dress replaced customary

[13] Hugh Kelly, "The Stone Cut Out of the Mountain. A Sermon preached at the opening of the Independent Methodist Chapel at North Shields, July 1, 1821," Newcastle-upon-Tyne, p. 15. Independent Methodists frequently employed millennial imagery and were not beyond literal interpretations of certain Biblical passages well into the nineteenth century. Their societies mingled with fringe Methodist sects famous for apocalyptic preaching. See J. F. C. Harrison, *The Second Coming* (New Brunswick, N.J.: Rutgers University Press, 1979). For a similar argument in an American setting, see Liston Pope, *Millhands and Preachers* (New Haven: Yale University Press, 1949), concerning factory workers in Gastonia, North Carolina.

behavior, and preachers demonstrated commitment to sectarian values by following a strict code of personal asceticism and refusing all pay for their work. Withdrawn from contemptible forms of worldliness, Independent Methodists encouraged a *ressentiment* that would create a more clearly defined, class-conscious community within industrial society.[14]

Sectarian sainthood changed with the times. The career of one Independent Methodist of Lowton (Lancs.), famous "beyond the precincts of [his] village" for an archetypal testimony, gave evidence of the upheaval taking place in the industrial north. John Roughly (b. 1817) was village born and bred, retaining a thick vernacular and a "quaint way" of speaking throughout his itinerancy as a sectarian raconteur. He came from a family of handloom weavers at Leigh, where he, like most laborers there, struggled through hard times in the 1830s. When he was eighteen, Roughly abandoned the loom and looked for other work. Uneducated, unemployed, and "possessed of a fine flow of animal spirits," he moved to Lowton. His prospects were not good: the reckless Roughly "became quite a desperado," popular in Lowton street life but lacking a steady occupation and a home. Experience schooled him in popular politics and reform, leading him to join a local Owenite group. Roughly was active in the cause until "rheumatic pains" and "a dry leprosy" forced him to enter the Manchester Infirmary.[15]

Through poverty, low life, radicalism, and then illness, Roughly gained "rich experience in Divine things." He also "acquired some practical knowledge of the treatment of fractures and disorders" while working as an orderly at the infirmary after his recovery, and the skill became the focus of his future public labor. Returning to Lowton, Roughly "went forth a changed man." The economic stability of the 1850s enabled him to find work, marry, and establish a family. In a newly industrialized environment, his commitment to the laboring

[14] Kelly, "The Stone," p. 9.
[15] "Memoir of John Roughly," *FGM*, 1874, p. 192.

poor came to include religious work. As a result of the sudden death of his daughter, Roughly began to attend cottage prayer meetings and converted to Independent Methodism in 1857. He then adopted the familiar dual role of preacher and nurse. "His services" as a medical practitioner "were often in request by persons who had met with accidents and other ailments" and were always "gratuitously rendered." Like female preachers and other popular evangelicals before him, Roughly tended bodies and souls.[16]

THE INDUSTRIALIZATION of northern England led to the emergence of new leaders among sectarian Methodists by mid-century. Mendicant preachers, migrant not by choice but necessity, spoke for religious laborers and artisans. With the growth of industrial towns and the gradual depopulation of the countryside, migration became an inevitable part of economic survival. Farm hands were migrant laborers in all but name before 1830; the uprooting of artisans gave even more striking evidence of the erosion of village life in later years. Once changeless figures in village society, shoemakers witnessed the decline of their craft and traditional security. Weavers experienced a more radical extinction. Through Independent Methodism, these new migrant preachers strove to reproduce the social values once fostered by their native villages.

Opportunities for agricultural work around Warrington were failing to keep up with a growing population. Lancashire farms, exceptionally small, provided little employment even at the beginning of the century. More than half the cultivated land in 1815 existed in parcels "of not more than from eight or ten customary acres to those of twenty, thirty, forty, fifty and sixty, up to a hundred"; the average farm ran just under seventy acres. Though these establishments once offered a chance of ownership to the enterprising laborer, such instances were rare after 1815. Many holdings, particularly in northern

[16] Ibid., pp. 301-3.

Cheshire, were devoted to dairying and thus needed few hands. Landless laborers faced additional hardship when late enclosures drove them out of their native districts and landlords pulled down cottages to facilitate improvements.[17]

Displacement from the land set many laborers upon the road to a preaching career. Jepheth Thompson (b. 1783) began migrating when he was eighteen. Born at Culcheth, a farming township outside Warrington, Thompson must have seen a dim future in his native district. He joined the army in 1801, a safe alternative to agricultural work. For twelve years, the Napoleonic wars kept him employed. Migrant, constrained to duty, and subject to rigid authority, Thompson gained the experience of a true sectarian "soldier" so that when he emerged from the army, "he was enabled to decide for God."

Thompson first found work outside Manchester, where he joined a Wesleyan chapel. Not long after, during the downturn of the 1820s, he moved to the outskirts of Lowton to work as a farm laborer. In twenty years of experience, ranging from military service to town industry and village labor, Thompson acquired religious conviction and social consciousness. He left the Wesleyans to preach for the Independents during his first year in Lowton. His sermons were "faithful, experimental, and practical." The laboring preacher lent immediacy to lessons of the Old Testament at the weaving village of Golborne, where he spoke on the domestic imagery of Psalm 27; and from Genesis 4:7, he invoked the example of Cain, the "tiller of the ground," whose humble offering went unrewarded.[18]

In their struggle against insecurity and poverty, laborer preachers became heroes among sectarians. In 1832, older members of the Independent Methodist Connexion "laid hands" upon a young follower from High Legh in recognition

[17] W. Stevenson, *A General View of the Agriculture of Lancashire* (London, 1815), p. 113; John Saville, *Rural Depopulation in England and Wales, 1851–1951* (London: Routledge & Kegan Paul, 1957), chap. 1; Arthur Redford, *Labour Migration in England, 1800–1850* 3rd ed. rev. (Manchester: Manchester University Press, 1976), p. 90.

[18] "Jepheth Thompson," pp. 87–8.

of his call to preach. Thomas Eyes (b. 1810) gave stark evidence of the adversity facing agricultural laborers during the 1820s and 1830s. He was nearly illiterate and "as was customary for farmers' boys," he was constantly on the move. He nevertheless performed astonishingly when he preached, speaking "without seeing the text," and "lining out" the hymns by memory:

> yet he preached with great zeal, generally at the top of his voice, and was well received, especially in the [Warrington] Circuit churches, the people meeting him, and here and there he was the means of their conversion.[19]

Eyes transformed the exactions of poverty into triumphs of self-denial and achievement. He became a celebrated teetotaller, partly out of principle but also as a matter of necessity: he found it advantageous after his marriage to a widow "to set a good example" for a nearly crippling number of stepchildren. Like Thompson, Eyes framed religious truth in vivid vernacular. Converted by a sermon based on Matthew 3:12 ("he will thoroughly purge his floor, and gather his wheat into the garner"), Eyes found similarly apt scriptural passages to illustrate his points. In Grappenhall, Culcheth, Leigh, Tattenhall, and other places around Lancashire and Cheshire, villagers found inspiration in the migrant laborer's message.[20]

Migrant laborer preachers offered proof of new hardships while providing plain truths of the past. By mid-century, they were valued in towns as much as in villages, where they brought messages from the countryside to transplanted cottagers. John Knowles (b. 1818) was a typical example, successful at organizing several societies far from his home. In his popular "village sermons," he "dealt mainly on the practical aspects of life," drawing insights from his own experience in getting a living and finding a home. Born at Carrington, Cheshire, Knowles had moved several times, first to the agricultural village of Warburton and then to Lymm. Like

---

[19] "Memoir of Brother Eyes," *FGM*, 1879, p. 307.
[20] Ibid., pp. 307–8.

Thompson, he tried fustian cutting as an alternative to farm labor, but disliking the work, returned to the fields as soon as his term expired. "Open-air employment," explained his obituary, "was more suited to his robust nature." Knowles, too, made virtue out of necessity. He became known for his remarkable pedestrian records in travelling to preach. Walking over 60,000 miles during his career, Knowles carried his village wisdom "to and from . . . Urmston, Stretford, Manchester, Ashton-under-Lyne, Oldham, Stockport, Lancaster, Oswestry, Bolton, Macclesfield, [and] Liverpool." The inveterate rural preacher also found an urgent call for his services in the growing factory town.[21]

Migrant laborer-preachers signaled the gradual proletarianization of other members of the laboring classes, including artisans. Growing demand and new technology changed craft production as well as agriculture, and artisans faced redundancy competing with cheap mass-marketed manufactures. Their skill, as well as their experience in political radicalism and reform, enabled them to protest change more effectively than laborers. Shoemakers, in particular, were outstanding advocates of working-class causes. Their central role in village life easily translated into prominent participation in Methodist sectarianism.

Shoemakers had always shown natural talent for speaking out. The proverbial warning "preaching cobblers make bad shoes" was, more accurately, a complaint against cobblers' many competing interests.[22] Owing to their habitual free thinking, shoemakers were often purveyors of dissent. In *Lives of Illustrious Shoemakers*, W. E. Winks included six Methodists, five of them preachers. They outnumbered most other occupational groups among sectarian Methodist preachers. "At one time there were twenty-one of them on the Driffield and Bridlington plans" in the East Riding of Yorkshire alone. Preaching

[21] "Memoir of John Knowles," *FGM*, 1889, pp. 336–40.
[22] Quoted in Eric J. Hobsbawm and Joan Wallach Scott, "Political Shoemakers," *Past and Present* 89 (1980), p. 90.

combined easily with their related services. One Primitive Methodist, eulogized as "The Philosopher" after his death, "practiced medicine on a rather large scale," alongside several other trades. Committed to social causes and the common people, shoemakers commanded positions of influence in popular culture.[23]

As cottage preachers and society leaders in the early nineteenth century, shoemakers affirmed their central place in village life. In Almondbury (Yorks.), where Methodism defined the independent culture of local weavers, Abraham Moss (b. 1750) acted as organizer and leader. The shoemaker's image as prophet and autodidact invested him with uncompromised authority. Followers gathered in Moss's shop to discuss current events and other matters, relying on the shoemaker's long-standing experience for direction and advice. Moss preached and led classes around Almondbury, sometimes walking as far as forty miles to an appointment, until his death in 1839.[24] When cottage religion constituted the only dissent from local gentry, self-employment enabled the shoemaker to assert such independence without risking his livelihood. Daniel Stones (b. 1787) helped to found a Primitive Methodist society in his native village of Alstonefield (Staffs.) during the 1820s.

[23] Hobsbawm and Scott, "Political Shoemakers," pp. 86–93 and passim; Henry Woodcock, *Piety Among the Peasantry* (London, 1889), pp. 71, 74–8. "They have, *as a class*, a reputation which is quite unique," Winks argued. "The followers of 'the gentle craft' have generally stood foremost among artisans as regards intelligence and social influence. Probably no class of workmen could, in these respects, compete with them fifty or a hundred years ago, when education and reading were not so common as they are now." W. E. Winks, *Lives of Illustrious Shoemakers* (1883), p. 232.

[24] Joel Mallinson, *Methodism in Huddersfield, Holmfirth, and Denby Dale* (London, 1898), pp. 20–44; Richard Roberts, *History of Methodism in Almondbury* (London, 1864), pp. 8–33. I am grateful to Dr. Patrick Joyce for his help in locating information on the Huddersfield area.

The granddaughter of Abraham Moss, Tabitha Moss (b. 1799), later became a leading Primitive Methodist in Almondbury. "In this place she was the first who opened a door for us, the first that got converted among us, the first that joined us, and the first that is gone to heaven from among us," her obituary recorded (*PMM*, 1825, p. 264).

Stones and his former master offered their homes as meeting places in the small dairying village, where their activity was sure to be an affront to local landlords.[25] Within the face-to-face relations of village life, shoemakers contributed essential advantages to autonomous popular activity.

Later shoemaker preachers cast a different image. No longer signifying either self-employment or free thinking, shoemaking became part of the general decline of skilled trades. The bond between village culture and shoemaking loosened as large numbers of semi-skilled "unsocialized" out-workers flooded the craft in village and town. While earlier shoemakers travelled only occasionally to preach, their successors in the 1830s and 1840s were constantly on the move. Unlike traditional journeymen, however, many came from other crafts and migrated in search of a steadier form of income. Their preaching careers reflected the changing world of the village cobbler.[26]

Primitive Methodist preacher William Pickard (b. 1802) worked first as a weaver at Bramley and then Rawden (Yorks.) before trying his hand at shoemaking. Forced out of one occupation, he encountered hardship in the next. "Many were the conflicts through which he had to pass," his obituary recorded, "having entered into business on the eve of commercial distress which pressed heavily on the manufacturing districts of England." Pickard tried to combat hard times by migrating to other places. He returned to Bramley, and moved again to Leeds and Bradford before he died prematurely in 1843.[27] Agricultural laborers, forced to leave the countryside

[25] "Memoir of Daniel Stones," *PMM*, 1828, pp. 348–51.

[26] Hobsbawm and Scott, "Political Shoemakers," pp. 106–10. Winks also lamented the disappearance of the traditional shoemaker. "The old Cobbler, like the ancient spinster and handloom weaver, is retiring into the shade of the boot and shoe factory." Winks, *Lives*, p. iv. Evidence suggests that this transition was taking place by the 1850s. See W. G. Rimmer, "Leeds Leather Industry in the Nineteenth Century," *Publications of the Thoresby Society* 46, Part 2 (1968): 136.

[27] "Memoir of William Pickard," *PMM*, 1844, pp. 375–7.

because of unemployment or physical disability, also tried shoemaking. Like Pickard, they met with new difficulties. Richard Cammack (b. 1836) left Heapham (Lincs.) for Hemswell in order to learn shoemaking because an injured ankle had "disqualified him . . . for farm service." As a Primitive Methodist exhorter, Cammack continued preaching in different societies when the demands of work forced him to move first to Springthorpe and then back to Heapham. Migration and poverty weakened his health, for Cammack became consumptive and died at twenty-six. Thomas Norman (b. ca. 1801) worked as an agricultural laborer in northern Cheshire before his apprenticeship to a shoemaker at Preston oth' Hill. Financial considerations probably entered his decision to become a salaried itinerant preacher for the Primitive Methodists in 1822, but after one year of strenuous travel, he became ill and died in Shropshire.[28]

The life of preacher James Seddon illustrates the extreme insecurity experienced by an Independent Methodist shoemaker. Seddon (b. 1817) grew up in poverty in Liverpool. "From an early age," he helped his father in shoemaking. Despite hardships, James applied his "naturally thoughtful disposition" to acquiring useful knowledge and a strong moral sensibility, and, at twenty, he became a local preacher for the Primitive Methodists. A strict ascetic code marked his behavior from these early years. In addition to preaching, Seddon also belonged to a "Youth's Temperance Society" and "became a strenuous advocate of teetotalism." Self-discipline and devotion to reformist causes characterized his life even before the end of his apprenticeship.[29]

Coming of age in 1838, Seddon embarked upon a responsible and rather ordinary course: he arranged a partnership with a shoemaker in Bolton, and, before moving, he married. Seddon's wife (and the ten children who followed) promised assistance in his work and, by necessity in so large a family,

[28] "Memoir of Thomas Norman," *PMM*, 1823, pp. 217–9; "Memoir of Richard Cammack," *PMM*, 1863, pp. 142–3.
[29] "Memoir of James Seddon, of Oldham," *FGM*, 1879, p. 302.

additional earnings of their own. But the hungry forties swept away whatever hope of security Seddon had. He was forced to leave Bolton and move to Birkenhead, and "from thence, he removed to Liverpool, and from thence to Prescot." Amidst all this upheaval, Seddon preached steadily for the Primitive Methodists. In each town, religion provided the continuity that was absent in his domestic circumstances and work.[30]

Religion in Prescot entered its own time of troubles around 1850. When Seddon arrived, "the Primitive Methodist cause [had] gone down." The area around Liverpool had been unresponsive to popular evangelicalism; despite numerous attempts by leading evangelists, a gulf remained between preachers and people. Poverty and the influx of immigrants undoubtedly contributed to organizational difficulties. And perhaps the dominating presence of local collieries, where paternalism and established Evangelicalism were strong, discouraged religious activity.[31] Independent Methodists, like the Primitives, experienced great difficulty in establishing a society in Prescot. Cottage meetings begun in 1818 had led to the erection of a chapel in 1823; but the society failed to secure preachers and sufficient funds and the chapel eventually closed. Warrington Independent Methodists planned to take advantage of the hiatus in religious activity following the decline of Primitive Methodism. When they learned that James Seddon had moved to Prescot, they set about implementing their scheme. In 1851, preacher and organizer William Sanderson visited Seddon and "gave him an explanation of [the Independent Methodist] polity, and asked him to cast in his lot with the Free Gospel people." Seddon agreed, and, in April, 1851, he joined the Connexion.[32]

Independent Methodism, a more radical form of sectari-

[30] Ibid., p. 302. On shoemakers' wives, see Rimmer, pp. 136–7.

[31] The odd assortment of personalities based at Liverpool probably contributed to Primitive difficulties. See H. B. Kendall, *History of the Primitive Methodist Church* 2 vols. (London, n.d.), 2:270.

More than two-thirds of the Prescot population were employed in mining in 1830. *New Lancashire Gazetteer* (1830), pp. 137–8.

[32]"Memoir of Seddon," p. 302.

anism, signified a further step towards uncompromised ascetic virtue. Unlike other forms of Methodism which relied upon full-time salaried preachers, Independent Methodism promised no financial security. Like the "truly Apostolic and primitive church," the sect promoted only those "able and willing to administer the Word of Life, without money and without price."[33] Seddon rejected worldly security and, with it, affiliation with an increasingly institutionalized religion. For the Primitive Methodist Connexion was following its Wesleyan ancestor in becoming more centralized and hierarchical. New methods of administration and a more professional generation of leaders appeared in the 1850s as town chapels grew in wealth and size. Independent Methodists, in contrast, prohibited all "distinctions of minister and laity," banning the use of "Reverend," and maintained a connexion free of bureaucracy. "Each church orders its own affairs" was its motto, directly derived from "Who hath despised the day of small things?" (Zechariah 4:10)[34]

Seddon's migration continued, along with financial distress: by the age of thirty-six, he had changed residences seven times, and misfortune had followed him everywhere. Two years after joining the Prescot Independent Methodists, "straitened circumstances" forced him to move to Liverpool. Shoemaking there proved "unsuccessful" after six months, when he returned to Prescot. Seddon's affiliation to the Independent Methodists rescued him, this time in a material way. In 1855, he became a missionary for chapels in eastern Lancashire, accepting gratuitous gifts and support in exchange for constant evangelism. This preaching interlude relieved, if only briefly, his penury. Seddon preached from town to town, settling for a time at Ashton-under-Lyne, and three years later, at Oldham.[35]

[33] Mounfield, *History*, p. 32.

[34] James Vickers, *A History of the Independent Methodist Connexion* (1905), p. 14. The two texts were part of the ceremonies at the Annual Meeting at Macclesfield in 1808.

[35] "Memoir of Seddon," pp. 302–3. Seddon's travels took him to Bolton,

At Oldham, the mendicant shoemaker became the leader of displaced laborers and migrant millworkers. Seddon had reached the height of his preaching career: his experiences and point of view enabled him to interpret the millworker's world of hardship and crisis. Overwhelmed by such oppression, Seddon urged a private victory through personal renunciation of worldliness. In his last sermon, he elaborated on a characteristic text from Paul's Epistle to the Hebrews, a depiction of his own struggle to survive:

> Wherefore seeing we also are compassed about with so great a cloud of witnesses, let us lay aside every weight, and the sin which doth so easily beset us, and let us run with patience the race that is set before us, looking unto Jesus, the author and finisher of our faith; who for the joy that was set before him endured the cross, despising the shame, and is set down at the right hand of the throne of God. [Hebrews 12:1-2]

A strict independent morality was his weapon against wickedness and oppression. Seddon's exhortation belonged to a world of craftsmen determined to protect their autonomy. The moral autonomy of Independent Methodism supplied a good approximation.[36]

Seddon's capability in addressing laborers' interests, despite his numerous economic defeats, made him eminently successful among Independent Methodists. Perhaps his frequent migration showed him the necessity of linking together scattered societies of the Connexion, for early in his career, he

---

Wigan, Lees, Rochdale, and Bury, as well as Ashton-under-Lyne and Oldham. His obituary included a catalogue of gifts presented to him by churches he had served: "At Sindsley he was presented with a watch in recognition of his labours among them. From the Warrington Circuit he received a splendid Family Bible, a large edition of the Connexional Hymn Book, and a purse of money at the close of his mission there. From the Bolton Circuit he received a letter expressing thanks to Almighty God for his services and speaking in glowing terms of the good that had accrued from his visit" (p. 305).

[36] Ibid., p. 304.

helped to formulate a Testimony of Union. Seddon also assumed the offices of president of the Oldham Circuit and vice-president of the Connexion for two successive years. Within this period, his wife and all but one of his ten children died of disease. Nevertheless, "he bore all these calamities with patient suffering and still continued to labour for the Master": deprived of his family, Seddon again arranged to travel as an evangelist. After preaching in the Warrington Circuit and through Yorkshire for a year, he returned to Oldham and shoemaking. His health was broken, however, and he died in 1879.[37]

THE MENDICANT SECTARIAN PREACHER was the tradition-bound artisan transformed by the emergence of capitalist agriculture and industry. Uprooted from his customary setting, he resumed his role as village philosopher by preaching in industrial towns. Independent Methodism thus enabled certain aspects of popular culture to survive in opposition to industrial society. The ideological independence of shoemakers was only one manifestation; weavers preserved other values and customs in sectarian Methodism. Religion reinforced the cultural autonomy they had enjoyed since the eighteenth century.

Weavers, like shoemakers, were distinctive figures in village life. Local politicians and champions of working-class interests in their own right, weavers also supported Owenism, Chartism, and Methodism. Their craft depended on an autonomous household economy and community spirit evident in rich cultural traditions. The economic and social status of handloom weaving, declining earlier and more dramatically than shoemaking, was under attack by 1800. While unfavorable commercial arrangements undermined their prosperity and security, weavers nevertheless sustained "a sense of lost status, as memories of their 'golden age' lingered; and with this, they

[37] Ibid., pp. 303–6; Mounfield, *History*, p. 38; Vickers, *History*, p. 52.

set a high premium on the values of independence."[38] Contemporaries regularly commented on the determined self-reliance of weavers. "The facility with which weavers changed their masters," Richard Guest remarked in 1823,

> the constant effort to find out and obtain the largest remuneration for their labour, the excitement to ingenuity which the higher wages for fine manufactures and skilful workmanship produced, and the conviction that they depended mainly on their own exertions, produced in them that invaluable feeling, a spirit of freedom and independence, and that guarantee for good conduct and improvement of manners, a consciousness of the value of character and of their own weight and importance.[39]

Further transformation of the textile industry rendered the independent ideology of sectarian Methodism increasingly important to weavers. As factory and power loom overtook workshop and handloom, weavers resisted giving up traditional ways of working and endured falling rates of payment and growing destitution. The political, social, and psychological aspects of their struggle, debated in an extensive historical literature, point to their insistence upon some degree of control over their craft.[40] For religious weavers, Independent Methodism presented a way of addressing this need through households and community while creating a symbolic independence from industrial society. Through its connection to the cottage economy, sectarian Methodism also provided an historical link to the village past.

The map of Independent Methodist outposts around Lancashire and Yorkshire reflected the convergence of the decline of handloom weaving and the rise of domestic-based worship.

---

[38] Edward P. Thompson, *The Making of the English Working Class* (New York: Vintage Books, 1963), p. 295 and chap. 9, passim.

[39] Richard Guest, *A Compendious History of the Cotton Manufacture* (Manchester, 1823; reprint ed., Totowa, N.J.: Frank Cass, 1968), p. 38.

[40] Thompson, *Making of the English Working Class*, chap. 9, esp. pp. 294–308; Bythell, *Handloom Weavers*, chap. 4.

As years passed, however, choices of meeting places marked the metamorphosis of the textile industry as worship moved from private cottages to abandoned weaving cottages and sheds. At Stretford, meetings began in the open air in 1820, later continued in an old barn, and, in 1824, finally settled in an empty weaving shed. The dilapidated building became known as "the White Chapel." The pattern was repeated in other Lancashire and Yorkshire villages. A society at Nelson, appearing slightly later, testified to the local decline of domestic industry. In 1852, the founders "rented a large room . . . over one or two cottages which had been used as a hand-loom weaving place, fallen into disuse through the introduction of power looms."[41] Rather than advancing to chapel building in later years, such societies instead retreated to domestic premises. At Golborne, a society gathered in a weaving shop in Mill Street in 1847 and later moved to a thatched cottage.[42] More than once, chapels proved ruinous to textile village societies; even at Nelson, the largest society in the Connexion by 1900, the first chapel was lost during financial difficulties in the 1870s. Independent Methodism was too closely tied to the livelihood of laboring communities to flourish during these years.[43]

Independent Methodism at Lowton, a small Lancashire township, reveals the interdependence of laboring life, economic change, and cottage religion. When meetings began in 1780, inhabitants of Lowton were engaged in agriculture and domestic handloom weaving. The scattered town altered its appearance over the next half-century as domestic industry and farming declined. Its population slowly rose and then fell after 1831. Spinning and fustian weaving attracted some labor to Lowton, but migration predominated, as the town lost its population to nearby industrial centers. In 1831, its population

[41] Mounfield, *History*, pp. 160, 81–3.

[42] Ibid., p. 69.

[43] Ibid., p. 162. The society was able to build a school two years later, and, in 1885, a larger "junior school" was built. But not until 1891 did members finally consent to laying the foundation of another chapel (pp. 162–3).

stood at 2,374; by 1851, it had fallen to 2,140 and remained below 2,500 until 1891. All textile production, besides a limited amount of domestic silk weaving, died out. "Covered for the most part with bricks and mortar," Lowton was serving as "a residential suburban retreat" for nearby industrial Leigh by the end of the nineteenth century.[44]

The small Independent Methodist society at Lowton weathered these changes with few alterations. Unlike local Wesleyans, who achieved "bricks and mortar" status as early as 1788, the Independents remained a cottage society. Originating at the Gilded Hollins Farm, meetings continued in domestic quarters for nearly seventy years. When a member donated land in 1793, the society built a school rather than a chapel. Numbers increased over the next few decades, so, in 1834, the Independents replaced the old Sunday School building with a larger one. In 1849, after generations of cottage meetings, the society finally erected a chapel.[45]

The preservation of cottage meetings throughout the economic transformation of Lowton was no coincidence. Chapel building entailed unwanted expense: the society was small, members were poor, and funds went first towards supporting the indigent and to Independent Methodist missions. Cost, however, explained only part of the unwillingness to build a chapel. The decline of cottage industry incited Lowton people to cling more tenaciously to traditions associated with domestic-based life. Cottage meetings, like handloom weaving, belonged to an inviolable personal domain demonstrating the survival of popular culture. The vicissitudes of Lowton's economic life would not penetrate such important territory. Advocating uncompromised self-reliance, Independent Methodist preachers invoked St. Paul's precepts. " 'Stand fast as the beaten anvil to the stroke,' " a Lowton preacher often intoned, at other times exhorting, " 'Finally, brethren, be ye steadfast,

---

[44] J. Corry, *History of Lancashire*, 2: 682; Edward Baines, *History, Directory, and Gazetteer of the County of Lancashire* (1825), 2: 718; *Victoria History of the County of Lancaster* (Oxford: Oxford University Press, 1906), 4:150–1 (hereafter *VCH*).

[45] *VCH*, 4:154; Mounfield, *History*, p. 67; *The Connexion*, March, 1980, p. 5.

immovable, always abounding in the work of the Lord.' "[46]
Sectarianism protected followers from becoming passive victims of change.

The ideology of Independent Methodism inspired different strategies aimed at self-determination. For some sectarian Methodists, the radical principles of seventeenth-century dissent provided a religious critique of contemporary society. Political radicals shared their anticlericalism, egalitarianism, and democratic principles, and economic marginalization in weaving villages sometimes led to both political and religious expressions of protest. At Bingley, for example, an Independent Methodist society grew out of Chartist meetings taking place in 1848.[47] Religion took a militant form, even when political activity declined. By answering weavers' demands for community and autonomy, cottage religion strengthened their stance against defeat.

Struggles in cottage industry and religion could lead to a life-long dedication to sectarian discipline. Born at Lowton in 1824, William Birchall came from a humble family of silk weavers. His mother "feared God . . . delighted in Christian communion," and sent her sons and daughter to the local Independent Methodist Sunday School. William's aptitude caught the attention of school officials, who encouraged him by promoting him to a teaching position. By then, work at home interfered with his studies. For a short time, he attended night school and "by rather extensive reading he . . . acquired considerable information." His education "rendered him good service" when his responsibilities increased. At twenty, he married, experienced conversion, and "in a few months" began to preach in the local Independent Methodist society.[48]

Sectarian Methodism became a means of resisting the proletarianization that was overwhelming handloom weavers after

[46] "Memoir of John Birchall," *FGM*, 1871, p. 246.
[47] Mounfield, *History*, p. 155.
[48] "Memoir of William Birchall," *FGM*, 1871, pp. 167–8. The memoirs of both Birchalls were written by their brother Joseph, also an Independent Methodist preacher.

1820. Through years of privation, Birchall never surrendered his autonomy and "never gave way to melancholy." He fought "greatly straitened circumstances" and "protracted afflictions . . . in his family" during the 1830s and 1840s, but discipline and morality guarded him against falling prey to the corrupt world of his oppressors. Birchall became noted for "the high stand which he took to maintain the purity of the church" in matters of principle and behavior. His determined self-reliance continued after he gave up handloom weaving in 1850. Capitalizing on his education, Birchall started a school and devoted his energies to the laboring community. Independent Methodism served him well again in his last years, when he supported himself and his family through mission work in nearby villages and towns. The Birchalls met with sudden death in 1866, when first a son, then three daughters, and finally William himself died within eight months, probably of contagious disease.[49]

William's brother John (b. 1826) found it more difficult to settle into life at Lowton Common. According to a third brother, John was "not possessed of the same adaptability to circumstances" as William. Though he also attended the Independent Methodist Sunday School, John preferred politics to religion: "he was for revolutionising society upon democratic principles." Given a limited formal education, he succeeded in broadening his vision with a remarkable range of reading. He delved into "the writings and speeches of political economists and lecturers" and occasionally "travel[led] eight or ten miles to be present at a political demonstration." By the late 1840s, John's "youthful zeal" had found little satisfaction in Lowton, and times were hard. Intending to make a new start, he married and moved to Manchester. But circumstances obviously worked against him and his life assumed the look of so many other uprooted weavers. After only "a year or two" in Manchester, he moved to Bedford, "and shortly after found his way back to Lowton Common."[50]

49 Ibid., pp. 168–70.
50 "Memoir of John Birchall," p. 245.

John Birchall reassessed his alternatives. No longer able to support himself and a growing family by handloom weaving, he took a job at a local cotton mill. Birchall struggled to prevent this loss of autonomy from signifying defeat; seeking to regain mastery of his situation, he shifted his attention to family, household, and, finally, religion. Birchall became involved in Independent Methodist cottage meetings, and religion became for him, as it had for his brother, a forum for self-expression. Within months of his conversion in 1852, he rose to the position of preacher. Energetic and yet "unassuming" in his manner, Birchall became "highly respected" in the Lowton society. "Sometimes during the delivery of a discourse," his brother recalled, "he would become enthusiastic with his theme, and seem as if under the influence of inspiration." His mottos vividly reflected his own experiences: " 'Having done all, thousands of times,' " he exclaimed, " 'stand yourselves like men, be strong in the Lord.' " After the death of his brother William, he returned to handloom silk weaving as a way of aiding his failing health. But when his daughter died a few years later, Birchall became totally disabled and finally died in 1871.[51]

Independent Methodism in Lowton provided a community for the displaced, the dissatisfied, and the unadaptable. People like William and John Birchall, who never relinquished a need for self-determination, moved from the world of cottage industry to that of cottage religion. For them, religious activity became part of a wider settling process in their lives; their attachment to their homes, families, and religious associations cushioned the effect of continuing uncertainties. Other weavers, however, rejected dogged persistence at the loom in favor of trial-and-error ventures in small trade. They, too, adopted the rugged individualism of Independent Methodism, but they capitalized on its portable aspect rather than its stability. Their faith admitted them to the supportive intimacy of successive societies and strengthened their resolve to struggle against adversity.

[51] Ibid., pp. 246–7.

Preacher John Holgate managed a heroic number of changes in occupation and residence during the first half of the century. Born in 1811 in Barrowford near Colne, Lancashire, he grew up in the heart of the old cotton manufacturing district. Handloom weaving in the Colne valley presented perhaps the starkest picture of decline after 1820: roughly three-fifths of the townships around Blackburn fell in population between 1821 and 1841, owing mostly to the migration of weavers, while country areas suffered similar though lesser losses.[52] First Primitive Methodism and later Independent Methodism flourished in these places, and Holgate was a member of both sects. Holgate worked as a handloom cotton weaver during the early part of his life. In his youth, he was profligate, but at nineteen he reformed. He signed the temperance pledge early in the movement (1830), and soon afterward converted to Primitive Methodism. The Barrowford society appointed him local preacher when he was twenty, and for the next ten years he took an active part in chapel life.[53]

In 1841, Holgate abandoned handloom weaving in order to escape pauperage. Nevertheless, "his life was chequered throughout, and he sometimes said that poverty seemed a near relation to him to the end of his days." Within the next fourteen years, Holgate moved five times and held at least four different jobs. He first relocated at Bradford, where he "commenced business as a bookseller." There he encountered Independent Methodists who welcomed him into their society and allowed him to resume his role of preacher. But his business venture evidently failed, for within the next year he moved to Knottingly, where he sold tea. Again he joined a local Independent Methodist society and acted as a local preacher. His financial circumstances seemed to improve, but Holgate refused to stop there. Two years later, he left Knottingly in order to establish a grocery shop in Thornhill, and, prudently enough, he also married. An Independent Meth-

[52] Bythell, *Handloom Weavers*, pp. 255–6; on Colne, see pp. 261, 166.
[53] "Memoir of John Holgate," *FGM*, 1877, p. 355.

odist society had just moved from a cottage into new quarters in a "school chapel," and Holgate contributed his efforts as preacher and Sunday School teacher in order to promote the cause at "Sodom," as the village was called. But the 1840s were hard times for small shopkeepers. By 1852, Holgate had lost all his savings. He again moved, this time to Rawfolde, Cleckheaton, and, three years later, he moved a final time to Dewsbury. His occupation from 1852 until his death in 1877 remains unknown, though he clearly spent a good deal of time in temperance work and might have made a living from it. Despite an altercation with society members at Dewsbury, he continued his affiliation with the Independent Methodists. By the time of his death, Holgate was famous for worldly wisdom as well as piety. His funeral attracted a great number of people, "composed of all grades of opinions, amongst whom was one of the leading secularists of the town," and an equally varied number of services took place in chapels and at the graveside. In many ways, Holgate had embodied the self-reliant, independent spirit of his age.[54]

MANY MENDICANT PREACHERS made the industrial town their final destination, where they founded Independent Methodist societies in an attempt to reconstitute village communities. Millworkers, like mendicant preachers, were often immigrants from the country who had witnessed the decline of cottage industry, small farming, and independent craft; insecurity and migration similarly characterized their lives. Many readily responded to the traditional features of cottage religion. Domestic meetings and pastoral care, including visiting the sick, schooling, and social activities, acquired added significance in the factory town. The democracy of Independent Methodism also became crucial in promoting sexual equality, which reunited families divided by work. Distinctly different from town chapels and churches, the sectarian Methodist society was closely identified with the economic and social lives of laborers.

[54] Ibid., pp. 355–7.

Women played an important part in dispensing pastoral care in the factory town. With its notorious appetite for female labor, textile industry constantly attracted distressed or poor women, and female preachers found renewed need for their services. A female preacher of Stockport (Chesh.) reflected the advance of industrialism in her own life and career. Born in 1811 at Manchester, Sister E. Butterworth experienced the "many trials and privations" of an industrial city "very early in life." In search of employment, her family moved to Heaton Mersey, near Stockport, where Butterworth attended a Wesleyan Sunday School and became converted. Her religious zeal eventually resulted in her exile from home, and, soon after, marriage to a fellow Wesleyan. But trouble followed when he "threw off the mask, and proved worthless." Butterworth's memoir made clear that her personal life, like her material circumstances, remained insecure.[55]

Such misfortune was preparation for a preaching career. When she and her husband moved to Compstal Bridge, Butterworth joined the Primitive Methodists and began to speak publicly. "Her fame was soon abroad in the districts round about—Tintwistle, Glossop, &c.—and thus for two or three years she continued most acceptably." But her marital problems worsened: by 1840, "her home life had become more than she could bear. All that she could earn by hard toiling was too little, and she separated from her husband, and with two small children came to Stockport." Forced into shameful isolation, Butterworth ceased preaching and lost all contact with the Primitive Methodists.[56]

Though withdrawn from religious involvement, Sister Butterworth entered a field close to urban evangelicalism: she became a nurse, first at the Stockport Infirmary and later at Sheffield and Swinton. When she returned to Stockport in 1852, she also returned to religion. "Feeling [not] very com-

---

[55] "Memoir of Sister E. Butterworth, of Stockport," *FGM*, 1880, pp. 88–9. Neither her given nor maiden name appears in Butterworth's obituary; Butterworth was the surname of her second husband.

[56] Ibid., p. 89.

fortable" with the local Wesleyan chapel, though typical in its respectability and suited to her new professional status, Butterworth joined the Independent Methodists. Within months, she was preaching again, as well as applying her "surgical and medical art" to "hundreds of poor people." Butterworth became a model urban cottage preacher, committed to the working classes but still oriented towards domestic care. For the last twenty-eight years of her life, she was "often . . . seen going with some article of clothing, food, or medicine to comfort some one in trouble or poverty." Later she married Luke Butterworth, a factory worker and, like herself, a prominent figure in the Independent Methodist society. In her public role and even her personal life, Butterworth maintained the principles of popular evangelicalism.[57]

Industrialism produced different varieties of female distress in the towns: orphans, abandoned wives, wives of indigent drunkards, poor spinsters, and widows faced unfamiliar hardships when the environment increased their misery and provided few mitigating services. In their remarkable thoroughness and candor, the obituaries in Independent Methodist magazines became ironic celebrations of survival. Loss of family, as well as marital discord, appeared more common, and work, if available, seldom relieved poverty. The responsibility of children added further complications, particularly if no relations lived nearby. For some working women in factory towns, the sectarian society held out their only opportunity for community and support.

In stark contrast to the pointless hardships of her earlier years, membership in an Independent Methodist society could impose order and meaning upon a female follower's life. Striking evidence appears in the obituary of Ann Hill, which, even if embellished, illustrates an attempt to confront considerable material and personal difficulty. Born in Wigan, Hill lived with neighbors after she was orphaned at eight. As a young girl, she worked in a mill during the day and at domestic industry at night. When she was twenty, she moved to her aunt's home

[57] Ibid., pp. 89–91.

in Oldham and found another job at a mill. Hill married a miner when she was twenty-eight, and for a few years they "lived comfortably" in a cottage in Oldham. But a strike at the pit forced her husband to look for other work, and after several years of migration and financial troubles, he fell into profligacy. Hill, like Butterworth, eventually left her husband; in 1835, she returned to Oldham with several children.[58]

As a single parent with no education, few skills, and apparently no surviving relatives (her aunt was not mentioned in these later years), Ann Hill must have been in difficult straits. Where she lived and what she did to support herself and her children were not recorded. When the death of a child occurred, she began to attend cottage meetings of a local Independent Methodist society, and after her conversion, her life took a new turn. Hill found "a home of her own" in a "cellar on Siderith Moor" and began to earn small sums by taking in linen work. Her daughter was "put out as a nurse, but ultimately got employment at the mill." These changes signified a degree of control over circumstances, control which Hill associated with cottage religion.[59]

Town churches and chapels did not supply the same services as the popular-based sectarian society. The pastoral care of Independent Methodism provided essential sociability, and visiting meant more than just evangelical or charitable solicitation. Henry Barlow (b. 1810), a builder and shopkeeper of Stockport, left the Baptist chapel to join the Independent Methodists because, he complained, the Baptist minister had visited him only once in nine years, and then only when Barlow had broken his arm while building the chapel.[60] More important, Independent Methodism incited working-class men and

---

[58] "Memoir of Ann Hill, of Greenacres Hill, Oldham," *FGM*, 1871, pp. 42–3.

[59] Ibid., pp. 43–5.

[60] "Memoir of Henry Barlow, of Stockport," *FGM*, 1888, pp. 402–3. Later in the century, the search for a distinct form of religion became part of a larger definition of a lower middle class. See Hugh McLeod, "White Collar Values and the Role of Religion," *The Lower Middle Class in Britain, 1870–1914*, Geoffrey Crossick, ed. (London: Croom Helm, 1977), pp. 61–88.

women to satisfy their own organizational needs in new environments. William Hill (b. 1811) "preached to the neighbours in his own house" outside Stockport and "kept a day school for children" that enabled him to quit his job at a mill. His marriage to an Independent Methodist preacher probably influenced his decision to stop preaching for the Methodist New Connexion; together the couple maintained a religious society that catered to the immediate needs of their working-class community.[61]

Cottage evangelicals often ignored the formalities of town churches in order to meet the needs of their members. The segregated neighborhoods of industrial towns led to a class-based evangelism, and Independent Methodists frequently violated denominational distinctions. Bolton Independent Methodists celebrated the career of a "general town Missionary" for his "willing horse" service on all occasions. Thomas Haslam, a spinner from Egerton, came to Bolton as an Independent Methodist in 1828 to work at a factory. His involvement in religion grew steadily: he first taught Sunday School, then joined the temperance society, and later "sustained the offices of president, preacher, leader of two classes, visitor in the school, [and] president of [the] sick society." With his fellow society members, Haslam practiced old-fashioned village evangelism. He tirelessly followed the behavior of every person, reproving and rebuking so much that "he was not always admired." Ubiquitous and confrontational, Haslam defied the anonymity of the factory town. His ministry extended beyond the Independent Methodist congregation to the entire "half of the town in which the chapel is situated." Haslam "was frequently called upon by people of different denominations to visit their sick and dying, baptize their children, to marry, and to bury" them. For the poor, the cost of institutional ritual was too great, and Haslam's services, true to sectarian principle, were always free.[62]

The experience of poverty in factory towns turned many

[61] "Memoir of William Hill, of Stockport," *FGM*, 1887, pp. 88–91.
[62] "Memoir of Thomas Haslam, of Bolton," *FGM*, 1871, pp. 247–9.

workers away from churches and chapels. Obituary pages were rife with accounts of financial conflicts, fascinating for their view into the inner workings of chapel administration, that resulted in conversions to Independent Methodism. John Sutton (b. 1796), a villager from Cheshire, broke with Manchester Wesleyans after a financial dispute. As class leader, he had received orders to "get more money" from his members. He refused, arguing that "he received and booked whatever the members of his class gave; and, beyond this, he was not willing to go." Sutton's unyielding stance led to his joining the Independent Methodists, famous for their "free gospel," who promoted him to the rank of preacher and chapel trustee. Points of financial principle, ignored or abandoned by town institutions, were elevated into high virtue by Independent Methodists.[63]

First-hand experience in self-run cottage meetings and a shared interest in small-scale religion enabled working-class dissidents to unite against offending chapels. The cause at Barnoldswick (Yorks.) began in just this way. The small factory town in the Colne valley barely weathered the fluctuations of the 1830s. A crisis in the Wesleyan church broke out in 1839, when local factory operatives and circuit officials disagreed over the quarterly collection. "Officials expressed surprise" at the meager offering of the Barnoldswick society, the church history reported, "and intimated that it would not satisfy the requirements." The story spread, resulting in bitter exchanges that led to the resignation of five class leaders. Members then began to meet on a new basis: a local "dissentient" opened his house for prayer, and the place "was soon crowded out" with worshippers. A vituperous war of sermonizing followed:

One of the ministers hearing of this, and finding his own Church almost empty, had the temerity to preach a sermon which has made history. The text was "Except these abide in the ship, ye cannot be saved." He skilfully manipulated his subject so as to compare the old Methodist body to the old ship, which of course was sound and

[63] "Memoir of John Sutton, of Manchester," FGM, 1872, pp. 366–8.

seaworthy, but held out no prospect for the seceders. This caused no consternation, but rather amusement, and became the talk of the village. One of the preachers, who preached the following Sunday in the cottage found a text, which he thought would be a suitable one for a reply sermon. It was "And now I exhort you to be of good cheer: for there shall be no loss of any man's life among you, but that of the ship." . . . From this time, one of the places was dubbed the "Old Ship" and the other the "New Ship."

The conflict between chapel and cottage, couched in Biblical terms, legitimized the cause of the secessionists. The new congregation delivered another rebuttal when they raised, with considerable sacrifice, a chapel of their own the next year. Built by the members themselves, the chapel cost £400. In a final gesture of dissent, a female preacher officiated at the opening service.[64]

In the village of Colne, members of the Primitive Methodist church became "much dissatisfied with the arrangements the officials and ministers made for their convenience" in 1851. Discontent grew until the circuit decided to sell the chapel to thirty rebellious members. For over six months, the group met without denominational affiliation, until the ubiquitous Independent Methodist missionary William Sanderson visited the town. According to Sanderson, "The enemies of a Free Gospel had circulated that I was an infidel, and warned people not to go near me." Sanderson therefore decided to attack the problem head-on:

I took my stand, and as the people came out of the mills for dinner I gave out the words "As concerning this sect, we know that everywhere it is spoken against." The people were amazed when I showed the sect I represented preached Christ as the only ground of a sinner's hope.[65]

[64] Mounfield, *History*, pp. 158–60.
[65] Vickers, *History*, p. 169.

He promised to prove Independent Methodism in accordance with the New Testament that evening in a sermon at Waterside Chapel. When the time arrived, the chapel was filled and Sanderson's two and one-half hour lecture proved convincing. The Colne body joined the Independent Methodist Connexion and thereafter aided in spreading the free gospel cause to other towns in the valley.[66]

In Lancashire, Cheshire, and Yorkshire, migration became the key factor in the continuing spread of cottage religion. The intensive industrialization of cotton towns, coupled with changes in the countryside, generated constant movement from village to town, which altered the context of cottage worship. In milltowns, Independent Methodism evolved as a theology of the dispossessed. Increasing awareness of a distinct cultural and class identity, particularly among displaced artisans, led to a shift in emphasis in the sectarian social critique. At a time when working-class political movements were growing in importance and strength, Independent Methodists withdrew from such developments and focused their energies on supportive efforts of their own. Their adherence to the founding principles of sectarianism ultimately distinguished them from other popular evangelicals. Though forces of political and social change gradually isolated the urban heirs of cottage religion, Independent Methodists succeeded, perhaps more than others, in preserving the cultural forms of early industrialism.

[66] Ibid., pp. 168–9; Mounfield, *History*, pp. 164–5. See also "Memoir of Bro. James Holt, of Colne," *FGM*, 1887, pp. 44–6. The newly founded church suffered from severe poverty in its early days and sorely felt the absence of an organ. But members managed without one: "When the hymn was given out, James Hartley, known as 'Happy,' whistled over the tune before the singing" (p. 165).

PART IV

POPULAR CULTURE AND
RELIGION

ELEVEN

"The Work of God at Filey": Popular Religion in a Yorkshire Fishing Village

POPULAR RELIGION adheres to no one definition; in different settings, in the hands of different people, the amalgam of belief that makes up its theology constantly changes.[1] The religion of the cottage must not be confined to comparisons with the chapel or to a discussion of population shifts from the country to the city, as though the grid of religious and social history moved along a preordained path. While comparison with modern institutional religion illuminates certain aspects of popular belief, it fails to reach those vital areas of experience that provide the most fundamental divide between popular religion and orthodoxy. In conceptualizing the religion of European peasants, Mircea Eliade argued against applying modern standards. "We must recognize," he pointed out, "that their religion is not confined to the historical forms of Christianity, that it still retains a cosmic structure that has been almost entirely lost in the experience of urban Christians."[2] A primary relationship to the cosmos, the basis of all primitive religions, gradually disappeared from modern re-

---

[1] I am indebted to Mr. John C. Crimlisk and his wife, Maisie, of Filey, Yorkshire, for extensive help in retrieving information concerning Filey. Much of the following discussion is based upon books, articles, and photographs lent to me by Mr. Crimlisk. I am also grateful for helpful comments on an earlier draft of this chapter given to me by Professor Karen Fields.

For a definitive discussion of popular religion in England, see James Obelkevich, *Religion and Rural Society* (Oxford: Oxford University Press, 1976), chap. 6.

[2] *The Sacred and the Profane* (New York: Harvest Books, 1959), p. 164.

245

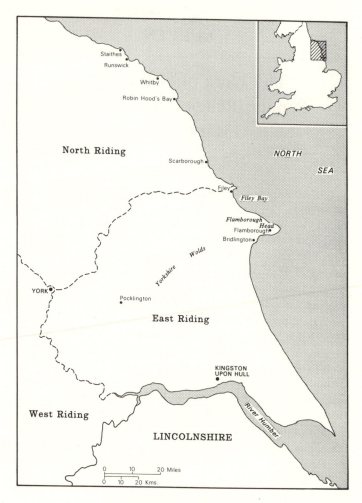

The East Riding of Yorkshire

ligion. Durkheim eloquently defended that quality of primitive belief that defies rational explanation:

> But the believers, the men who lead the religious life and have a direct sensation of what it really is, object to this way of regarding it, saying that it does not correspond to their daily experience. In fact, they feel that the real function of religion is not to make us think, to enrich our knowledge, nor to add to the conceptions which we owe to science . . . but rather, it is to make us act, to aid us to live.[3]

The daily experience of nineteenth-century cottagers often took place in a realm qualitatively different from modern industrial society, a realm in which religious ritual and belief were essential to survival itself. That is not to say that villagers failed to comprehend material change. Their response to the coming of modern society was to adopt multiple layers of consciousness enabling them to participate in both old and new worlds while preserving their attachment to popular culture.

The records of Primitive Methodism therefore provide only a narrow means of access into the world of a fishing village. Sectarian Methodism coexisted with and revitalized the "cosmic structure" of popular religion in Filey, but it was not entirely conterminous with it. Much of the old culture continued to exist alongside aspects of the new, though seldom with the conscious sanction of Primitive Methodism. The fisherfolk had religion in "three layers," an observer once noted: they were ardent Primitive Methodists, they gave the local church its due, and they were steadfastly superstitious.[4] Primitive Methodism took root in Filey because of the basic beliefs it shared with primitive religion: cottage religion, with its emphasis upon the sanctification of the household, democratic

[3] *The Elementary Forms of Religious Life*, J. W. Swain, trans. (New York: The Free Press, 1915), pp. 463–4.

[4] "The Fishermen of old Filey," *Yorkshire Post*, 26 October 1961.

social relations, and inspired theology, syncretized with the superstitions and customs of the village. Primitive Methodism flourished as changes in the fishing industry and the social composition of Filey undermined the popular culture of the fishing community. Cottage religion strengthened the indigenous traditions and belief of villagers while ushering them into modern industrial society.

Since medieval times, history had favored Filey by leaving it alone. The road leading to the village, used for fortification in Roman times, long since lay outside the main network of the county. On the far edge of the township, an Early English church had fallen into similar disrepair. The small village was perched on an awesome cliff overlooking the North Sea; only the experienced native could negotiate the path to and from the sands below. At the beginning of the nineteenth century, the population hovered around five hundred, with a majority of the inhabitants earning their living from the fishing industry. Women outnumbered men in Filey, a fact that betrayed the brutishness of coastal life. Villagers measured their ages by the number of storms since their kinfolk were lost and made room in their cottages for widows and children left homeless by unpredictable gales. "They scowl at strangers with a suspicious eye," wrote Crabbe of the East Coast fisherfolk; strong ties of tradition and belief bound them together in ways that were unfathomable to the outsider.[5]

Fishing was the source of this rigorous insularity and the channel through which Filonians touched a primitive past. The industry kept fishing families in constant communication with the forces of an uncontrollable universe. "Methods and boats" of the East Coast fishery "had changed little since the Viking era" and promised no more ease or success than superstition

[5] Rev. A. N. Cooper, *Across the Broad Acres* [i.e., Yorkshire] (Hull, 1908), pp. 28–9; John Cole, *The History and Antiquities of Filey* (Scarborough, 1828), p. 6; *Victoria History of the County of York* (Oxford: Oxford University Press, 1913), 3:489 (hereafter *VCH*); K. J. Allison, *The East Riding of Yorkshire Landscape*, The Making of the English Landscape Series (London: Hodder & Stoughton, 1976), p. 40.

and folkways could provide.[6] Neither were Filonians open to suggestion from others. "Some charitable summer visitors, and one or two kind neighbours" founded a friendly society for Filey fishermen in 1811, owing to the bad times caused by the Napoleonic wars. But the fishermen inhabited a world different from their philanthropic betters; with no immediate use for the fund, the fishermen refused to make payments.[7] The religion of the nineteenth century would meet with similar disinterest. The fishing families entered the age of improvement with methods of survival and codes of behavior peculiarly their own.

Popular religion encompassed the activities of household, family, and work in Filey. Through shared superstitions, social customs, and holiday celebrations, religion invested these areas of life with a charged "human" and "moral" quality. Religion generated and in turn emanated from the actions of the collectivity:

> On the surface, popular religion was a mass of particulars without logic or a unifying myth. Yet it is possible to infer from the particulars certain general modes of perception and response—the outlines of a collective mentality.[8]

Religion became visible in what Durkheim called "common action": it emerged in the material world of getting a living and maintaining a community. The ways in which Filonians worked and socialized were the basis of religion and thus provide a means of reconstructing the popular culture of Filey.[9]

[6] Arthur Godfrey, *Yorkshire Fishing Fleets* (Skipton: Dalesman Books, 1974), p. 12.

[7] Cole, *History*, pp. 127–8; Paul Davis, *The Old Friendly Societies of Hull* (Hull: Brown & Sons, 1926), p. 17.

[8] Obelkevich, *Religion and Rural Society*, p. 306; Durkheim, *Elementary Forms*, pp. 465–6.

[9] This definition of culture implies a unity of outlook more than common experience *per se*. "The core of culture lies in how people conceptualize their relations to each other—the claims people make on each other, the deferences towards each others claims, and the concerns and caring people have for one

The boats of Filey were at the heart of the fishing culture; rhythms of work as well as social relations within the village depended upon the vessel used by the fishermen. The most common type at Filey, the coble (pronounced "cobble"), was the key to the local character. The simple craft was "nothing more or less than a clinker built [i.e., planked] version of a skin boat" claiming an ancestry stretching back to the Vikings.[10] Like the fisherman, the coble was bold in design but very vulnerable. Small in size (averaging around twenty by five feet) and completely open, the coble was no match for a North Sea storm. Yet the boat came with essential advantages. Only a small craft like the coble could launch out from and land at the shallow beach at Filey; larger boats required a deeper harbor and an easier means of unloading. The coble was particularly well suited to independent in-shore fishing and thus kept the fishermen employed all year round. Unlike fishermen of neighboring villages, Filonians never worked at jobs meant to supplement their earnings from the sea. The limited size of the coble, moreover, permitted a small and therefore more flexible crew. As few as three men could navigate it, and two or three ordinary fishermen (often brothers or in-laws) could afford to buy one. The coble both shaped and responded to the fierce independence of Filey fishermen. Identifiable by its color, the boats from Filey were the gayest and brightest on the East Coast.[11]

---

another." See Gerald M. Sider, "The ties that bind: culture and agriculture, property and propriety in the Newfoundland village fishery," *Social History* 5 (1980), p. 21 and passim.

[10] *The English Coble*, Maritime Monographs and Reports, no. 30, Cdr. J. E. G. McKee, ed. (London: Trustees of the National Maritime Museum, 1978), p. 4. "The word has been in use for over a thousand years, spelt in more ways than it can be pronounced . . . *cuople* is similar to the Celtic *ceubal* (Welsh) and *caubal* (Breton) meaning ferry boat or skiff." Cf. E. Thurston Hopkins, *Small Sailing Craft* (1931), p. 65, quoted in *The English Coble*: "The coble is splendidly English and splendidly unique" (p. iv).

[11] The importance of boat design cannot be overstated. "Generally speaking, types of fishing craft have been adopted to meet specific ecological and economic conditions, both maritime and terrestrial," and thus determine later

Fishing from cobles was punctuated by seasonal work from a second kind of craft, the yawl. Towering over the coble in size and cost, the yawl required a different system of ownership and management: "masters" (who were often part-owners) directed five to seven crewmen on expeditions lasting for weeks or months at a time. The movement of different species of fish dictated the itinerary of the fishermen. "Spring fishing" from yawls opened the fishing year: while storms and frigid temperatures still prevailed, fishermen and a number of wives and children sailed south, often as far as Yarmouth, one hundred forty miles down the coast, to catch cod, ling, skate, haddock, and halibut. Women remained on shore, repairing and treating nets every three weeks, while the fishermen worked out of sight of land. The season lasted from three to four months, enabling the boats to return to Filey "after Good Friday" in time to prepare for the arrival of the herring in June. Then both yawl and coble entered the early season north of Filey; but by September, the fish moved beyond the reach of the smaller boats so that coble fishermen again joined the crews of the yawls. The herring fishing continued at great distances from shore until the end of November. From then until the following spring fishing, the yawls remained at Scarborough. During these winter months, Filey fishermen relied upon earnings from early-morning coble expeditions and periodic ventures in the lively smuggling trade of the East Coast.[12]

Long-standing customs governed the work of both coble and yawl. Personal negotiation and family ties determined the

adoption of technology and expansion of commercial contacts. Shepard Forman, *The Raft Fishermen: Tradition and Change in the Brazilian Peasant Economy* (Bloomington, Indiana: University of Indiana Press, 1970), p. 9. At Filey, cobles "have for centuries been built to no plan except the owner's needs." Ted Gower, comp., *Filey* (Skipton: Dalesman Books, 1977), p. 19; "Craft with a Viking Spirit," *Yorkshire Post*, 20 November 1962; *The English Coble*, p. 41.

[12] Jack Dykes, *Smuggling on the Yorkshire Coast* (Skipton: Dalesman Books, 1978); Godfrey, *Yorkshire Fishing Fleets*, pp. 111–2; George Shaw, *Our Filey Fishermen: with Sketches of their Manners and Customs, Social Habits and Religious Condition* (London, 1867), pp. 110–3; Cole, *History*, pp. 93–7.

composition of yawl crews. Despite his lesser wealth, the fisherman without a share in the yawl still brought nets, lines, and expertise to the larger boat. Yawls also carried one or two cobles contributed by members of the crew. As a cooperative unit, the yawl decided the schedule of its expeditions and the grounds it fished. Together the crew sold its catch and then divided the proceeds by shares. The process of selling, according to outsiders, was "most mysterious"; idiosyncratic manners, symbolic language, and seemingly arbitrary decisions resulted in an exchange that appeared more begrudging than grateful. The fishermen were "a very bold, hardy, robust race of men" not given over to the ways of life on land.[13]

The stalwart fisherman was a member of a large enterprise: his household was the basic unit of work, family, and cultural life in the village and the source of essential assistance. Wives, widows, sisters, and daughters managed every aspect of work outside the boat. "It is a maxim with them," recorded one historian, " 'that a woman at weant work for a man is nea worth yan.' The men have only to catch the fish, their labour, as a rule, being over as soon as the boat touches the sand."[14] Women tanned and repaired nets, made baskets, tended to domestic animals, knitted indestructible guernsey jerseys (some lasted up to forty years), and, most important, greeted the fishermen on the shore in order to haul the fish up the cliff to the village. A visitor to Filey remarked on the extraordinary coordination of activity on the beach, noting that upon the return of the fishermen, "their wives immediately descended with large pitchers of some hot stuff, which, by its smell, might be anything one chose to imagine. They also brought large baskets, which they immediately filled with fish and placed on their heads. Carrying thus the best part of a hundredweight, they toiled up the zigzag [path] to the village. The result," he added, "was that they had good figures and

[13] Rev. Arthur Pettitt, *The Filey Hand-Book* (Sheffield, 1868), pp. 45–7; Cole, *History*, pp. 107–8.

[14] Rev. Arthur Pettitt, *Guide to Filey* (Sheffield, 1868), p. 59.

an upright bearing, but were rather too drudged and weath-
erbeaten for what townspeople would call good looks."[15] Filonians held to a different standard. "Riding the stang," the
archaic nighttime custom of heckling wife-beaters, continued
well into the nineteenth century at Filey. The entire community had a stake in the welfare of a good fisherwoman.[16]

Women also gathered bait, a time-consuming occupation
that demanded "rough and hazardous" travel up and down
the coast. The Filey "flither lasses" were well known by their
distinctive colorful dress and their noticeable *esprit de corps*.
"From December to June these hardy workers ransack the
rocks," a guidebook explained,

> to the Northward, for flithers (limpets). The supply on
> the Brigg is very small, compared with the demand of the
> Fishery. The Gristhorpe rocks afford some assistance, so
> that they, too, are thoroughly cleared to meet the need.
> To shorten the distance, and to reach some portions of
> these rocks at all times, the bait-gatherers descend the cliff
> . . . by means of a rope, fastened, when required, to a very
> small and unsafe-looking stake at the top of the crack
> down which they go. For about forty feet they have to
> hang about this rope, and gain what additional help they
> can by planting their feet against the perpendicular cliff-
> side . . . The fisherwomen, when they have filled their
> three baskets, called "mawns," come up by the same dan-
> gerous means.[17]

[15] Rev. Thomas Mozley, *Reminiscences Chiefly of Towns, Villages and Schools*, 2
vols. (London, 1885), 1:450.

[16] Cole, *History*, p. 144. The economic importance of women in fishing villages
has been noted elsewhere by anthropologists; their role is often central to the
economic management of the industry. "One of the notable features of the
Kelantan peasant life," Raymond Firth pointed out, "is the freedom of women,
especially in economic matters. Not only do they exercise an important influence on the control of the family finances, commonly acting as bankers for
their husbands, but they also engage in independent enterprises, which increase
the family supply of cash." *Malay Fishermen* (London: Kegan Paul, 1946), p.
80.

[17] Pettitt, *Hand-Book*, p. 41.

The "lasses" were in fact as rugged as their relations manning the cobles:

> Five feet five inches in height, square in the shoulder, stalwart and swarthy, of no particular age, for young girls soon became women and the older women retained a wiry youth about them.
>
> Barefooted or wearing what could only by courtesy be called shoes (these for the sharper parts of the coast), kilted in coarse woollen, dull red, dark blue, or grey, jacketed in some indescribable upper garment that could hardly be called a coat, still less anything else, ladened with a creel, armed with a knife, crowned with a head gear in the shape of a bonnet, but tilted first over the keen eyes, round part topmost, and black curtains flapping over back hair in a double knot behind—such was the picture of the "flither lass."

The flither girls did not hesitate in demonstrating the traits of native character and clannish loyalty owned by all Filonians:

> Her manners were of the rough and ready description, her dialect a lingo not to be understood of the inland people, but having a cadence of its own. . . . It was a primitive dialect, full of keen idioms, and strong descriptive words, with a dash of salt-water phrases and remarkable capacities of objurgation. He would be a bold man . . . who could stand for five minutes the fire of a Filey flither girl's tongue, even if not enforced by a sprinkling of empty shells from the collective forces of the sisterhood.[18]

Fishergirls rarely married out of the fishing community. The only departure from a native sisterhood resulted from seasonal fishings, when crewmen married women from neighboring coastal villages. So much interdependence in social and work relations created a highly endogamous community, manage-

[18] "The 'Flither Girls,' " *Scarborough Mercury*, 2 July 1958.

254

able only through the application of a vast array of nicknames.[19]

A panoply of popular religious belief bound together community and family life in Filey. Through holiday observances, the village marked the passing of fishing seasons and registered its plea for good fortune. Christmas was a time of important preparation for the coming year; a program of superstitions, customs, and traditions ensured that the fisherman's household remained intact. Several weeks before the holiday, women initiated the season by engaging in a ritualized form of begging. The holiday gave occasion for palliating the unequal distribution of wealth in the village, a gesture especially appreciated during the inactive months of deepest winter:

> The lower order of females [carry] from door to door little square boxes of pasteboard, in which is placed a wax doll, as an image of Christ, surrounded by evergreens, with apples or oranges. The boxes are called *Vessel cups*. The women sing a carol, and are rewarded with a few halfpence: to send them away empty is to forfeit the luck of the whole year.

The women acted as liaisons between the fishing families and the rest of the village, reaffirming traditional social relations between classes while obtaining money for seasonal celebrations. The wealthier classes shared in the ritual, recognizing that their luck, too, depended upon joining in the exchange.[20]

The domestic celebrations of Christmas Eve similarly strengthened the fishing household. Every action throughout the holidays carried import for the season: the yule candle (usually a gift from the chandler) and the yule clog, if handled properly, brought a year of good luck. "A fragment of the [clog] thrown into the fire is said to quell the raging storm," according to custom. Assembling at table, cutting the pie, and

[19] Gower, *Filey*, p. 16; A. N. Cooper, *Filey and Its Church* (Filey, 1889), p. 40.
[20] Cole, *History*, p. 136.

snuffing the candles also demanded careful execution. No act was performed "before the proper time," which occurred only when all members of the family gave their solemn attention. The united household, assembled in its entirety only on such special occasions, conferred good fortune upon the fisherman.[21]

The customs of Christmas Day reaffirmed the importance of the woman's place in the household while honoring the role of the fisherman. On that morning, women belonged at home:

> They were . . . very particular when Christmas morning arrived, to allow no person to go out of the house till the threshold had been consecrated by the entrance of a male, and should one of the opposite sex come in, the event causes the utmost horror and alarm. On no account would they give a light out of the house, or throw out the ashes, or even sweep up the dust, there being, as they believed, no chance of a good fishing to such persons as committed those practices, and wilfully acted against their own interests.

Restricted behavior was unknown to flither girls and fishwives except for these moments; their deference to custom proved its importance. All awaited the dramatic entrance of the fisherman, who reenacted a return to domestic security after a safe expedition.[22]

Filonians also celebrated holidays directly related to the fishing calendar. Just before the spring season in February, fishermen and their families observed important preparatory customs. The yawls left Scarborough sometime in January and received extensive "fitting out" at Filey prior to sailing. Meanwhile, masters and fishermen assembled their equipment and crews on shore and, once employment was secured, celebrations began. On the Sunday before departure, "Boat Sunday," festivities took place, attended by "all [the fishermen's] friends

[21] Ibid., pp. 136–7.
[22] Shaw, *Our Filey Fishermen*, p. 11.

from the neighbouring villages" who wished to "bid them farewell." On the eve of departure later that week, each boat crew sent a piece of sea-beef to selected friends to whom they, in turn, wished good will. The fishermen finally joined their respective households for a last supper, when "those who are going away and those who remain meet to enjoy good cheer." The various assemblies of old and new "business" relations, as well as kin, eased tension created by the regrouping and selection of crews. Farewell suppers made way for amicable relations during and after the fishermen's absence.[23]

The abbreviated household engaged in customs that revealed latent attitudes towards other members of the community while reinforcing the solidarity of the fishing families. With the heads of their families away at sea, the young men of Filey naturally assumed greater responsibility. Ironically, one of their first "duties" entailed prank playing: "on the third Saturday night after the boats sailed for the Yarmouth fishing," the boys of the village "seized all the unemployed wagons and carts they could find and drag[ged] them to the cliff top, leaving them there to be taken away by the respective proprietors on the following morning." According to the villagers, this act "drove the herrings into the nets." In fact, the prank was aimed at local traders, a middling class distinct from the poorer fishing families of the village. As the only members of the family who enjoyed some exemption from business relations in the village, the boys were free to show the hostility that the fisherfolk felt towards the traders. The boys' actions spoke for their absent fathers, who supposedly gained from the trick against the merchants.[24]

As an elaborate system of unifying custom and belief, popular religion flourished outside the Filey Church. "Happy they would be," complained a local antiquarian of the fishermen, "if the many providential deliverances they experience made

[23] Cole, *History*, p. 143. For an excellent study of ritual in social and economic relations of a fishing village, see Gerald M. Sider, "Christmas Mumming and the New Year in Outport Newfoundland," *Past and Present* 71 (1976): 102–25.
[24] Shaw, *Our Filey Fishermen*, p. 15.

a suitable impression on them. These men see the works of the Lord and his wonders in the deep in the highest degree." The Parish Church, meanwhile, offered few attractions: besides registering births, marriages, and deaths, its custodians seldom saw fisherfolk cross its threshold. St. Oswald's occupied a suitably well removed spot some distance from the village. While the original Filey settlement (including the fishermen's cottages) lay along the shore and spread towards the south and westward, the Church stood north of the village behind the ravine and in fact fell outside the boundary of the East Riding. Its remoteness worked its way into a local saying. If a fisherman were near death (and hence on his way to the grave), his friends would acknowledge it by remarking, "He will soon be in the North Riding."[25] The expression served as a euphemism for the Church as well as for death itself. Nineteenth-century religious historians had harsher though similarly perceptive words for the institution. "So far from exerting any practical influence on the lives of the bulk of the fishermen," one fulminated, "[the Church] might as well have been in another world as in another Riding."[26]

Neither could Wesleyan Methodists, upon their arrival in 1806, heal the breach between formal religion and the people. Hecklers greeted a Wesleyan street preacher "with a volley of dried fish" on one occasion and, on another, forced a pig into a prayer meeting. Popular support did not follow this routine opposition. A society finally formed in 1810, but remained small even after years of proselytizing. When the group built a chapel in 1811, a member of Parliament donated the funds while a local gentleman gave the land for the venture. The Old Methodists ultimately represented a sector of the middle class that withdrew from the Established Church, as well as from the fishing culture, through organized religion.[27]

Primitive Methodists initially encountered similar resistance

---

[25] Cooper, *Across the Broad Acres*, p. 4; Cole, *History*, pp. 107–8.

[26] H. B. Kendall, *The History of the Primitive Methodist Church*, 2 vols. (London, n.d.), 1:103.

[27] Shaw, *Our Filey Fishermen*, pp. 16–8; *Rambles About Filey* (London, 1867), pp. 18–9. The membership of the society was numbered at fifteen in 1823.

and lack of support among the fishing families. While their missions proceeded apace in nearby Scarborough and Flamborough, Filey remained unimpressed. Unlike the neighboring villages, Filey constituted a more homogeneous fishing community that was much harder to penetrate. "[Filey] had been frequently attempted by our preachers and as frequently given up without hope of success," reported William Howcroft, an itinerant farm laborer, "until about the beginning of March, 1823, when one soul was awakened under brother Peart, then in the Bridlington branch."[28] Experience had taught Primitive Methodists never to question the mechanics of a revival; as there had been no particular explanation for Filey's resistance, there need not be a reason for success. But beneath the revival lay factors generating an awareness of change in the fishing village. The acceptance of Primitive Methodism marked the entrance of Filey into a new age.

The most notable change in Filey after 1800 was a distinct rise in population. Between 1801 and 1811, the village grew slightly but significantly from 505 to 579; during the next ten years, the population multiplied by 33.5 percent to 773. In the space of twenty years, the village had increased by over 53 percent. Reasons for this growth, which seems to have occurred primarily within the fishing community, are difficult to determine. Clearly the growing demand for food in nearby towns and in London affected the East Coast fishing industry. The Yarmouth fishery expanded after 1813, when dealers agreed to supply London merchants with "great quantities of fish." Filey fishermen responded by intensifying their work from cobles, while the number of yawls remained the same. The decades after the Napoleonic wars marked the height of small-scale fishing in the numerous villages along the Yorkshire coast. In the Northeast, Runswick, Robin Hood's Bay, Flamborough, and Filey shared in a general rise in activity.[29]

---

[28] "On the Work of God at Filey," *Primitive Methodist Magazine*, 1823, p. 256 (hereafter *PMM*).

[29] Godfrey, *Yorkshire Fishing Fleets*; Dr. Cortis, *An Historical Account of the Herring Fishery on the North-East Coast of England* (Filey, 1858), p. 4. I owe thanks to Mr. J. Crimlisk for bringing this pamphlet to my attention. *Second Report of*

Less visible changes altered the nature of the industry itself. Since the late eighteenth century, the government had encouraged the spring herring fishery at Yarmouth and other ports by rewarding bounties for quantities of fish caught within stipulated dates. The system did not apply to fishing at Filey, however, until around 1820, when the Edinburgh Board of Fishery introduced another schedule of payments for summer fishing. Under the new arrangement, fishermen obtained payment for every ton of fish caught within ninety days between June and October. Boats remained at sea almost constantly, returning only once "at the end of [every] week to deliver their Ling and Cod to the fish salters for cure." At each landing, crews also sold other kinds of fish, such as turbot, halibut, and haddock, "on the sands to the highest bidder." But their greatest efforts were devoted to fulfilling quotas and meeting deadlines. The Board of Fishery agreement, added to the spring fishing at Yarmouth, brought the total amount of time occupied by contracted fishing to more than half the year.[30]

The threat to traditional fishing challenged the customs and folkways of the village. The bounty system imposed a different standard of time upon the fishermen, who were accustomed to consulting nature and crew mates in determining schedules. Their work habits defied external authority. Informed by secret lore and family tradition, the "old hands" on board imposed their own set of rules that promised to protect them from changing times. Line-baiting and sailing preparations "would stop if someone mentioned a pig," and "if a fisherman met a pig on his way down to the boats he would turn back and refuse to go." At sea, fishermen took the time to insert coins into the corks of the nets, in order "to show that they can *pay for the fish*." A multitude of customary laws shielded the Filey fishermen against regimentation.[31]

the Association for the Relief of the Manufacturing and Laboring Poor, relative chiefly to the General Supply of fish in the metropolis and the interior, 1815; VCH, 3:489.

[30] Arthur M. Samuel, The Herring: Its Effect on the History of Britain (London, 1918), pp. 156–61; Cole, History, pp. 95–6; Cortis, "Herring Fishery," p. 4.

[31] Shaw, Our Filey Fishermen, pp. 12–3; Cooper, Across the Broad Acres, p. 23; Gower, Filey, p. 16; Forman, The Raft Fishermen, pp. 65, 72.

Villagers on shore had less control over new circumstances. Changes in seasonal fishing upset the rhythms of village customs and diminished the importance of the natural calendar. Fishing families could not avoid admitting new factors of time and alien authority into the social life of the village. The growth of the fishing population undermined their traditional ways of working and sharing. For a longer period of the year, fisherwomen were left in charge of a community that was becoming increasingly unsettled. Fishing families struggled harder to survive from fishing alone. The wealth of the community did not grow with the population, proven by the unchanging number of yawls at Filey. A greater number of fishermen and their sons competed for places on the yawls; those who remained in the village during the Yarmouth fishery depended upon the less remunerative work from cobles. As the demands of industrial towns transformed the fishing industry of the East Coast, the quality of economic and social life in Filey changed. The collective system of popular religion and customs began to disintegrate.[32]

Primitive Methodism united the fishing community against the pressures of change by harnessing the form and content of popular culture. Preaching was not the best means of communicating attitudes and values championed by popular religion; rumor, on the other hand, could convey an essential hint of insubordination and covert derision. A yarn concerning an exchange between Primitive Methodists and the local coast guard officer, Mr. Gordon, played a large part in winning the favor of the fisherfolk. A band of preachers had gone fishing late at night. Mr. Gordon, in his role as customs officer, was out in search of smugglers. He caught sight of the coble in the distance and hollered, "Who goes there, what have you gotten?" The preachers remained unruffled and called out in

[32] On the transition of traditional fishing communities into modern fishing centers, see Chris Baks and Els Postel-Coster, "Fishing Communities on the Scottish East Coast: Traditions in a Modern Setting," *Those Who Live From the Sea: A Study in Maritime Anthropology*, American Ethnological Society Monograph no. 62, M. Estellie Smith, ed. (St. Paul, Minn.: West Publishing Co., 1977), pp. 23–40.

somber tones, "The water of life!" Gordon fled in fear. "The story got out," recorded one preacher, "and greatly amused the fishermen, who long after used to hail Gordon with, 'Well maister, what sort of prize did ye tak when ye met t' Ranter Parson?' " The incident forged an alliance between the preachers and the people against a superior proven, in the eyes of both parties, to be a fool.[33]

With the arrival of "Praying Johnny" Oxtoby, cultural and class distinctions became clearer. The "rustic evangelist, whose prayers and homely exhortations were couched in the broad East-Riding dialect, [became] the chief outstanding figure" in the revival.[34] Oxtoby captured the attention of the fishing community and "laid bare" the tenets of cottage religion. "You mun shout," a converted fisherman explained to his sister, "it's all a matter of shouting." Filonians readily adopted boisterous practices that earned them the notorious epithet of "Ranters." "A great many more were awakened, and stirred up to seek the Lord," reported a preacher after the coming of Oxtoby. But with no Primitive Methodist society to join (for "Praying Johnny" had not established one), some converts yielded to the entreaties of local Wesleyans. A class apart from the fisherfolk, the Old Methodists threatened to appropriate the popular revival. Others in the village recognized the danger:

> ... some friends in the town who were well-wishers to our cause, though not joined with us, being grieved to see the Old Methodists entering into our labours, and gathering the fruits, sent off to Bridlington with all speed, to solicit brother Oxtoby to return, desiring him to stay with them a few days, to assist in getting souls into liberty and form a society.

Soon installed in various cottages around Filey, Oxtoby launched a revival in which "souls were awakened every day."[35]

---

[33] Shaw, *Our Filey Fishermen*, p. 20.

[34] Kendall, *History*, 2: 106.

[35] "On the Work of God at Filey," p. 256; Cooper, *Across the Broad Acres*, p. 224.

As a popular preacher, "Praying Johnny" Oxtoby celebrated all the traits of a hardy, self-made Yorkshireman. Born in 1767 at Little Givendale, near Pocklington, Oxtoby was still very young when his family was forced to leave their small farm. His parents sent him to live with an uncle in nearby Warter, where he was raised "in the midst of very humble surroundings." Oxtoby's education was meagre. After a short stint at the village school, he began to work as an agricultural laborer and earned a small but regular wage. He attended the village Church (but never got "true religion") and developed the habit of steadily saving a small portion of his salary each payday. By 1804 (after over twenty years), Oxtoby could call himself "the master of his own movements." At just this time, he had a spiritual crisis. Having encountered travelling Wesleyan Methodists in a nearby village, Oxtoby began to ruminate about religion and finally experienced conversion under a sermon entitled "Saving Faith." His transformation moved him to visit every home in the surrounding area "to talk and pray with the families." Gradually he broke down opposition until nearly every house expected the regular appearance of "Praying Johnny." According to some, Warter "began to wear a different aspect," and finally the villagers built a chapel on land donated by Oxtoby himself. In 1818, Oxtoby left Warter to travel through Lincolnshire and the East Riding with several other Wesleyan lay evangelists. During this last decade of his life, Oxtoby transferred his allegiance to the Primitive Methodists. As their missionary, he entered Filey in 1823.[36]

Oxtoby's way would not be easy. Filonians resented the condescension of ecclesiastics and other professionals, whose educated expertise lacked practicality and profundity. In the case of medical doctors, for example, such talent did more to alienate than impress. Though failing to comprehend the meas-

[36] "Memoir of John Oxtoby," PMM, 1831, pp. 9–13, 44–8, 142–8; G. Shaw, The Life of John Oxtoby ("Praying Johnny") (Hull, 1894); Kendall, History, 1:365–70.

uring stick of the fishing village, an unsympathetic observer
described their predilections with accuracy:

> If a doctor announced that he had studied by the light of
> the moon, or that for many years he had carefully read
> the stars, he was considered wonderfully clever. But the
> best recommendation was that he had not studied at all,
> but received his knowledge by a certain divine intuition:
> thus to be a seventh Son was to be born a man of healing;
> but the seventh son of a seventh son was an infallible
> physician.[37]

Similar standards applied to travelling theologians: their
claims to authority would require support from some agent
greater than mankind, as well as a sense of the greater good
of the entire village. Individual achievement, personal virtue,
and feminine humility would not suit the needs of fishermen
and flither girls.

Oxtoby offered the kind of expertise most valued by the
fishermen and women. Without much education or wide
travel, he had arrived at a general *modus operandi* for trials of
life. When Primitive Methodist founder Hugh Bourne met
Oxtoby in 1820, he "was surprised at his having attained so
deep experience with so little information":

> In his dialect [Oxtoby] was very provincial; and much of
> his preaching consisted in giving accounts of what he had
> seen of the work of God when he was at this place, and
> that place; and as the work was frequently breaking out
> under him, he was constantly furnished with something
> fresh.[38]

Oxtoby was not without weaknesses; but the very defects decried by Bourne were championed by natives of Filey. The
village responded to his strong language, his prophetic utter-
ances, and his skill in the art of healing. According to legend,

[37] Shaw, *Our Filey Fishermen*, p. 13.
[38] "Remarks by Hugh Bourne," *PMM*, 1831, pp. 46–7.

the highly respected minister John Flesher once asked Oxtoby "why the results of their preaching were so different." Oxtoby supposedly answered, "Oh, thou leads the people to the tree of knowledge, and I leads them to the tree of life." To Oxtoby, religion evolved from experience, not rational exegesis. His authentic theology reasserted the tenets of primitive religion.[39]

Filey immediately hailed Oxtoby as a prophet. A mere visit or word from the singular figure transformed bystanders into followers and generated a powerful spirit of community among the fishing families. In each instance, Oxtoby reminded villagers of their role in a collective enterprise. His talent for house-to-house visiting proved a valuable asset in the fishing community. Like Filonian customs affirming ties between households, visiting maintained a sense of mutual concern. Oxtoby's power to heal, moreover, at once generated and ben-efited from the impetus of the religious revival. When visiting a fisherwoman whose legs were "stiff and hard, as though they had not a joint in them," Oxtoby uttered a characteristic proph-ecy. "Thou wilt get better," he intoned, "and be able to walk as ever thou did, for the Lord has told me so." His straight-forward message from above brought forth a quick recovery below. Soon "she could run up and down the cliff with as heavy a load upon her head as any fisherman's wife in the place."[40] The healing served the entire community while en-hancing the appeal of the extraordinary preacher.

Oxtoby's prophecies also lent a sense of immortality to the collective spirit of the village. Seeing a young man standing idly in a doorway, Oxtoby approached him and placed his hand on his shoulder, saying "Thou must get converted, for the Lord has a great work for thee to do." Oxtoby's pro-nouncement came true: John Wyvill (b. 1801) attended a prayer meeting with a friend that evening and caught the mantle of the popular preacher. "Both of them being excellent singers," Wyvill's obituary explained, "they assisted the

[39] Kendall, *History*, 1:368.
[40] Shaw, *Our Filey Fishermen*, pp. 24-5.

preacher . . . and in a short time were both converted to God."
Wyvill maintained a fast commitment to Filey; he soon became
an outstanding local preacher, and when the Connexion offered to promote him to the itinerancy, he declined. His identification with the fishing community was an inseparable part
of his work in the ministry.[41]

Primitive Methodism preserved the household customs of
popular religion. "There has always been a strange social element in the Church-life of Filey," a minister observed some
years later, "and a marked domesticity in its devotions."
Though a chapel was built at the end of 1823, more souls were
saved in class meetings (always held in houses) than in the
modern sanctuary.[42] Visiting preachers commented on domestic rituals peculiar to Filey. The fishing families established
the custom of holding a prayer meeting on the eve of the
funeral "at the house where the corpse is laid." "In many
instances, the results have been most beneficial upon the
friends and acquaintances of the departed," noted one
preacher, "and many conversions have taken place in connection with them."[43] At the center of the fishing culture,
the household and its religion continued to promote autonomy and distinguish the fishing community from the world
around it.

[41] "Memoir of John Wyvill," *PMM*, 1866, pp. 542–5; Shaw, *Our Filey Fishermen*, p. 35–7. Wyvill always remembered his prophetic beginnings. Upon the
death of Oxtoby, he eulogized the preacher in the flyleaf of his class book: "A
saint indeed was Father John / And humbly with his God he walk'd; / He lived
by faith in Christ the Son, / And daily with his Saviour talk'd; / And now he's
gone His face to see, / A fadeless crown to him is given; / May I my Jesus
faithful serve, / And meet John Oxtoby in heaven. Amen." [Shaw, *Our Filey
Fishermen*, p. 36.]

[42] Rev. R. Harrison, quoted in Kendall, *History*, 2:106.

[43] Shaw, *Our Filey Fishermen*, p. 50. The fishermen also adopted the hymn
"There is a land of pure delight," by Isaac Watts, as their own. Other customs
followed at funerals included the use of women pallbearers for the services of
deceased women and the superstitious practice of leaving a chapel window
open during the service itself. See "Memoir of Jenkinson Haxby," *PMM*, 1909,
pp. 238–9; Gower, *Filey*, p. 18.

Popular evangelicalism thus enabled Filey fishermen and their families to defend themselves against profound changes taking place in the life of the village. The next decade witnessed an abrupt curtailment of growth: between 1821 and 1831, the population of Filey rose by only 3.8 percent, reflecting the paralysis of the fishing industry as well as the beginning of depopulation in agricultural areas surrounding the village.[44] Though operating as extended families, the households of fishermen were nevertheless small. Faced with harder times, family networks became more important as a means of controlling economic activity. The disappearance of drinking customs occurred not only because of sectarian strictures; culture and economy were inextricably linked in the fishing village, and the decline of drinking (at least in the form of public ritual) indicated increasing concern about the performance of productive roles.[45] Through Primitive Methodism, fishing families exchanged certain customs for "new" ones. By enforcing the cooperative aims of the household economy, religion contributed to the economic as well as the cultural survival of the village.

Decisive changes in the fishing industry occurred throughout Yorkshire during the 1830s. The use of trawlers revolutionized the industry in coastal towns. Their appearance marked the beginning of large-scale capitalization of fishing: new larger boats demanded greater investment, bigger crews, and deeper harbors. Small villages like Filey, as well as Staithes, Scarborough, and Whitby, could not compete with wealthier ports more advantageously located. Though Filey eventually adopted larger yawls (the smaller ones were totally abandoned

[44] VCH, 3:489; Allison, The East Riding Landscape, pp. 148–51. I also owe thanks to Mr. J. Crimlisk for his summary of the Filey Census of 1841 and for details concerning the households of his fishing ancestors.

[45] "One of the most common arguments among kinsmen concerns excess drinking, since drunkenness can prevent a fisherman from going to sea and can result in a loss of income for his entire family." Forman, The Raft Fishermen, pp. 85–6. On Filey drinking customs and their decline, see Shaw, Our Filey Fishermen, p. 50.

by 1850), lack of a good harbor prohibited the village from fully entering the new era of fishing. The expansion of the industry subjected the small fisherman to an uncompromising system of free enterprise. During the next two decades, Filey fishermen confronted hard times that were, like the ever-present elements, beyond their control.[46]

Religion remained as a source of power and a means of resistance. Against the domination of big boats, Primitive Methodism channeled the independent spirit of the fishermen into a defiant "work stoppage" called Sabbitarianism. For the first decade following the arrival of Primitive Methodism, the entire fishing community, converts included, continued to work on Sunday. The traditional method of fishing demanded irregular periods of work and leisure, and Sundays necessarily went unobserved. Fishermen on large boats likewise never rested on Sunday. According to a contemporary, "Their masters justify their sinful practice by asserting that there is no Sunday in ten fathoms of water, particularly as they are out of sight of land." Given the pressures of financial need and time, neither fishermen nor masters wanted to lose a day at sea. Eventually, however, Primitive Methodist fishermen chafed at the practice. Their motives sprang from a mixture of piety and obstinancy: the first demonstration against Sunday fishing occurred during the spring season, when most Filey men migrated south to Yarmouth in larger boats belonging to wealthier masters who were not, obviously, Primitive Methodists. Three Primitive fishermen (two of them related by marriage) arranged to borrow a small yawl requiring

[46] The main purpose of fishing regulations, according to one authority, was to protest the injustices forced upon "the poorer classes of our fishermen," with their "qualities of originality, resourcefulness, and hardihood." The "capitalisation of the industry" proved to be incompatible with the small fishing village. See James Johnstone, *British Fisheries: Their Administration and their Problems. A Short Account of the Origin and Growth of British Sea-Fishery Authorities and Regulations* (London, 1905), p. vii; E. W. H. Holdsworth, *Deep-Sea Fishing and Fishing Boats* (London, 1874), pp. 250-71; F. G. Aflalo, *The Sea-Fishing Industry* (London, 1904), pp. 225, 254-6.

only a crew of three. They likewise travelled to Yarmouth, "and to the astonishment of the others," they "ceased to desecrate the Lord's day." Their protest inspired others. Soon three more fishermen (sons of one of the pioneers) found a small boat, named it the *Three Brothers*, "and henceforth . . . [kept] the Sabbath, without fear of vexation from owners or any one else." Divine Providence settled the issue for the entire Primitive Methodist community when the *Three Brothers* competed against two Scarborough boats and won, 110,000 herrings to 25,000, even though they had sat out on Sunday. Wesleyans later followed suit and likewise ceased Sunday fishing, but posterity credited the Primitives with the courage and special favor that made possible their revolt. "If there was twea [two] herrings in the sea," a local proverb claimed, "Ranter Jack would be seaar to git yan [one] on em."[47]

Along with changes in the fishing industry, Filey also witnessed the transformation of the family economy. As coordinators of the multifarious activities taking place on shore and as overseers of family finances, women felt the changes in the village most acutely. Unemployment forced their sons to seek work outside fishing, and the declining wealth of the community threatened the welfare of their children and village widows. New fishing methods, schedules, and boats displaced women from their traditional roles as assistants on the sands and in marketing. That fishermen began to join benefit societies suggests that customary support systems for men as well as women were no longer operable. As the traditional community altered its behavior, women lost their power to influence the well-being of the village.[48]

[47] Shaw, *Our Filey Fishermen*, pp. 44–7. See also David R. M. White, "Environment, Technology, and Time-Use Patterns in the Gulf Coast Shrimp Fishery," *Those Who Live From the Sea*, pp. 195–214. Religious historians and anthropologists have long debated the illusive "work ethic" of the fishing village, weighing evidence of Sabbath-breaking against charges of indolence. See Sider, "Christmas Mumming," p. 108.

[48] In other settings, women have been instrumental in controlling financial matters in the modernization of fishing communities. See B. Christensen, "Mo-

The link between cottage religion and popular tradition
enabled women to assert control of the household in a new
way. In the home, they oversaw the traditions and customs
preserved by the new religion, now fortified by the additional
observances of Primitive Methodism. In the community, they
emerged as avid missionary workers. Women again acted as
liaisons between the fishing families and the wealthier classes
of the village; their role in popular customs at Christmas now
became more systematic and continual under the auspices of
Primitive Methodism. Collecting money from around the village, the fisherwomen then redistributed it throughout the
fishing community. During the winter, they gave "away large
sums . . . while visiting the sick, the aged, and the poor," and
they took up additional subscriptions for widows and children
following disasters at sea.[49] The financial affairs of Primitive
Methodism fully involved women in the economy of the village; as their role as producers diminished, they reasserted
themselves as managers of the welfare of the entire fishing
community.

While other villages produced local female preachers, Filey's
leading sister was known as the "Queen of the missionary
collectors." Ann Cowling, later known as "Nanny Jenk," was
born at Filey in 1804. Her introduction to religion occurred
in 1823, when she heard "Praying Johnny" Oxtoby preach at
a cottage service. She soon became a class leader (a position
she retained until her death) and remained active in the society
throughout her twenties. At twenty-nine, she married another
Primitive Methodist, John Jenkinson, a fisherman who shared
her commitment to the Ranters' cause. With a household of
her own, Nanny was able to extend her involvement: she

tor Power and Women Power: Technological and Economic Change Among
the Fanti Fishermen of Ghana," *Those Who Live From the Sea*, pp. 71–95. Ultimately, women were displaced by the new techniques of fishing. For a critical
interpretation, see Audrey Chapman Smock, "The Impact of Modernization
on Women's Position in the Family in Ghana," *Sexual Stratification*, Alice Schlegel, ed. (New York: Columbia University Press, 1977), pp. 192–214.

[49] Shaw, *Our Filey Fishermen*, p. 51.

opened her house to visiting preachers "and . . . any of the friends" who needed assistance. More important, she now could claim kinship with a considerable part of the Primitive Methodist community. Her own family, first of all, joined the chapel following her conversion, including her brother Thomas, also a fisherman, who later became a boat partner with her husband, John. On the Jenkinson side, the family tree grew to gigantic proportions: John's father, William (b. 1783), also converted to Primitive Methodism under Oxtoby and "immediately opened his house for the entertainment of the ministers." As a humble fisherman, "Willy" refused all positions except trustee and doorkeeper of the local chapel. Several of his sons, however, became leading spokesmen of the community. George Jenkinson (Nanny's brother-in-law) acted as class leader and local preacher. At his death, old father Willy boasted of no fewer than one hundred Primitive Methodist relatives. The Jenkinsons wielded considerable influence in Filey and together exercised control over the character of the religion they practiced. As an historian remarked of Flamborough, a similarly endogamous fishing community, "A preacher must be careful what he says about the people, or he will soon get into trouble."[50]

Nanny Jenk profited from this vast network, but connections alone could not provide the legendary sums she collected in her missionary work. The key to her success lay in her acumen as a fishwife. When William Clowes visited Filey on a preaching tour, he discovered the mechanics of her method:

> . . . the contributions were good, and in Mrs. Jenkinson's missionary box there was about £8. It was some time before I could find out how our good sister contrived to get so much money. At last I found that she was highly esteemed by the fishermen, and that engaging [her] to pray for them while they were fishing, they pledged themselves

[50] Ibid., p. 30; "Memoir of William Jenkinson," *PMM*, 1866, pp. 566–7. Henry Woodcock, *Piety Among the Peasantry* (London, 1889), p. 62.

to give her for a missionary box a per centage over a certain quantity of fish caught.[51]

Superstition, kinship, and faith melded in a strange practice that resembled missionary collecting only in name. Nanny Jenk no doubt added a note of intimidation to her persuasive appeals on the sands.

The retreat to small-scale fishing and the continuing independence of popular culture simply pulled Filey fishing families out of the path of the Victorian age. Alongside the fishing village, another "culture" was growing: in 1835, Birmingham solicitor J. W. Unett began "the systematic development" of Filey as a resort area. Enormous villas and stuccoed terrace houses appeared along the cliff top south of the fishermen's cottages, as prosperous merchants from the West Riding and Hull secured their places on "The Crescent" overlooking the sea. When the railway reached Filey in 1846–47, it benefited tourism more than the fishing industry. Flither girls lined up on the platform to board the train for Scarborough (charitable ladies often provided their fares), but they seldom stopped to pose for "the hand-camera." Filey fisherfolk, unlike their more compromising neighbors at Whitby and Flamborough, "were a class apart" from their modern-day counterparts. Their distinctive dress, their refusal to board the "smacks" (trawlers), and their ancestry stretching back for generations marked them as dogged survivors of a time gone past.[52]

Filey fishing families also clung to their old religion. Their only gesture in the direction of modernity appeared in 1880, when a group of singing fishermen formed and began to travel throughout the North. "The Filey Fishermen" met with spectacular success, even though their message resonated less in the great towns than in their native village. "They just ring out the old experimental gospel," reported one admirer, along

---

[51] Shaw, *Our Filey Fishermen*, p. 31.

[52] Aflalo, *The Sea-Fishing Industry*, p. 225; Ernest Dade, "The Old Yorkshire Yawls," *Mariner's Mirror* 20 (1934): 186; Allison, *The East Riding Landscape*, pp. 248–9.

with "the old Methodist [hymn] favourites" and "many modern sacred songs which smack of the sea," such as "Does your anchor hold?" and "Throw out the life-line." The Fishermen carried on the work at Filey, remindful of the inscription on John Oxtoby's grave:

> For chronicles like these may in an age
> Be lost, and in oblivion pass away.[53]

[53] Kendall, *History*, 1:370 (epitaph by William Howcroft); "The Filey Fishermen," *PMM*, 1905, pp. 153–4.

TWELVE

Afterword

OVER THE COURSE OF a half-century, popular religion rendered visible the experiences and values of laboring women and men. Through preaching, sectarian laborers repudiated church and chapel, redressed the errors of a new industrial society, and sanctified the world of the cottage. Gradually, their strategy declined in extensiveness and power. The conditions that fostered cottage religion were changing as rural England assumed a different face. New religious ideologies lent a different meaning to their actions and new political activity revised and extended a critique of industrial capitalism. The shape of class relations in villages and towns finally altered the dialogue between cottagers and their contemporaries.

The decline of cottage religion stemmed from gradual changes in the wider context of Victorian society as well as in sect organization. The prosperity of the mid-century inevitably affected the dynamics of evangelicalism. The most obvious manifestation of increasing wealth was widespread chapel building, especially among Primitive Methodists. In 1847, their societies met in 1,421 chapels and 3,340 rented chapels and rooms (or houses). By 1868, chapels outnumbered rented places, 3,235 to 3,034. The largest growth in new chapels built occurred between 1850 and 1879, peaking between 1863 and 1872, when 1,191 chapels were erected. The Potteries, the birthplace of Primitive Methodism, boasted as many as thirty-one chapels by 1900. Though bricks and mortar never precluded sectarian practices and belief, the trend toward institutionalization was unmistakable in a more complex administration.[1]

[1] H. B. Kendall, *History of the Primitive Methodist Church*, 2 vols. (London, n.d.),

Numerical growth contributed to the development of formal administration and greater centralization among the sects. The Primitive Methodist Connexion expanded from a membership of 16,394 to one of 75,967 between 1821 and 1841, and hierarchical management followed the rise in adherents and chapels. A growing number of administrative officers, a prolific London-based publishing house, and even the monthly magazine reflected new concerns and new wealth. Bible Christians experienced a similar growth in organizational sophistication. While the traditional division between urban evangelism in London and cottage religion in the West Country continued, the balance between chapel and cottage had tipped. In their struggle for worldly recognition, the sects were beginning to resemble the established institutions they once criticized.[2]

Sheer numbers and chapel building did not necessarily spell the end of cottage religion, but continuing industrialization and urbanization inevitably encouraged formalization as village evangelists came in contact with large towns. As early as 1824, Primitive Methodists remarked on the difficulties created by urban populations, constant immigration, and the confusion of city neighborhoods. Preacher Nathaniel West advised itinerants to draw up maps, charts, and visitation records, which, no matter how simple, pointed to new administrative control.[3] Small villages no longer exercised the same influence on town religion; often such localities became satellites of urban centers, and chapels, like other village institutions, took cues from larger centers. So fundamental an innovation as the railway affected relationships between country and town. Though influence flowed in both directions, patterns of communication were never again the same.[4]

2:456. On the trend towards denominational status, see James Obelkevich, *Religion and Rural Society* (Oxford: Clarendon Press, 1976), pp. 248–58.

[2] Alan D. Gilbert, *Religion and Society in Industrial England* (London: Longman, 1976), p. 31.

[3] "Advice to Travelling Preachers," *Primitive Methodist Magazine*, 1824, pp. 73–4.

[4] At Belper, for example, the North Midland Railway, completed by 1840,

With chapels, pulpits, and administration came new concerns: later generations of sectarian Methodists desired a more professional ministry far different from the lay cottage preaching of earlier years. Prescribed behavior and speech began to replace spontaneity and inspiration. "Some in Hull and in the country are much offended by my plain preaching," complained Primitive evangelist Parkinson Milson in 1847. "And 'who are they? Reprobates?' No! . . . they are professors of religion—some of them class leaders and local preachers."[5] Both the laity and connexional authority promoted increasing sophistication. The establishment of Primitive Methodist academies and colleges, while offering opportunities to some, effectively excluded those who had pursued preaching in a desultory way. The gulf between preacher and people became more marked than ever as fewer common laborers took up the calling and instead obeyed exhortations to lead the exemplary lay life. Implicit in this separation was the suggestion that preaching was open only to the select few. "If we cannot preach with the eloquence of the lips," claimed a president of the Primitive Methodist Connexion late in the century,

> we can testify by the even more persuasive eloquence of the life. . . . Pure living, upright conduct, practical obedience to the law of Christ, is the most effective testimony for Christianity that any man can bear, and the most effective contribution he can make to the stability and progress of the nation to which he belongs.

A new rhetoric, associated with new centers of power, guided the aspirations of common followers.[6]

The power of the pulpit attracted preachers less interested in domestic evangelism. Objections to family visiting rose in

---

proved "as significant in its impact . . . as had been the coming of Strutt." R. J. Millward, *Belper in Bygone Years* (Belper, 1977), pp. 7–8. See also Andrew Charlesworth, *Social Protest in a Rural Society*, Historical Geography Research Series, Number 1 (1979).

[5] G. Shaw, *Life of Parkinson Milson* (London, 1893), p. 44.

[6] Rev. Thomas Mitchell, "A Statesman's Retrospect," *Sermons by Primitive Methodist Preachers* (London, 1903), p. 22.

the 1830s in the great towns, where Primitive Methodists involved in other ministerial responsibilities found domestic duties too difficult, tiring, and time-consuming.[7] Independent Methodists also noted a decline in "domestic religion" in the 1850s. While more successful than other sects in preserving a nonprofessional ministry, Independents observed a growing division between institutional and family religion. "Whatever stir be made congregationally or ministerially will still leave the church but partially awakened," argued *The Free Gospel Advocate* in 1852, "till the *families* of the righteous become the scenes of religious concern and of spiritual instruction." The pulpit, it warned, threatened to displace "the domestic constitution."[8]

Perhaps the clearest evidence of the waning of cottage religion was the decline of female preaching. Hardly any biographies eulogizing women preachers appeared in connexional magazines after 1865; those that did, recognized women who had begun their careers early in the century. No official notice was made of this change, other than the occasional nostalgic comment about former times. "In those days," one writer complained, "the people were not so much hampered by excess of church regulations, nor by a spurious modesty. It was common in their social worship to invite any, whether male or female, who had a psalm or exhortation, to give it." An Independent Methodist was more explicit. One reason for "the languid state of some of the Churches," he lamented in 1891, was the new reticence of women. "Our sisters have in many cases ceased to pray in public. Time was in our experience when the sisters were as open and free in the prayer-meeting as anyone." By the end of the century, even informal speech by women was infrequent, while female preachers were rare "exceptions to the general rule."[9]

The disappearance of female preachers was intimately re-

[7] "On Family Visiting," *PMM*, 1832, pp. 106–7.

[8] "Family Religion," *Free Gospel Advocate*, 1852, p. 95.

[9] Wilson Barrett, "Women's Work in the Church," *PMM*, 1888, p. 100; "An Appeal to the Sisters," *Free Gospel Magazine*, 1891, pp. 73–4; William Jessop, *Methodism in Rossendale* (Manchester, 1881), p. 192.

lated to more general changes in working-class life. The household economy, with its many home-based sources of income and production, was also disappearing. The decline of domestic industry in the countryside and the spread of wage labor seriously eroded the household's economic functions. With these developments, female preachers lost their base of support and power. Like artisans, these women were representatives of an earlier era of social and economic organization. Though neither they nor artisans disappeared altogether, their demands and complaints became less pertinent to the central values of Victorian society.[10]

In an ironic shift of emphasis, the domestic ideals of cottage religion conspired with the values of Victorian society to confine more prosperous working-class women to the household. Despite different origins and experiences, sectarians had arrived at assumptions that were fundamental to middle-class culture. "There can be no question," asserted a Primitive Methodist of the 1880s, "but that the home is woman's primary sphere of action."[11] New standards of respectability and behavior, defining the public world as male and the domestic world as female, replaced the more flexible ways of earlier years. Greater financial security altered the meaning of domestic religion. Widespread chapel worship removed women from their central place in cottage religion while assigning them to a *domus* that was no longer a true center of laboring life. Once a strategy for survival, the call for familial solidarity became an activity pursued by mothers in private homes; instead of preaching to the entire community, working-class women were expected to preach to their children. While middle-class women moved into the public arena through philanthropy and reform movements, their working-class sisters lost

[10] On the decline of Cornish Methodism and its relationship to the decline of artisanal trades, see Gilbert, *Religion and Society*, pp. 146–7. On the household wage economy, see Louise A. Tilly and Joan W. Scott, *Women, Work, and Family* (New York: Holt, Rinehart and Winston, 1978), Part II.

[11] Barrett, "Women's Work in the Church," p. 100; *A Mother's Sermons for her Children* (Kirkby Lonsdale, 1829).

the power to speak—in both domestic and public spheres—that came through the pulpit.

The meaning of religion itself, particularly for the working classes, was also changing. As an essential arm of Victorian culture, established religion endeavored to overwhelm its competitors and adopted many of the features of popular evangelicalism. According to a supporter of village Methodism, cottage evangelists had provoked others into action and thus had sacrificed their unique position.[12] But the dialectic between the two forms of religion was more subtle than this. The Church appropriated the very images of cottage religion and consigned them to a symbolic function within a hegemonic religious ideology. The pious poor, with their plain speech and unsophisticated resolve, became examples to more fortunate Victorians as well as to the poor themselves. "Happy cottagers" figured large in the prolific literature of tract and missionary societies. These saints had no thoughts or will of their own, and their speech reflected an exaggerated humility. The content of one tract revolved around the cottager's diet of crusts of "barley-bread" and "herby pies." "I never desire better," a poor woman is made to say. "Better is a little with the fear of the Lord, than the great treasure and trouble therewith. Better is a dinner of herbs, where Christ is at the table, than a stalled ox, and hatred therewith." Through an unwelcomed assimilation into the consensus of Victorian religion, pious peasants forfeited the power to speak, decry, and offend.[13]

As champions of distinctively popular religion, cottage evangelists encountered trying times after 1850. Those who survived lost much of their leverage in addressing the problems of industrial society. The experiences of sectarian saints no longer widely resonated among laborers and other *menu peuple*. The 1840s marked the end of a half-century of political and social conflict, and as popular unrest diminished, so did the

---

[12] John Colwell, *Sketches of Village Methodism* (London, 1877), p. 139.
[13] *The Happy Cottagers* (London: Religious Tract Society, [1830?]).

strength of the sectarian critique. Itinerant preachers henceforth appeared less threatening to village authorities. Though
occasional harassment continued, the last arrest of a Primitive
Methodist preacher occurred in 1843 and nearly coincided
with the first year (1842) of a decline in membership. Now an
accepted part of the village landscape, popular preachers lost
some of their appeal.[14]

Fewer sectarian Methodists recalled the original conditions
that inspired domestic religion. Societies knowing nothing of
the religion of the cottage were evolving in milltowns; a growing number owed their origins to missions promoted not by
country evangelists, but by townspeople. At Sindsley, millworkers founded a society in 1838 after moving from Roe
Green, near Manchester, where steam power had replaced
handlooms and forced emigration. The group met in a room
at the mill until 1846, when a "powerful revival" and subsequent expansion led to the building of a chapel and school.
Many members were natives of other milltowns with experience of nothing but industrial labor and migration. Old-style
preachers occasionally addressed the Sindsley society, but with
the passing of displaced villagers, a generation of preachers
molded by different experiences appeared in factory towns.[15]
Meanwhile, societies in old weaving villages declined. Cottage
meetings at Flockton (Yorks.) led to the building of a chapel
in 1853; but owing to the "unfavourable geographical position" of the village, "some miles from any business centre,"
many members "had to remove on account of work." Similarly,
at Skelmersdale, meetings began in 1884 in a double cottage
celebrated as "the cradle of all the Free Churches of Skelmersdale." Independent Methodists occupied the cottage after
Wesleyans, Primitives, and Congregationalists had successively
established causes there. But the prognosis of the mining village society was dim: though a "school-chapel was built in 1889,

---

[14] Owen Chadwick, *The Victorian Church*, 2 vols. (New York: Oxford University Press, 1966), 1:388.

[15] "Manchester: Our Circuit Retrospective," *FGM*, 1883, pp. 122–9.

... the flooding of the collieries ... led to many removals" and the society was still shrinking in 1905. Sectarian Methodism, by definition, became associated with decline and extinction.[16]

And yet cottage religion continued in isolated parts of England and Wales. In rural areas, villagers preserved the traditional arrangements of cottage societies despite the national trend towards chapel building. Primitive Methodists in Preston (Wilts.) met in cottages belonging to two eighteenth-century farmhouses from 1830 to 1907, when members finally decided to erect a corrugated iron chapel.[17] The Welsh Revival of 1904–5 gives similarly suggestive evidence of the persistence of sectarian Methodism in industrializing societies. And to the discerning eye, promoters of plebeian righteousness and humble virtue were still at work in the Salvation Army missions in late nineteenth-century cities. But the heyday of cottage evangelism, when all its components worked in unison, had passed. Cottage religion had flourished during a brief period of early industrialization and social change in the countryside. It lost its power as the prophecies of its sons and daughters became, in the words of the Scriptures, the outmoded dreams of old men.

[16] Arthur Mounfield, *A Short History of Independent Methodism* (Wigan, 1905), pp. 179–80; 153.
[17] *Victoria History of the County of Wiltshire*, E. Crittal, ed. (London: Institute of Historical Research, 1978), 9:93, 103.

BIBLIOGRAPHY

Manuscript Sources

Methodist Archives and Research Center, John Rylands Library, Manchester:
Bourne, Hugh. "Journal"; correspondence of Mary Barritt and
    Zachariah Taft; correspondence and diaries of Methodist
    ministers.

Hull Local History Room, Central Library: Primitive Methodist Circuit
    lists.

Leeds Central Library: Wray, J. "History of Methodism in Leeds";
    Leeds Central Library, Sheepscar: Leeds Circuit Quarterly
    Preachers' Meeting Minutes; Primitive Methodist Leeds Circuit
    class books and registers.

Private Collections: Crimlisk, Mr. John C., Filey, Yorkshire. Books,
    manuscript material, assorted pamphlets; Dews, Mr. D. Colin,
    Leeds; Wood, George, Primitive Methodist Preacher, "Sermons."

Official Publications

Board of Agriculture Reports

Brown, Robert. *General View of the Agriculture of the West Riding of
    Yorkshire*. Edinburgh, 1799.
Davis, Thomas. *General View of the Agriculture of Wiltshire*. London,
    1813.
Farey, John. *General View of the Agriculture and Minerals of Derbyshire*.
    3 vols. London, 1811, 1815, 1817.
Mavor, William. *General View of the Agriculture of Berkshire*. London,
    1808.
Pitt, W. *General View of the Agriculture of Staffordshire*. London, 1796.

BIBLIOGRAPHY

Plymley, Joseph. *General View of the Agriculture of Shropshire.* London, 1803.

Stevenson, W. *General View of the Agriculture of Lancashire.* London, 1815.

Strickland, H. E. *General View of the Agriculture of the East Riding of Yorkshire.* London, 1812.

Tuke, John. *General View of the Agriculture of the North Riding of Yorkshire.* London, 1800.

Worgan, G. B. *General View of the Agriculture of Cornwall.* London, 1811.

Vancouver, Charles. *General View of the Agriculture of Hampshire.* London, 1813.

PERIODICAL PUBLICATIONS

Newspapers: The Leeds Mercury; The Leeds Times; The Times.

Denominational Periodicals: Bible Christian Magazine; Free Gospel Advocate; Free Gospel Magazine; Methodist Magazine; Primitive Methodist Magazine; The Primitive Methodist Preachers' Magazine; Primitive Methodist Quarterly Review.

Other: The Folk-Lore Record; Yorkshire Folk-Lore.

OTHER PRINTED SOURCES

Religious Histories and Tracts

Antliff, William. "Woman: Her Position and Mission." London, 1856.

Beckworth, William. *A Book of Remembrance. Being Records of Leeds Primitive Methodism.* London, 1910.

Bourne, F. W. *The Bible Christians.* London, 1905.

Bourne, Hugh. *History of the Primitive Methodists, giving an account of their rise and progress up to the year 1823.* Bemersley, 1823.

————. "A Treatise on Baptism, In Twelve Conversations, with Five Original Hymns." Bemersley, 1823.

Colwell, John. *Sketches of Village Methodism.* London, 1877.

Dale, R. W. *The Old Evangelism and the New.* London, 1889.

Deed Poll of the Primitive Methodist Connexion, Dated, Feb. 4, 1830. Bemersley, 1837.

Extracts from the Minutes of the 22nd Annual Conference of the Bible Christian Church. Devon, 1840.

A Female. "An Appeal to the Consciences of Christians, on the Subject of Dress." Darlington, 1815.

Fletcher, G. Arthur. *Records of Wesleyan Methodism in the Belper Circuit, 1760–1903.* Belper, 1903.

Forms for the Administration of Baptism; the solemnization of matrimony; maternal thanksgiving after child-birth; et. al. Newcastle-upon-Tyne, 1859.

General Minutes of the Conferences of the Primitive Methodist Connexion. Bemersley, 1836.

H., J. G. *History of Methodism in North Devon.* London, 1871.

Hannam, E. P. *Prayers and Selections from Scripture, for Wives and Mothers.* London, 1835.

Holland, Bernard G. "The Doctrine of Infant Baptism in Non-Wesleyan Methodism." Occasional Publications of the Wesley Historical Society. New Series, no. 1., 1970.

Horne, C. Silvester. *A Popular History of the Free Churches.* London, 1903.

Hulbert, Charles A. *Annals of the Church and Parish of Almondbury, Yorkshire.* London, 1882.

Knill, R. "The Influence of Pious Women in Promoting a Revival of Religion." Religious Tract Society. Narrative Series. London [c. 1835].

Lyth, John. *Glimpses of Early Methodism in York and the Surrounding District.* York, 1885.

Mallinson, Joel. *Methodism in Huddersfield, Holmfirth, and Denby Dale.* London, 1898.

Minutes of the First Conference of the Preachers in Connexion with William O'Bryan. 1819. Devon, 1825.

Mounfield, Arthur. *Short History of Independent Methodism.* Wigan, 1905.

Parrott, Rev. John. *A Digest of the History, Polity, and Doctrines of the Primitive Methodists.* 2nd ed. London, 1864.

Patterson, Arthur H. *From Hayloft to Temple. The Story of the Primitive Methodism in Yarmouth.* London, 1913.

Pyke, R. *A Golden Chain.* London, 1913.

Roberts, Richard. *History of Methodism in Almondbury.* London, 1864.

Robinson, William. *An Essay on a Lay Ministry*. London, 1832.

Shaw, George. *Our Filey Fishermen*. London, 1867.

Sibree, James. *Fifty Years' Recollections of Hull*. Hull, 1884.

S[impson], M. E. "An Address to Farm Servants, who had been confirmed, many of whom had soon after joined the Primitive Methodists or Ranters." London, 1862.

A Sketch of the history and proceedings of the Deputies appointed to protect the civil rights of the Protestant Dissenters, to which is annexed a summary of the laws affecting Protestant Dissenters. London, 1813.

Smith, Samuel. *Anecdotes, Facts, and Biographical Sketches connected with the Great Revival of the Work of God in . . . the Primitive Methodist Connexion*. London, 1872.

Steele, Anthony. *History of Methodism in Barnard Castle and the Principal Places in the Dales Circuit*. London, 1857.

Tonks, William C. *Victory in the Villages: The History of the Brinkworth Circuit*. London, 1907.

Townsend, W. J.; Workman, H. B.; Eayrs, George. *A New History of Methodism*. 2 vols. London: Hodder and Stoughton, 1909.

Ward, J. *Historical Sketches of Methodism in Bingley and the Circuit*. Bingley, 1863.

Vickers, James. *History of Independent Methodism*. Wigan, 1920.

Walker, J. U. *A History of Methodism in Halifax and Its Vicinity*. Halifax, 1836.

Woodcock, Henry. *Piety Among the Peasantry: Being Sketches of Primitive Methodism on the Yorkshire Wolds*. London, 1889.

Wray, J. Jackson. *Nestleton Magna. A Story of Yorkshire Methodism*. London, 1885.

Sermons and Hymnals

Bourne, Hugh. *A Collection of Hymns, for Camp Meetings, Revivals, &c.* Bemersley, 1822.

———. Another edition. Bemersley, 1827.

———. A General Collection of Hymns. Bingham, 1819.

———. *Large Hymn Book, for the Use of the Primitive Methodists*. Bemersley, 1824.

———. *Large Hymn Book*. 6th ed. London, 1848.

Carr, Ann, and Williams, Martha. *A Selection of Hymns for the Use of the Female Revivalists*. Dewsbury, 1824.

———. *A Selection of Hymns, for the Use of the Female Revivalists.* Leeds, 1828.

———. *A Selection of Hymns, for the Use of the Female Revivalists.* Leeds, 1838.

A Collection of Revival Hymns, Adapted to Popular Airs. Bishop Auckland, 1844.

Dorricott, I., and Collins, T. *Lyric Studies: A Hymnal Guide, Containing Biographical Sketches of the Authors . . .* London [1891].

Hymns for Methodist Cottage-Services, and for Prayer-Meetings. London, n.d.

Kelly, Hugh. "The Stone Cut out of the Mountain." Newcastle-upon-Tyne, 1821.

Mower, Arthur. "On Vocal Music Considered as a Branch of National Education." Central Society of Education Papers. London, 1837.

O'Bryan, William. *A Collection of Hymns, For the Use of the People Called Arminian Bible Christians.* Devon, 1824.

The Primitive Pulpit, Being Original Sermons and Sketches by various ministers of the Primitive Methodist Connexion. London, 1857.

Watts, Isaac. *Divine Songs, in an easy language, for the use of Children.* Glasgow, 1814.

Wesley, John. *A Collection of Hymns, for the Use of the People Called Methodists.* London, 1877.

Biographies, Collected Biographies, and Autobiographies

Barfoot, J. *A Diamond in the Rough; or Christian Heroism in Humble Life.* Being jottings concerning that remarkable peasant preacher, William Hickingbotham, of Belper, Derbys. London, 1874.

Beaumont, Joseph. *Memoirs of Mrs. Mary Tatham, Late of Nottingham.* London, 1874.

Bede, Seth. *Seth Bede, "The Methody."* London, 1859.

Bourne, F. W. *A Centenary Life of James Thorne, of Shebbear.* London, 1895.

———. *The King's Son; or, A Memoir of "Billy" Bray.* London, 1871.

[Bramwell.] *Memoir of the Life and Ministry of William Bramwell . . . by members of his family.* London, 1848.

Bramwell, William. "A Short Account of the Life and Death of Ann Cutler." Sheffield, 1796.

Brooks, Johanna. *A Handmaid of the Lord.* London, [1868].

BIBLIOGRAPHY

Buoy, Charles Wesley. *Representative Women of Methodism*. New York, 1893.

Clowes, William. *The Journals of William Clowes, a Primitive Methodist Preacher*. London, 1844.

Coulson, John E. *The Peasant Preacher: Memorials of Mr. Charles Richardson, A Wesleyan Evangelist, Commonly Known as the "Lincolnshire Thrasher."* London, 1866.

Davison, John. *The Vessel of Beaten Gold; or, a Memoir and Correspondence of the Late Miss Mary Burks, Preacher in the Primitive Methodist Connexion*. Grimsby, 1840.

Dews, D. Colin. "Ann Carr, The Female Revivalists, and the Leeds Jumping Ranters." Unpublished paper, 1980.

Dodd, James. *The Village; and other poems: religious and miscellaneous*. London, 1853.

Eldridge, C. O. *Local Preachers and Village Methodism*. Rochdale, 1895.

Farningham, Marianne. *A Working Woman's Life*. London, 1907.

Forster, E. M. *Marianne Thornton*. New York: Harcourt Brace, 1956.

Freeman, Charles B. *Mary Simpson of Boynton Vicarage: Teacher of Ploughboys and Critic of Methodism*. East Yorkshire Local History Society Publications, no. 28. York, 1972.

Freeman, Henry. *A Memoir of the Life and Ministry of Ann Freeman*. London, 1828.

Garbutt, Jane. *Reminiscences of the Early Days of Primitive Methodism in Hull*. Hull, 1886.

Herod, George. *Biographical Sketches of some of those preachers of the Primitive Methodist Connexion*. London, n.d.

"Hugh Bourne; or, Piety and Usefulness." Religious Tract Society. Narrative Series. [c. 1835.]

Ireland, Jonathan. *Jonathan Ireland the Street Preacher. An Autobiography*. London, n.d.

James, John Angell. *Female Piety: or the Young Woman's Friend and Guide through Life to Immortality*. London, 1852.

Keeling, Annie E. *Eminent Methodist Women*. London, 1889.

Kendall, C. *Life of the Rev. William Sanderson, Primitive Methodist*. London, 1875.

Lightfoot, John. *The Power of Faith ... the Life and Labours of Mrs. Mary Porteus*. London, 1862.

Lyth, John. *The Living Sacrifice; or, a Short Biographical Notice of Sarah Bentley, of York*. York, 1848.

M'Allum, Daniel. *Memoirs of the Life, Character, and Death of the Rev. H. Taft.* Newcastle, 1824.
———. *Remains of the Late Rev. Daniel M'Allum [sic], M.D.* London, 1829.
Michell, William J. *Brief Biographical Sketches of Bible Christian Ministers and Laymen.* 2 vols. Jersey, 1906.
Petty, John. *Memoir of the Life and Labours of Thomas Batty: one of the early Primitive Methodist Preachers.* London, 1857.
Russell, K. P. *Memoirs of the Rev. John Pyer.* London, 1865.
Russell, Thomas. *Autobiography of Thomas Russell.* London, n.d.
Shaw, George. *Life of John Oxtoby ("Praying Johnny").* Hull, 1894.
———. *Life of Parkinson Milson.* London, 1893.
Simpson, John. *Recollections and Characteristic Anecdotes of the Late Rev. Hugh Bourne.* London, 1859.
Sykes, John. *William Schofield.* Huddersfield, 1882.
Taft, Mrs. Mary. *Memoirs of the Life of Mrs. Mary Taft.* 2 parts. London, 1827.
Taft, Zachariah. "Bible Religion Illustrated." Whitby, 1820.
———. *Biographical Sketches of the Lives and Public Ministry of Various Holy Women.* Vol. 1., London, 1825. Vol. 2., Leeds, 1828.
———. "The Scripture Doctrine of Women's Preaching: Stated and Examined." York, 1820.
———. "Thoughts on Female Preaching. With Extracts from the Writings of Locke, Martin, &c." Dover, 1803.
Walford, John. *Memoirs of the Life and Labours of the late venerable Hugh Bourne.* Edited by W. Antliff. London, 1855.
Warren, Samuel. *Memoirs and Select Letters of Mrs. Anne Warren.* London, 1827.
Wilkinson, John T. *Hugh Bourne, 1772–1852.* London: Epworth, 1952.
———. *William Clowes, 1780–1851.* London: Epworth, 1951.
Williams, Martha. *Memoirs of the Life and Character of Ann Carr.* Leeds, 1841.
Winks, William E. *Lives of Illustrious Shoemakers.* London, 1883.

Local Histories, Works of Folklore, etc.

Aflalo, F. G. *The Sea-Fishing Industry.* London, 1904.
Baines, Edward. *History, Directory, and Gazetteer, of the County of Lancaster.* 2 vols. London, 1825.

BIBLIOGRAPHY

Baines, Edward. *The Social, Educational, and Religious State of the Manufacturing Districts*. London, 1843.

Clarke, Stephen. *Clitheroe in its Railway Days*. Clitheroe, 1900.

Cobbett, William. *Rural Rides*. 1830. Harmondsworth: Penguin Books, 1967.

Cole, John. *History and Antiquities of Filey*. Scarborough, 1828.

Cooper, A. N. *Across the Broad Acres*. Hull, 1908.

———. *Filey and Its Church*. Filey, 1889.

Cortis, Dr. *An Historical Account of the Herring Fishery on the North-East Coast of England*. Filey, 1858.

Cox, J. C., ed. *Memorials of Old Derbyshire*. London, 1907.

———. *Three Centuries of Derbyshire Annals*. 2 vols. London, 1890.

Davies, D. P. *A New Historical and Descriptive View of Derbyshire*. Belper, 1811.

Eliot, George. *Scenes from Clerical Life*. 1858. Harmondsworth: Penguin Books, 1973.

Fairfax-Blakeborough, J. *Yorkshire Village Life, Humour and Characters*. London, n.d.

Glover, Stephen. *The History, Gazetteer, and Directory of the County of Derby*. Vol. 1., Derby, 1829. Vol. 2., Derby, 1836.

Hawker, James. *A Victorian Poacher: James Hawker's Journal*. Oxford: Oxford University Press, 1978.

Henderson, William. *Notes on the Folk-Lore of the Northern Counties of England and the Borders*. London, 1866.

Lockwood, Ernest. *Colne Valley Folk*. London, 1936.

Morris, M.C.F. *Yorkshire Folk-Talk*. London, 1911.

Nicholson, John. *Folk Lore of East Yorkshire*. London, 1890.

Pettitt, Arthur. *The Filey Hand-Book*. Sheffield, 1868.

———. *Guide to Filey*. Sheffield, 1868.

Samuel, Arthur M. *The Herring: Its Effect on the History of Britain*. London, 1918.

Smith, William. *History of Morley*. Morley, 1876.

Sudgen, John. *Slaithwaite Notes of the Past and Present*. 3rd ed. Manchester, 1905.

Sykes, John. *Slawit in the 'Sixties*. Huddersfield, 1926.

Wedgwood, Henry Allen. *People of the Potteries*. 1877–81. Reprint. Bath: Adams & Dart, 1970.

Willott, Charles. *Historical Records of Belper*. Belper, 1885.

Wright, Peter. *The Yorkshireman's Dictionary*. Skipton: Dalesman Books, 1980.

BIBLIOGRAPHY

Secondary Sources

Acquaviva, S. S. *The Decline of the Sacred in Industrial Society.* Translated by Patricia Lipscomb. Oxford: Basil Blackwell, 1979.

Allison, K. J. *The East Riding of Yorkshire Landscape.* The Making of the English Landscape Series. London: Hodder & Stoughton, 1976.

Anderson, Michael. *Family Structure in nineteenth century Lancashire.* Cambridge: Cambridge University Press, 1971.

———. "Sociological History and the working-class family: Smelser revisited." *Social History* 3 (1976): 317–34.

Anderson, Olive. "Women Preachers in Mid-Victorian Britain: Some Reflexions on Feminism, Popular Religion and Social Change." *Historical Journal* 11 (1969): 467–84.

Barber, B. Aquila. *A Methodist Pageant.* London: Holborn, 1932.

Barrell, John. *The Dark Side of the Landscape.* Cambridge: Cambridge University Press, 1980.

———. *The Idea of the Landscape and the Sense of Place.* Cambridge: Cambridge University Press, 1972.

Barton, David A. *Discovering Chapels and Meeting Houses.* Aylesbury, Bucks.: Shire Publications, Ltd., 1975.

Baxter, John. "The Great Yorkshire Revival, 1792–6: A Study of Mass Revival among the Methodists." In *Sociological Yearbook of Religion,* vol. 1. London: SCM Press, 1968.

Benet, Francisco. "Sociology Uncertain: the Ideology of the Rural-Urban Continuum." *Comparative Studies in Society and History* 6 (1963): 1–23.

Best, G.F.A. "The Evangelicals and the Established Church in the Early Nineteenth Century." *Journal of Theological Studies* 10 (1959): 63–78.

———. *Temporal Pillars.* Cambridge: Cambridge University Press, 1964.

Braun, Rudolf. "The Impact of Cottage Industry on an Agricultural Population." In *The Rise of Capitalism,* edited by David Landes. New York: Macmillan, 1966.

Brown, Ford K. *Fathers of the Victorians: The Age of Wilberforce.* Cambridge: Cambridge University Press, 1961.

Brundage, Anthony. "The English Poor Law of 1834 and the Cohesion of Agricultural Society." *Agricultural History* 48 (1974): 405–17.

Burke, Peter. *Popular Culture in Early Modern Europe*. London: Temple Smith, 1978.

Bythell, Duncan. *The Handloom Weavers: A Study in the English Cotton Industry During the Industrial Revolution*. Cambridge: Cambridge University Press, 1969.

Calhoun, C. J. "Community: toward a variable conceptualization for comparative research." *Social History* 5 (1980): 105–29.

Chadwick, Owen. *The Victorian Church*. 2 vols. New York: Oxford University Press, 1966.

Chambers, J. D., and Mingay, G. E. *The Agricultural Revolution, 1750–1880*. New York: Schocken Books, 1966.

Church, Leslie. *The Early Methodist People*. New York: The Philosophical Library, 1949.

———. *More About the Early Methodist People*. London: Epworth, 1949.

Church, Roy A. *Economic and Social Change in a Midland Town: Victorian Nottingham, 1815–1900*. London: Frank Cass, 1966.

Colls, Robert. *The Collier's Rant: Song and Culture in the Industrial Village*. Totowa, N.J.: Croom Helm, 1977.

Cunnington, C. Willett. "Costume and the Countryman." *Derbyshire Countryside* 16 (1946): 44–5.

Currie, Robert; Gilbert, Alan; Horsley, Lee. *Churches and Churchgoers: Patterns of Church Growth in the British Isles Since 1700*. Oxford: Clarendon Press, 1977.

Daniel, Clarence. *Derbyshire Customs*. Skipton: Dalesman Books, 1976.

Davies, Horton. *The English Free Churches*. 2nd ed. London: Oxford University Press, 1963.

———. *Worship and Theology in England: from Watts and Wesley to Maurice, 1690–1850*. 5 vols. Princeton, N.J.: Princeton University Press, 1961–70.

Davis, Natalie Zemon. "Some Tasks and Themes in the Study of Popular Religion." In *The Pursuit of Holiness in Late Medieval and Renaissance Religion*, edited by Charles Trinkaus with Heiko A. Oberman. Leiden: E. J. Brill, 1974.

———. "Women on Top." In *Society and Culture in Early Modern France*. Stanford: Stanford University Press, 1975.

Dolbey, George W. *The Architectural Expression of Methodism: The First Hundred Years*. London: Epworth, 1964.

Donnelly, F. K. "Ideology and early English Working-class History: Edward Thompson and his critics," *Social History* 2 (1976): 219–38.

Dooling, D. M., ed. *A Way of Working*. New York: Anchor Press, 1979.

Dunbabin, J.P.D. *Rural Discontent in Nineteenth-Century Britain*. London: Faber & Faber, 1974.

Durant, William. *The Story of Friars' Green Church*. Warrington: The Guardian Press, 1951.

Durkheim, Emile. *The Elementary Forms of the Religious Life*. Translated by Joseph W. Swain. 1915. Reprint. New York: The Free Press, 1965.

Dykes, Jack. *Smuggling on the Yorkshire Coast*. Skipton: Dalesman Books, 1978.

Eisenstadt, S. N. *Modernization: Protest and Change*. Englewood Cliffs, N.J.: Prentice-Hall, 1966.

Eliade, Mircea. *The Sacred and the Profane: The Nature of Religion*. Willard R. Trask, trans. New York: Harvest Books, 1959.

Evans-Pritchard, E. E. *Theories of Primitive Religion*. Oxford: Clarendon Press, 1965.

Evans, Eric J. *The Contentious Tithe: The Tithe Problem and English Agriculture, 1750–1850*. London: Routledge & Kegan Paul, 1976.

Everitt, Alan. *The Pattern of Rural Dissent: the Nineteenth Century*. Department of English Local History Occasional Papers, No. 4. Leicester: Leicester University Press, 1972.

Faulkner, Harold U. *Chartism and the Churches*. New York: A.M.S. Press, 1968.

Fitton, R. S., and Wadsworth, A. P. *The Strutts and the Arkwrights, 1758–1830*. Manchester: Manchester University Press, 1958.

Forman, Shepard. *The Raft Fishermen*. Bloomington, Indiana: University of Indiana Press, 1970.

Foster, John. *Class Struggle and the Industrial Revolution*. London: Methuen, 1974.

Gay, John D. *The Geography of Religion in England*. London: Duckworth Press, 1971.

Gilbert, Alan D. *Religion and Society in Industrial England*. London: Longman, 1976.

Ginzburg, Carlo. "High and Low: the theme of forbidden knowledge in the 16th and 17th Centuries." *Past and Present* 73 (1976): 28–41.

Glock, Charles Y., and Stark, Rodney. *Religion and Society in Tension*. Chicago: Rand McNally & Co., 1965.

Godfrey, Arthur. *Yorkshire Fishing Fleets*. Skipton: Dalesman Books, 1974.

Goody, Jack; Thirsk, Joan; Thompson, E. P. *Family and Inheritance: rural society in Western Europe, 1200–1800.* Cambridge: Cambridge University Press, 1976.

Gowland, D. A. *Methodist Secessions. The Origins of Free Methodism in three Lancashire Towns: Manchester, Rochdale, Liverpool.* Manchester: Chetham Society, 1979.

Halévy, Elie. *England in 1815.* 1913. Translated by E. I. Watkin and D. A. Barker. London: Benn, 1960.

Hammond, J. L., and Hammond, Barbara. *The Village Labourer.* 1911. Reprint. London: Longman, 1978.

Hammond, Nigel. *Rural Life in the Vale of the White Horse, 1780–1914.* Reading: William Smith, 1974.

Harte, N. B., and Ponting, K. G., eds. *Textile History and Economic History: Essays in Honour of Miss Julia de Lacy Mann.* Manchester: Manchester University Press, 1973.

Hey, D. G. "The Pattern of Nonconformity in South Yorkshire, 1660–1851." *Northern History* 8 (1973): 86–118.

Hobsbawm, Eric J. "From Social History to the History of Society." *Daedalus* (Winter, 1971): 20–45.

———. *Labouring Men: Studies in the History of Labour.* London: Weidenfeld and Nicolson, 1964.

———. *Primitive Rebels: Studies in Archaic Forms of Social Movement in the 19th and 20th Centuries.* New York: Norton, 1959.

Hobsbawm, Eric J., and Rudé, George. *Captain Swing.* London: Lawrence and Wishart, 1970.

Hobsbawm, Eric J., and Scott, Joan W. "Political Shoemakers." *Past and Present* 89 (1980): 86–114.

Hoch-Smith, Judith, and Spring, Anita, eds. *Women in Ritual and Symbolic Roles.* New York: Plenum Press, 1978.

Holderness, B. A. " 'Open' and 'Close' Parishes in England in the 18th and 19th Centuries." *Agricultural History* 20 (1972): 126–39.

Hoskins, W. G. *Devon.* London: Collins, 1954.

———. *The Making of the English Landscape.* London: Hodder & Stoughton, 1955.

Howe, Daniel W. "The Decline of Calvinism: An Approach to Its Study." *Comparative Studies in Society and History* 14 (1972): 306–27.

Hufton, Olwen. "Women and the Family Economy in Eighteenth-Century France." *French Historical Studies* 9 (1975): 1–22.

Inglis, Kenneth S. *Churches and the Working Classes in Victorian England.* London: Routledge & Kegan Paul, 1963.

———. "Patterns of Religious Worship in 1851." *Journal of Ecclesiastical History* 11 (1960): 74–86.

Jarratt, Arthur. *"Lang Sarmons" with other poems and stories in the East Yorkshire Dialect.* Hull: A. Brown & Sons, 1974.

Johnson, Marion. *Derbyshire Village Schools in the Nineteenth Century.* Newton Abbot: David & Charles, 1970.

Jones, Gareth Stedman. "From historical sociology to theoretical history." *British Journal of Sociology* 27 (1976): 295–305.

Joyce, Patrick. *Work, Society and Politics.* New Brunswick, N.J.: Rutgers University Press, 1980.

Kendall, Holliday Bickerstaff. *The Origin and History of the Primitive Methodist Church.* 2 vols. London, n.d.

Kent, John. "American Revivalism and England in the Nineteenth Century." Papers Presented to the Past and Present Conference on Popular Religion, 7 July 1966.

Lanternari, Vittorio. *The Religions of the Oppressed.* Lisa Sergio, trans. London: Macgibbon & Kee, 1963.

Laslett, Peter. *The World We Have Lost.* New York: Charles Scribner, 1965.

Laqueur, Thomas W. *Religion and Respectability: Sunday Schools and Working-Class Culture, 1780–1850.* New Haven: Yale University Press, 1976.

Levine, David. *Family Formation in an Age of Nascent Capitalism.* New York: Academic Press, 1977.

Lewis, I. M. *Ecstatic Religion: An Anthropological Study of Spirit Possession and Shamanism.* Harmondsworth: Penguin Books, 1971.

Linebaugh, Peter. "The Tyburn Riot Against the Surgeons." In *Albion's Fatal Tree: Crime and Society in Eighteenth-Century England.* New York: Pantheon Books, 1975.

Macfarlane, Alan. *Reconstructing Historical Communities.* Cambridge: Cambridge University Press, 1977.

Malcolmson, Robert W. *Popular Recreations in English Society.* Cambridge: Cambridge University Press, 1973.

Mann, Julia de Lacy. *The Cloth Industry in the West of England from 1640 to 1880.* Oxford: Clarendon Press, 1971.

Martin, David. *A Sociology of English Religion.* New York: Basic Books, 1967.

Martin, Ernest W. *The Shearers and the Shorn*. London: Routledge & Kegan Paul, 1965.

Marx, Karl. *Pre-Capitalist Economic Formations*. Translated by Jack Cohen. Edited by E. J. Hobsbawm. New York: International Publishers, 1965.

McLeod, Hugh. "Class, Community and Region: The Religious Geography of Nineteenth-Century England." In *Sociological Yearbook of Religion*, vol. 6. London: SCM Press, 1973.

McKee, J.E.G., ed. *The English Coble*. Maritime Monographs and Reports, no. 30. London: Trustees of the National Maritime Museum, 1978.

Medick, Hans. "The Proto-industrial Family Economy: the structural function of household and family during the transition from peasant society to industrial capitalism." *Social History* 3 (1976): 291–318.

Mendels, Franklin F. "Proto-industrialization: The First Phase of the Industrialization Process." *Journal of Economic History* 32 (1972): 241–61.

Mills, Dennis R., ed. *English Rural Communities: The Impact of a Specialised Economy*. London: Macmillan, 1973.

Mingay, G. E. *Enclosure and the Small Farmer in the Age of the Industrial Revolution*. London: Macmillan, 1968.

————. *English Landed Society in the Eighteenth Century*. London: Routledge & Kegan Paul, 1963.

Mitchell, Henry H. *The Recovery of Preaching*. London: Hodder and Stoughton, 1977.

Moore, Robert. "The Political Effects of Village Methodism." In *Sociological Yearbook of Religion*, vol. 6. London: SCM Press, 1973.

Obelkevich, James. *Religion and Rural Society: South Lindsey, 1825–1875*. Oxford: Clarendon Press, 1976.

Overton, John H., and Relton, Frederic. *The English Church from the Accession of George I to the End of Eighteenth Century*. London: Macmillan, 1906.

Palliser, D. M. *The Staffordshire Landscape*. London: Hodder & Stoughton, 1976.

Patterson, W. M. *Northern Primitive Methodism*. London, 1909.

Phythian-Adams, Charles. *Local History and Folklore: a new framework*. London: Bedford Square Press, 1975.

Pinchbeck, Ivy. *Women Workers and the Industrial Revolution, 1750–1850*. 1930. Reprint. Totowa, N. J.: Frank Cass, 1977.

Ponting, Kenneth G. *A History of the West of England Cloth Industry*. London: Macdonald, 1957.

Pope, Liston. *Millhands and Preachers*. New Haven: Yale University Press, 1942.

Power, E. G. *A Textile Community in the Industrial Revolution*. London: Longman, 1969.

Redford, Arthur. *Labour Migration in England, 1800–1850*. 3rd ed. rev. Manchester: Manchester University Press, 1976.

Rimmer, W. G. "The Industrial Profile of Leeds, 1740–1840." *Publications of the Thoresby Society* 50 (1967): 130–57.

———. "Occupations in Leeds, 1841–1951." *Publications of the Thoresby Society* 50 (1967):158–78.

———. "Working Men's Cottages in Leeds, 1770–1840." *Publications of the Thoresby Society* 46 (1960): 165–99.

Ritson, Joseph. *The Romance of Primitive Methodism*. London, 1909.

Rule, John G. "Some Social Aspects of the Cornish Industrial Revolution" in *Industry and Society in the South-West*, edited by Roger Burt. Exeter: University of Exeter Press, 1970.

Samuel, Raphael. *Village Life and Labour*. London: Routledge & Kegan Paul, 1975.

Sandeen, Ernest. *The Roots of Fundamentalism*. Chicago: University of Chicago Press, 1970.

Saville, John. *Rural Depopulation in England and Wales, 1851–1951*. London: Routledge & Kegan Paul, 1957.

Schlegel, Alice, ed. *Sexual Stratification: A Cross-Cultural View*. New York: Columbia University Press, 1977.

Scott, Joan W., and Tilly, Louis A. "Women's Work and the Family in Nineteenth-Century Europe." *Comparative Studies in Society and History* 17 (1975): 36–64.

Shanin, Teodor. *Peasants and Peasant Societies*. Harmondsworth: Penguin Books, 1971.

Semmel, Bernard. *The Methodist Revolution*. New York: Basic Books, 1973.

Sider, Gerald M. "Christmas Mumming and the New Year in Outport Newfoundland." *Past and Present* 71 (1976): 102–25.

———. "The Ties that Bind: Culture and agriculture, property and propriety in the Newfoundland village fishery." *Social History* 5 (1980): 3–36.

Sizer, Sandra S. *Gospel Hymns and Social Religion*. Philadelphia: Temple University Press, 1978.

Smelser, Neil J. *Social Change in the Industrial Revolution, 1770–1840*. London: Routledge & Kegan Paul, 1959.

Smith, Alan. *The Established Church and Popular Religion, 1750–1850*. Seminar Studies in History. London: Longman, 1971.

Smith, M. Estellie, ed. *Those Who Live From the Sea: A Study in Maritime Anthropology*. American Ethnological Society Monograph no. 62. St. Paul, Minn.: West Publishing Co., 1977.

Stigant, Paul. "Wesleyan Methodism and Working-Class Radicalism in the North, 1792–1821." *Northern History* 6 (1971): 98-116.

Swift, Wesley F. "The Women Itinerant Preachers of Early Methodism." *Proceedings of the Wesley Historical Society* 28–29 (1952–3): 89–94; 76–83.

Tamke, Susan S. *Make a Joyful Noise Unto the Lord: Hymns as a Reflection of Victorian Social Attitudes*. Athens, Ohio: Ohio University Press, 1978.

Thirsk, Joan, ed. *The Agrarian History of England and Wales*, vol. 4. Cambridge: Cambridge University Press, 1967.

———. "Industries in the Countryside." In *Essays in the Economic and Social History of Tudor and Stuart England*, edited by F. J. Fisher. Cambridge: Cambridge University Press, 1961.

Thomas, Keith. *Religion and the Decline of Magic*. Harmondsworth: Penguin Books, 1971.

Thomis, Malcolm I. *The Luddites*. Newton Abbot: David & Charles, 1970.

Thompson, David M. "The Churches and Society in Nineteenth-Century England: A Rural Perspective." In *Popular Belief and Practice*, Studies in Church History, vol. 8, edited by G. J. Cuming and Derek Baker. Cambridge: Cambridge University Press, 1972.

———, ed. *Nonconformity in the Nineteenth Century*. London: Routledge & Kegan Paul, 1972.

Thompson, Edward P. *The Making of the English Working Class*. New York: Vintage Books, 1963.

———. "On history, sociology and historical relevance." *British Journal of Sociology* 27 (1976): 387–402.

Thompson, F.M.L. *English Landed Society in the Nineteenth Century*. London: Routledge & Kegan Paul, 1963.

Tilly, Louise A., and Scott, Joan W. *Women, Work, and Family*. New York: Holt, Rinehart, and Winston, 1978.

Troeltsch, Ernst. *The Social Teaching of the Christian Churches*, 2 vols. 1911. Reprint. New York: Harper Torchbooks, 1960.

Victoria History of the Counties of England.

Walker, R. B. "Religious Changes in Cheshire, 1750–1850." *Journal of Ecclesiastical History* 17 (1966): 77–94.

Walsh, John. "Methodism and the Mob in the Eighteenth Century." In *Popular Belief and Practice*, Studies in Church History, vol. 8, edited by G. J. Cuming and Derek Baker. Cambridge: Cambridge University Press, 1972.

———. "Methodism at the End of the Eighteenth Century." In *A History of the Methodist Church in Great Britain*, vol. 2. London: Epworth, 1965.

———. "Origins of the Evangelical Revival." In *Essays in Modern English Church History*, edited by G. V. Bennett and J. D. Walsh. New York: Oxford University Press, 1966.

Ward, W. R. *Religion and Society in England, 1790–1850.* New York: Schocken Books, 1973.

———. "The Religion of the People and the Problem of Control, 1790–1830." In *Popular Belief and Practice*, Studies in Church History, vol. 8. Cambridge: Cambridge University Press, 1972.

———. "The Tithe Question in England in the Early Nineteenth Century." *Journal of Ecclesiastical History* 16 (1965): 67–81.

Warne, Arthur. *Church and Society in Eighteenth-Century Devon.* Newton Abbot: David & Charles, 1969.

Webb, R. K. *Modern England.* New York: Dodd, Mead, & Co., 1971.

Weber, Max. *The Sociology of Religion.* Translated by Ephraim Fischoff. 1922. Boston: Beacon Press, 1963.

Wells, Roger A. E. "The Development of the English Rural Proletariat and Social Protest, 1700–1850." *Journal of Peasant Studies* 6 (1979): 115–39.

White, R. J. *Waterloo to Peterloo.* London: 1957.

Williams, Raymond. *The Country and the City.* London: Chatto & Windus, 1973.

Wilson, Bryan R. *Magic and the Millennium.* New York: Harper & Row, 1973.

———, ed. *Patterns of Sectarianism.* London: Heinemann, 1967.

Wilson, D. "Belper Nailers." *Derbyshire Countryside* 50 (1943): 21–2, 26.

Woodforde, John. *The Truth About Cottages.* London: Routledge & Kegan Paul, 1969.

Yelling, J. A. *Common Field and Enclosure in England, 1450–1850.* London: Macmillan, 1977.

BIBLIOGRAPHY

Unpublished Theses

Cox, Jeffrey L. "The Social Origins of the Decline of Religion in England, 1880–1930." Ph.D. thesis, Harvard University, 1978.

Elliott, Charles M. "The Social and Economic History of the Principal Protestant Denominations in Leeds, 1760–1844." D. Phil. thesis, Oxford University, 1963.

Rule, J. G. "The Labouring Miner in Cornwall c. 1740–1870. A Study in Social History." Ph.D. thesis, Warwick University, 1971.

Stigant, Edward P. "Methodism and the Working Class, 1760–1821: A Study in Social and Political Conflict." Master's thesis, Keele University, 1968.

INDEX

Acts, 97
Adam Bede, 64, 70
Adler, Rachel, 36
afterlife, 131, 200
agricultural depression, 107–8, 109,
 163
agricultural laborers, 216–19, 221–
 2; as preachers, 216–19
agriculture, transformation of, 216–
 19
alienation, 65
America, emigration to, 117–18
American revivalism, 12, 88, 90
Anglican Church, *see* Church of
 England
anticlericalism, 134, 143–4, 163, 209
anti-Methodism, *see* persecution
Antinomianism, 35, 140, 156–7
Arkwright family, 161
Arminian Methodist Connexion
 (Derby Faith Methodists), 72
artisans, 216, 219, 226; religion
 and, 219
atheism, 126

baptism, 153
Baptists, 153n, 237
Barritt, Mary, 55–64, 71, 93, 109,
 188
Belper, 163–83; growth of, 165;
 Strutts family in, 164–6
Bemersley, 81
benefit societies, 269
Berkshire, 109–11. *See also* Brink-
 worth Circuit
Bible, justification for female
 preaching in, 71, 190
Bible Christians, 21, 26, 121–3,
 140–58; Bible Christian Confer-
 ence, 151, 157; female preachers

of, 140; growing authoritarianism
 of, 156–7; origins of, 144; persecution of, 154; polity of, 151; theology of the oppressed in, 145
Booth, Catherine, 50
Bosanquet, Mary (Mrs. John
 Fletcher), 50, 51, 61–2
Bourne, Hugh, 31, 38, 45, 94, 208,
 264; as carpenter, 81; defense of
 female preaching, 95–7; life of,
 79–87; works: *History of the Primi-
 tive Methodist Church*, 82; "Re-
 marks on the Ministry of
 Women," 95–7
Bramwell, William, 53–4, 55, 57,
 57n; works: *Life of Ann Cutler*,
 60–1
"bride of Christ," 199
Brinkworth Circuit, 111, 133–4
Brothers, Richard, 4n
Brunswick Chapel, 194
Bulwer, Edward Lytton, 7
Bunting, Jabez, 62n
Bunyan, John, 80
Butler, Josephine, 50

camp meetings, 88–91, 133, 173; as
 attack on authority, 74; break
 from Wesleyanism and, 88–91; legal restrictions and, 89
Captain Swing, 109
Carr, Ann, 187–204; childhood of,
 187–8; founding of Female Revivalists, 192–3; free evangelism
 of, 192, 194–5; funeral of, 200;
 style of, 189–90; success of,
 203–4
catechism (Church of England),
 124, 141
Cathars, 32

female preachers (*cont.*)
folk belief and, 137–8; homelessness of, 117–18, 163; images of,
112–16, 162–3; industrialism and,
161–2, 174, 178–82, 235–6; laboring life and, 50, 65; marriage
and, 40, 58–9, 179; origin of, 51–
2, 55, 91–8; persecution of, 59–
60, 131–2, 135–6, 148, 149; style
of, 53–4, 147, 189–90; Wesleyan
restriction against, 55, 91–3. *See
also* Female Revivalists; names of
individual preachers
"Female Preacher's Plea, The," 150
Female Revivalists, 29–30, 33–4,
187–204; chapels of, 203–4;
founding of, 192–3; Friendly Society, 203, 204; membership of,
201–3; social mobility and, 202.
See also Carr, Ann; Leeds
Filey (Yorks.): boats of, 250–2;
changes in fishing industry, 259–
60, 267–9; Church of England in,
257–8; culture of, 247–9; fishing
customs in, 255–7; growth of,
259–60; holiday industry in, 272;
Primitive Methodists in, 259, 262,
263–6; transformation of, 267,
272; Wesleyan Methodists in, 258,
262; women in, 248, 252–5, 268–
72. *See also* Oxtoby, John
"Filey Fishermen, The," 272–3
Fletcher, Rev. John, 51, 61, 81
"flither lasses," 253–4, 272
folk culture, 24, 137–8
folklore, religion and, 32, 77, 88–9
food, *see* fasting
Forster, E. M., 48
Fox, George, 87, 209
framework knitting, 69, 164
free evangelism, 192–3, 194–5
free gospel, 238, 239
Freeman, Henry, 153–8
French Revolution, 4, 18, 74

friendly societies, 177–8, 249
Frome, 118–19
funerals, 200, 212

Gaunt, Elizabeth, 38–40
Gilbert, Alan, 89
Ginzburg, Carlo, 5
gleaning, 38–9
gossip, 34, 66
Great Yorkshire Revival, 54

Halévy, Elise, 3–5
handloom weaving, 210, 215
Harriseahead, 82
Harrison, J.F.C., 4n
healing, 70–1, 137–8, 264, 265
High Legh, 207
Hill, Octavia, 50
Hobbes, Thomas, 18
Hobsbawm, Eric J., 103, 109
holiday customs, in Filey, 255–7
hosiery, 69, 190
household: customs of, 266; fishing,
255–7; importance of, 9, 22, 31–
2, 115–17, 249, 252; laboring, 10,
22; religious importance of, 31–3,
108, 148, 209
household economy, 31–2; decline
of, 111, 269, 278; definition of,
31n; religion and, 104; women
and, 34–5, 115–16
Hufton, Olwen, 40
hymns, 29–31, 30–1n, 128, 129–30,
135, 173, 195–200, 272–3
hypocrisy, 34, 68

illness, 70, 77, 137–8, 146–7, 215
independence, value of, 47, 104,
175–6, 207, 220, 225, 227, 232,
234
Independent Methodism, 21; break
from Wesleyan Methodism, 207–
8; female preachers of, 235–6;
free gospel of, 238, 239; govern-

O'Bryan, William, 144, 149–50, 152, 153
Okell, Betty, 207
Old Testament, 36–7, 60, 87, 217
oral tradition, 51
orphanhood, 117–18
Owenites, 4n, 215
Oxtoby, "Praying Johnny," 262–6, 270, 273

paternalism, 168–9
Peacock, Hannah, 76–7
persecution: of Bible Christians, 154; of Primitive Methodists, 126–7, 133–5, 280; of Wesleyans, 92
philanthropy, 52, 183; women and, 9–10, 51
Phillips, Peter, 76–7, 78, 86, 95, 209–10
piety: female, 50, 62, 93–4; middle-class, 93–4; plebeian, 45, 70–1; Victorian, 48
pilgrimage, 28–30, 104; in hymns, 29–30, 198–200
Pilgrim's Progress, 80
politics and religion, 3–5, 17–18, 20, 230, 231, 241, 274
Poor Laws, 108, 117
popular culture, 11, 35, 168–9, 220, 221, 249–50n, 261
popular medicine, 77, 137–8, 210, 264
popular religion, 144, 170–2, 247, 249, 255, 279; definition of, 245
potteries, 80, 107
Primitive Methodism, 21, 29–30, 41–3, 79, 82, 109–39, 170–4, 177–8, 261–2, 280; as household religion, 109–39; decline of cottage religion in, 223–4, 274–7; female preaching and, 7, 38–41, 91–8, 109–39, 178–83, 190, 192–3, 194–5; Independent Methodism and, 208, 223; Wesleyan

Methodism and, 23–7, 51, 79–95, 167. *See also* Bourne, Hugh; Clowes, William; female preachers; names of individual female preachers
prophecy, 60, 171, 264–6
propriety, 11, 35, 92–3
prostitutes, 196
Psalms, 211, 212–13, 217
public and private, 33–5, 90, 94

Quaker Methodism, 74–7, 207. *See also* Independent Methodism
Quakers, 76, 81, 156, 157

railway, 183, 272
Ranters, 262. *See also* Primitive Methodism
reform, 9–10
religion: class and, 61–2, 97, 106, 215, 274; family strife and, 55–6, 201; modern, 76–7, 86–7, 183, 245, 247; of the oppressed, 97, 104, 145, 213; politics and, 3–5, 20, 230, 231, 241, 274; privatization of, 11, 278–9; social and economic change and, 21, 34, 104–8; work and, 31–3, 47, 213, 249
respectability, 6, 48, 124, 199, 278
ressentiment, 211–12, 213n, 215
revivalism, 52–5, 82, 84, 167, 280
"Riding the Stang," 253
Rosaldo, Michelle Zimbalist, 34
Rudé, George, 109
rural customs, 54, 101–2, 159, 171–2
rural industry, *see* cottage industry; domestic industry; village industry
rural society: disruption of, 106, 107–8, 111, 145, 174; poverty and, 38, 102–3, 114

Sabbitarianism, 268–9
sacraments, 153, 154, 156

INDEX

St. Paul, 49, 60, 96, 149, 225, 229–30
Salvation Army, 281
sectarianism: definition of, 33; decline of, 157; seventeenth-century, 76, 81, 87, 153, 230
sermons, 25–6, 33, 65, 210–11, 239–40
servants, 65, 97, 125–7, 125n, 202
sexual equality, 51–2, 234
sexual repression, 31
Shebbear, 144
shoemakers, 216, 219–26
Sidmouth, Lord, 89
silkweaving, 107, 120, 121–2, 230, 232
small farmers, 104, 105, 111–12, 114–15, 141, 142–3
Smith, Bonnie G., 9
Smith, Elizabeth, 123–39
social control, theories of, 3–5
Song of Deborah, 37
Southcott, Joanna, 4n, 144
Southwest, 109–39
squirearchy, 103–4, 134
Staffordshire, 67, 79–80, 105
Strutt family, 161, 164–6, 168–9, 172, 175, 180, 182, 183; paternalism of, 168–9; religion and, 165, 168–9
Sunday schools, 41–2, 48, 93, 170, 201, 229, 235
superstitions, 247, 257–8
syncretism, 32

Taft, Mary, see Barritt, Mary
Taft, Zachariah, 58–60, 61, 63–4, 188
teetotalism, 203n, 214–15, 218, 222
temperance, 203n, 233
testimony, religious, 147–8
textile industry, 52–3, 159, 161–2, 227; female preachers and, 187, 191–2, 202–3; women and, 118–20, 161–2

theology of the oppressed, 97, 104, 145, 213
Thomas, Keith, 8
Thompson, E. P., 4–5, 17–18
Thorne, James, 144, 145, 153, 156
time and religion, 84, 175–6, 260–1
tithes, 103, 134
Tomlinson, Elizabeth (Mrs. Betsey Evans), 64–72, 162
trances, 77, 137–8

unemployment, of women, 107, 145, 190–1
Unett, J. W., 272
unmarried women, 66, 107–8, 177–8
uprootedness, 191–2, 195
urban life, 187, 245, 275

Victorianism, 3, 6, 11, 47, 48, 88–98, 101
vicar of Lichfield, 46
village: relationship to town, 183, 275; values of, 11, 183, 205–6, 208–9, 216, 218, 227, 234
village culture, 54, 173
village industries, 106–7, 118–20, 159, 161–2. See also cottage industry; domestic industry
village scold, 54
Virgin Mary, 95
visionaries, 94, 97–8, 214
visiting, 42n, 43–5, 53, 56, 66, 94, 154–5, 263, 276–7

Wales, 127–9; Methodism in, 32, 281
Walsh, John, 5n, 17n
Ward, W. R., 87
Warrington, 74, 205–7, 210
Watkins, Ruth, 120
Watts, Isaac, 29, 196
weaving, 24, 76, 164, 280
Weber, Max, 211–12n, 213n
Wesley, John, 4, 7, 17, 22, 29, 31,

307

LIBRARY OF CONGRESS CATALOGING IN PUBLICATION DATA

Valenze, Deborah M., 1953–
Prophetic sons and daughters.

Bibliography: p.
Includes index.
1. Women clergy—England—History—19th century.
2. Methodist Church—England—History—19th century.
3. England—Church history—19th century. 4. England—
Religious life and customs. I. Title.

BR759.V34 1985   274.2'081'088042   85-42755
ISBN 0-691-05455-X (alk. paper)

DEBORAH M. VALENZE has taught at Smith College and
Worcester Polytechnic Institute